PERFORMANCE ASSESSMENT FOR FIELD SPORTS

It has become standard practice for students of sports and exercise science to follow modules in performance assessment. But where should they start in their appraisal of a player's performance? What criteria are important, and why? What tools are now available to help achieve this task? *Performance Assessment for Field Sports* comprehensively addresses all these questions.

This is the first book dedicated to the assessment of performance in field sports such as soccer, rugby, hockey and lacrosse. It provides detailed and up-to-the-minute information about the laboratory and field-based methods which can be used to assess and identify improvements in individual and team performance. Features include:

- over 80 diagrams, photos and tables
- a look at emerging performance assessment technologies such as virtual reality and ingestible sensors
- contributions from three of the world's foremost sports scientists.

Integrating sports science theory, new research and technology, and their practical application in a user-friendly manner, *Performance Assessment for Field Sports* contains everything students need to understand the relationship between theory and practice in field sports performance. This is a crucial text for students of all levels on courses involving sports science, kinesiology, human movement science, sports performance or sports coaching.

Christopher Carling is Head of Sports Science at Lille Football Club and undertakes medical research in elite youth soccer for the Clairefontaine National Institute of Football.

Thomas Reilly is Director of the Research Institute for Sport and Exercise Sciences at Liverpool John Moores University. He is President of the World Commission of Science and Sports.

A. Mark Williams is Professor of Motor Behaviour at the Research Institute for Sport and Exercise Sciences, Liverpool John Moores University.

PERFORMANCE ASSESSMENT FOR FIELD SPORTS

CHRISTOPHER CARLING, THOMAS REILLY AND A. MARK WILLIAMS

Routledge
Taylor & Francis Group

LONDON AND NEW YORK

First published 2009
by Routledge
2 Park Square, Milton Park, Abingdon, Oxon, OX14 4RN

Simultaneously published in the USA and Canada
by Routledge
270 Madison Avenue, New York, NY 10016

Routledge is an imprint of the Taylor & Francis Group, an Informa business

Typeset in Zapf Humanist and Eras by
Keystroke, 28 High Street, Tettenhall, Wolverhampton
Printed and bound in Great Britain by
Antony Rowe, Chippenham, Wiltshire

British Library Cataloguing in Publication Data
A catalogue record for this book is available from the British Library

Library of Congress Cataloging-in-Publication Data
Carling, Christopher, 1972–
    Performance assessment for field sports : physiological, and match
notational assessment in practice / Christopher James Carling, Thomas Reilly
and A. Mark Williams.
        p. cm.
    1. Sports—Physiological aspects. 2. Physical education and
training—Physiological aspects. 3. Sports sciences—Research—Methodology.
I. Reilly, Thomas, 1941– II. Williams, A. M. (A. Mark), 1965– III. Title.
    GV711.5.C34 2009
    613.7′1—dc22   2008021958

ISBN 978–0–415–42685–5 pbk
ISBN 0–415–42685–5 pbk

ISBN 978–0–415–42684–8 hbk
ISBN 0–415–42684–7 hbk

ISBN 978–0–203–89069–1 ebk
ISBN 0–203–89069–8 ebk

CONTENTS

FIGURES

X

figures

TABLES

xii

tables

ACKNOWLEDGEMENTS

Many thanks to the companies Fifth Dimension Technologies, Fusion Sports, Inmotio, GPSports, OmegaWave Technologies, Simi Reality Motion Systems, Sportstecinternational, Sport-Universal Process, University of Michigan Virtual Reality Lab and Virtual Spectator for their contributions.

CHAPTER ONE

INTRODUCTION

Excelling in the performance of his or her chosen sport is the major aim of any elite athlete. The drive to win, the desire to succeed and the ambition to push beyond the present limits of performance are all essential features of achieving excellence in elite sport. Athletes must constantly strive to attain peak levels of performance to reach and subsequently stay at the top. In field sports, players must now move faster, anticipate better, demonstrate greater levels of technical and tactical ability and persist longer than competitors from the past. The commitments made by club, coach and player in attempting to attain perfection undeniably necessitate an extensive amount of time and financial contribution, especially as the gap between winning and losing grows ever smaller. The foundations for training and

1

competing can no longer be based on simple subjective views of how well athletes perform or on traditional methods passed from one generation of coach to another.

Fundamental to elite performance in field sports is the need to capture, analyse and evaluate information on key areas such as the physical or technical capacities of players. This information on the numerous characteristics of sports perform-ance is the foundation for providing feedback on how the player or athlete is performing. In turn, this feedback leads to the development of informed coaching interventions centred on evidence-based practice within daily training and preparation for match-play. When the opinions, experiences and know-how of elite practitioners are supplemented with these informed coaching methods, the combined approach may prove critical in finding that extra margin between success and failure.

In this introductory chapter we look at the role and benefits of sports science and performance assessment within field sports. We examine the role that technology is playing in assessing how players perform. In the remainder of this chapter, the various complexities and concerns in the field of performance assessment are considered.

THE ROLE OF SPORTS SCIENCE SUPPORT AND RESEARCH IN CONTEMPORARY ELITE SPORT

Practitioners within contemporary elite sport are constantly questioning their understanding and knowledge of the key elements of performance. If athletes are to attain world-class levels of performance, information from the continuous assessment of training and competition must be made available to aid in the evaluation of how players are performing and progressing. To this end, many countries now possess a nationwide framework of state-of-the-art sports science support services to coaches which are designed to help foster the talents of elite athletes and improve how they perform. Two notable examples are the Australian Institute of Sport (www.ais.co.au) and the English Institute of Sport (www.eis2win.co.uk). The Australian Institute of Sport has been highly successful and is regarded internationally as a 'world best practice' model for development of elite athletes (Farrow and Hewitt, 2002). Such centres provide the framework for delivery and application of multi-disciplinary support services that are now deemed essential by contemporary coaches and athletes if sporting excellence is to be achieved and maintained. The wide range of support services on offer to elite athletes at these centres includes applied physiological, biomechanical and motor skills testing as well as medical screening and consultations. The provision of other services such as nutritional advice, performance analysis, psychological support, podiatry, strength and conditioning, sports vision and lifestyle management analysis is also readily available.

Contemporary coaching staff involved in elite field sports such as soccer and rugby, are regularly supported by a comprehensive team of backroom staff that boasts strength and conditioning specialists, psychologists and dieticians. Sport scientists are frequently employed to aid in the delivery of the diverse spectrum of support services mentioned above and to carry out research of an applied nature aimed at directly enhancing the performance of athletes. A sports scientist will conduct experiments, make observations, assess, evaluate and interpret data and communicate findings (provide feedback) on coaching, training, competition and recovery practices, in all areas of elite performance.

The astonishing growth of sport and exercise science into a recognised academic area and accreditation schemes (such as those offered by the British Association of Sport and Exercise Sciences or BASES) to ensure gold-standard quality assurance (Winter et al., 2007a) have undoubtedly played an essential role in making sure that practitioners are supplied with the necessary skills to ensure the provision of top-class scientific support. Testament to informed good practice in contemporary sports science support is the recent publication by the British Association of Sports and Exercise Sciences (BASES) of two sourcebooks providing comprehensive and practical guidelines for sports and exercise testing (Winter et al., 2007a, 2007b).

A recent survey amongst contemporary elite coaches provided evidence that practitioners felt personal experience in coaching is no longer sufficient for developing elite athletes and an elite coach should have appropriate knowledge of the sport sciences (Williams and Kendall, 2007a). The recognition, acceptance and understanding of scientific techniques and strategies to enhance sports performance have therefore progressively, and willingly, been incorporated into coaching practices and world-class preparation programmes. This integration has been achieved through practitioners increasing their understanding of sports science and sports scientists beginning to understand better the needs of sport. Only then can the application of scientific principles play a significant role in enhancing player performance. In his comprehensive review of how science can enhance sports performance, Meyers (2006) stated that it is the merging of sports science with coaching that will allow today's athletes not only to excel and compete at higher levels, but also allow the athlete to prevent injury and maintain health. He continued by describing how a more comprehensive approach to coaching through science provides the coach and athlete with greater control, preparation, accountability and, most importantly, measurable progress.

The provision of sports science support has led to the emergence over the past two decades of a significant body of research into the host of factors contributing towards optimal performance in sport (Williams and Hodges, 2005). This increased research activity has been particularly evident in field sports such as soccer (association football) and Rugby Union where the importance of research and applied work has become increasingly accepted in the professional game. Whilst coaches are the intended beneficiaries of the outcomes of a large proportion of sports science research, references in the literature on coaching include claims that a 'gap' has existed between research and coaching practice (Goldsmith, 2000). This gap may have been due to a commonly held belief by sports scientists that 'coaches did not know what questions to ask the sports scientists', and conversely, coaches believed that 'sports scientists kept answering questions that no one was asking' (Campbell, 1993)! It may also have been due to a lack of dissemination of research findings through coaching clinics and sports-specific magazines, and the need for more appropriate 'lay' language in the information dissemination process (Williams and Kendall, 2007b).

Nevertheless, in recent years, there has been a proliferation of textbooks, scientific journal special issues and empirical research articles focusing on the application of scientific research notably within the various codes of football. If one examines scientific research over the last decade on soccer alone, a glut of comprehensive reviews has been published on the physiology (Impellizzeri et al., 2005, Stølen et al., 2005), psychology (Gilbourne and Richardson, 2005, Williams and Hodges, 2005), biomechanics (Lees and Nolan, 1998) and interdisciplinary (Reilly and Gilbourne, 2003) aspects of soccer. These scholarly works have attempted to translate scientific knowledge and expertise into a form usable by practitioners in order to have a meaningful impact on performance and learning. At the elite end of sport, the link between research and coaching practice needs to indicate that coaches incorporate the outcomes of sports science research (Williams and Kendall, 2007b).

Those working in the field of sports science are increasingly faced with the need to demonstrate that their work impacts on policy and professional practice (Faulkner et al., 2006). In exercise physiology and fitness testing, the outcomes of research projects have been adopted as fundamental elements of elite training programmes in the field sports. Similarly, the benefits of sports science disciplines such as match analysis are now widely recognised as being critical in laying the foundations for evaluating and understanding competitive performance in a wide range of field sports. Therefore, the acceptance over recent years of sports science support and research is unsurprising considering the performance-enhancing role that they can offer elite coaches who are continually searching for a competitive edge.

4

THE ROLE OF PERFORMANCE ASSESSMENT IN FIELD SPORTS

Performance in field sports is more difficult to appraise than it is in individual sports due to its highly dynamic and complex nature. In individual sports, such as track-and-field or cycling, the competitor who passes the winning line first, achieves the best time, jumps highest or longest or throws the missile furthest is victorious. Competitors can be judged according to precise measures of performance such as their rank order in finishing, or the time taken or distance achieved during competition. In field sports, contests are decided by a single determinant of victory, scoring more goals or points than the opposing team. The coach of a team winning a game can rightly claim that this simple objective of scoring more than the opposition has been achieved. Thoughts can be refocused on moving on and planning and preparing for the next game and securing another victory.

Coaches may therefore base their preparation and evaluate progress on the number of wins or losses with little regard for more objective means of defining specific indices of athleticism, which ultimately determine performance (Meyers, 2006). Yet, there is a distinction between the outcome (e.g. winning or losing) and the performance by which it was achieved (Carling et al., 2005). Since chance may play a role in the scoring or conceding of goals, for example, an 'own-goal' or a fluke deflection or a decision by the game officials, coaches recognise that the team they deemed to have been the best (e.g. in terms of possession and scoring chances created) does not always win the game.

This kind of comment raises questions about what is the basis for judging performance and whether there are any clear criteria used as evidence. The concept of performance can range in complexity from the parsimonious to the multivariate and the issues are most complex when it comes to analysing performance in field games (Reilly, 2001). Unless objective, specific and reliable means of assessment are used, evaluation and interpretation of performance will remain essentially subjective. In such contexts, the assessment of how well the team is playing and how much individuals could and actually do contribute to team effort, especially as there is no definitive index of each player's performance, presents a major challenge to the coaching staff and sports scientist.

The major objectives of coaching are to help athletic performers learn, develop and improve their skills. Information that is provided to athletes (more commonly known as feedback) about action is one of the most important factors affecting the learning and subsequent performance of a skill (Franks, 2004). The provision of feedback is part of the traditional cyclical coaching process involving the analysis, evaluation, planning and conducting of interventions. Failure to provide feedback about the proficiency with which players perform, or simply basing and planning coaching interventions on subjective observations on how a player is performing can reduce any chances of improvement (Carling et al., 2005). Coaching actions to monitor, evaluate and plan performance effectively must therefore be based on systematic, more quantifiable, reliable, objective and valid approaches for gathering and analysing information.

To be successful in field sports, players generally require many attributes and competencies including high levels of endurance, muscle strength, flexibility, agility, speed and coordination, as well as technical and tactical know-how. The primary concern of coaches is to develop and optimise all these skills in training in order to enhance performance and to harness individual capabilities to form an effective unit. Training for field sports may be placed in an ergonomics context as this signifies that a development programme is designed to prepare the individual for the demands of the game by aiming to raise his or her capabilities, thereby enhancing performance (Reilly, 2007). An ergonomics model of training allows the training process to be considered as interfacing with the demands of the game on the one hand and with the capabilities of players on the other. For example, field sports impose a wide range of physical demands on players who must possess the necessary fitness to cope with these requirements. Team selection must also be incorporated into such a model as there is a need to choose the most appropriate team for a forthcoming contest. An example of an ergonomics model for the analysis of soccer is illustrated in Figure 1.1.

It is important to know if a training intervention has been effective and whether the team as a whole has benefited. In addition, the identification of individual weaknesses and the need to take positional differences into account must be fitted into the ergonomics model. There is also a need to explain the mechanism of action of the various attributes within performance and determine which one(s) might make worthwhile differences in the way players perform. This can be partly achieved if monitoring, analysis and evaluation are undertaken to assess

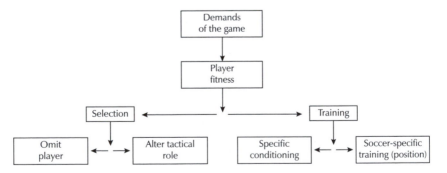

Figure 1.1 An ergonomics model for the analysis of soccer (adapted from Reilly, 2005)

developments in physical, mental, tactical or technical skills (Robertson, 2002). Whilst testing can provide a good indication of the general and sport-specific capacities of players, individual results cannot always be used to predict performance in match-play because of the complex nature of performance in competition (Svensson and Drust, 2005). Sports scientists are used to dealing with precise, quantifiable, numerical data, and although these are indicators of an athlete's potential to perform, actual performance within a team-sport framework is still a relatively abstract concept (Mujika, 2007).

Coaches and sports scientists generally use performance assessments to evaluate four major facets of player performance; these are physical, mental, tactical and technical skills. It is also worth mentioning that performance assessment has direct relevance in the clinical setting for the diagnosis and prognosis of conditions as well as being used to evaluate the effectiveness of medical or exercise interventions that are designed to be therapeutic (Winter et al., 2007b). The main features of sports performance mentioned beforehand must be broken down further to allow a more discriminate evaluation of the key elements of performance. For example, assessment of physical capabilities may include the evaluation of a variety of areas such as the aerobic capacity, muscular endurance and strength, flexibility and speed of the player. Mental skills assessment may cover the anticipation skills or personality traits of a player. Tactical analysis could involve simply looking at the system or style of play employed by a team. A combination of data from the evaluation of the various features of performance may also be employed to increase the practitioner's understanding of the subsequent effect on specific determinants of performance. For example, a coach may look at success rate in certain tactical situations such as when challenging for the ball (e.g. in terms of a won/loss percentage). This information can then be complemented by data from fitness testing, for example, on the vertical jump capacity or upper-body strength of the player compared to the normative value of the squad. In addition, the capture and evaluation of the player's decision-making or anticipation capacities could be carried out to determine how well he or she reads the game or formulates tactical decisions.

As mentioned earlier in this chapter, the information provided from formal assessments can be used to provide individual profiles of respective strengths and weaknesses in many aspects of performance. By establishing a starting point for performers according to pre-identified strengths and weaknesses, coaches can plan and prescribe optimal training interventions and strategies to prepare for competition. Individual baseline information is important as scientists need to consider the degree of inter-individual variability in the responses and adaptations to training (Mujika, 2007). The monitoring of progress across the season via frequent and regular testing can be implemented to provide an objective evaluation of the impact of training on performance thereby appraising the effectiveness of the

7

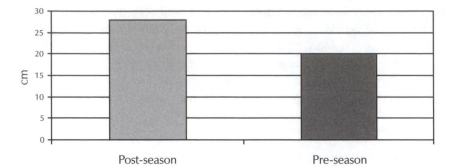

Figure 1.2 Comparison of post-season and pre-season vertical jump performance in a group of American Football players (drawn from data of Salci et al., 2007)

interventions. A comparison of post-season and pre-season vertical jump performance in a group of American Football players is illustrated in Figure 1.2. A coach can observe a significant difference in performance between the two periods which may suggest the need for an off-season conditioning programme to maintain fitness.

A profile of data obtained from fitness testing can also be juxtaposed alongside the physiological responses to match play (such as heart rate or concentration of blood lactate) highlighting the extent to which players can impose demands on themselves and provide pointers as to when they are underperforming in matches by not meeting the requirements of the game (Reilly, 2005). Such information may be further complemented by the inclusion of motion analysis data to assess the player's work rate profile such as the total distance run and/or recovery time between sprints which are related to the maximal aerobic power of elite soccer players (Carling et al., 2005). Therefore, a player with a high aerobic power but whose average heart rate during the course of the game is inferior to that obtained from measures on team-mates combined with a lower work rate may be deemed as under-performing in competitive conditions. A summary of the many reasons and purposes of testing and assessing the performance of participants in field sports is presented in Table 1.1.

Whilst performance assessment is mainly employed to identify individual strengths and weaknesses in various sporting skills, one can see from the list in Table 1.1 that it can also play a role in other areas such as player rehabilitation and health and the development or detection of talented young performers. During a rehabilitation programme, for example, it is important to monitor the progress of a player and by comparing base-line data obtained from initial assessments (when the player was healthy) useful information can be provided on when a player should best return to

Table 1.1 Reasons for assessing performance in sports

1. To establish a baseline profile for each player and the squad as a whole.
2. To identify individual strengths (to build on) and weaknesses (to be improved).
3. To provide feedback to players on their own capacities and act ergogenically by influencing their motivation to improve.
4. To evaluate objectively the effectiveness of a specific training intervention in terms of progress (improvement or failure to improve).
5. To evaluate objectively the effectiveness of other training-related interventions such as a nutritional or psychological development programme.
6. To monitor progress during rehabilitation or determine whether an athlete is ready to compete.
7. To identify a relationship between individual performance capacities and the actual demands of competition.
8. To monitor the health status of a player.
9. To assist in identifying talented soccer players.
10. To attempt to create performance norms according to age category, stage of development, special populations, playing position and sport.
11. To monitor and evaluate the progression of youth players.
12. To place players in an appropriate training group.
13. To examine the development of performance from year to year.
14. To enable future performance to be predicted.
15. To provide data for scientific research on the limitations of performance.

full training and competition and how far he or she is from peak level. Isokinetic measurement of muscle performance in particular now plays an essential role across a wide range of field sports in assessing the player's rehabilitation, as well as in screening and injury prevention from the point of view of muscle strength and balance. Information from performance assessments can help practitioners to determine the type, quantity and rate of training (extremely important during rehabilitation) as well as determining competitive strategies such as the rate or pattern of play (Meyers, 2006). More effective preparation can be achieved through minimising training errors and providing greater control over coaching interventions.

Assessment can also serve as a vehicle to promote excellence in young players and provide guidelines for talent identification (Stratton et al., 2004). Noteworthy examples are research projects for defining norms in fitness levels according to age in elite youth soccer players previously described by Carling (2001) and Balmer and Franks (2000) for French and English Academy players respectively. Balmer and Franks (2000) collected values for 5- and 15-m sprints from a pool of over 400 English Academy players. From these results, the authors established normative data on short sprint times providing the basis for a comprehensive database and a reference tool for youth team coaches. Future data from player assessment could be compared against these norms resulting in above average, below average or

Table 1.2 Fitness tests and national squad performance standards for netball (Grantham, 2007)

Fitness test	National netball squad performance standard
Vertical jump	58 cm
10-m sprint test	<1.77 s
777 agility test	<4.3 s
Multi-stage fitness test	12-5 (level & shuttle reached)
Speed-endurance test (mean)	<10 s

average performance categorisation. Along similar lines is the creation of desired performance standards for different levels of achievement. These standards may be defined for aspiring players performing at levels ranging, for example, from County to National. An example of fitness tests and desired national squad performance levels for English netball players is illustrated in Table 1.2.

HOW HAS TECHNOLOGY AFFECTED SPORTS ASSESSMENT?

Utilising the most efficient and valuable sources of information to support decision-making is a constant challenge for coaches. They must aim to collect, organise and analyse information as well if not better than the rest of their competitors. The means and equipment employed by coaches play an essential part in this process and these have all been affected in some way or other by developments in technology. From a purely performance point of view, modern technology makes it possible for coaches to gather, analyse and integrate information and resources more effectively in order to improve training, decision-making and collaboration (Katz, 2001). Individuals must always look at their own personal 'knowledge gaps' and seek out the latest techniques and resources to help create better-informed coaching decisions. Success at the highest level in sport requires a drive and determination to be the best at everything that one does and information derived from technology can be both a key strategic resource and a competitive one (Lawlor, 2003).

In an age driven by technology, it is inevitable that sports science and medical support services have been subject to the constant changes brought on by a myriad of technologies. Many sports generally have embraced technology and are now at the cutting edge of research and development, allowing athletes to push back the boundaries of performance. As the stakes get higher, even the very best coaches are being coerced into embracing this cultural change with the realisation that they would be well served to extract information from every available source in their quest for success. Technology applied to sport is playing an important role both in the daily training and competition environment, and its use and application can be seen to accelerate with each successive season.

Technology within elite sport has manifested itself in a variety of ways from the advanced equipment and facilities now used by athletes within competition to the implementation of scientific training-support schemes used by coaches to prepare teams for competition. Information technology (IT) is a notable example used to aid the analysis and management of information when making organisational and administrative decisions at both strategic and operational levels within elite sports organisations. For example, applications of IT are dramatically changing the nature of management practices and business strategies in sport due to the rapid development and integration of computer networking services (e.g, Internet, videoconferencing) and specialised software (e.g. customer databases).

From the point of view of the assessment of sports performance, coaches commonly use several methods of gathering information on training and competition. Robertson (2002) listed these as questionnaires, notation (e.g. match analysis), video and tests (e.g. fitness tests). Technological advances have, to a certain extent, affected all these particular methods of assessment. The constantly improving portability and unobtrusiveness of equipment employed for data collection within performance assessment combined with user-friendly and powerful computer interfaces for processing data are allowing many sports-monitoring interventions to step into new territories. For example, the ability to extend testing from the laboratory to the field has enhanced the specificity and validity of the evaluation methods (Svensson and Drust, 2005).

A significant advancement in the field-assessment of metabolic responses to exercise has been the development of online breath-by-breath respiratory gas analysers. Online gas analysers are replacing the cumbersome Douglas Bag for measuring gas expired composition in laboratory conditions. Portable gas analysers operated by short-range telemetry have also gained acceptability due to increased portability and the opportunity for obtaining instantaneous feedback in field settings. Similarly, the capacity to measure cardiac responses to exercise in the field has undergone radical evolution. Using lightweight heart-rate monitors, accurate data on exercise intensity and training load can be collected simul-taneously for a large group of players. Data are now transmitted over long distances for storage on a computer laptop where dedicated software can then be utilised to retrieve and analyse the information instantaneously. The intensity of training can then be adjusted accordingly.

Major enhancements in contemporary sports performance are also being obtained when different types of technology are combined. For example, there may be a need for enhanced knowledge and understanding of the optimal requirements for kicking a rugby ball in terms of speed, force, timing and technique. The relationship between data on muscle activity, force and power obtained from testing on an isokinetic dynamometer could be combined with a three-dimensional video analysis of the kicking technique. An evidence-based plan for enhancement of kicking could then be designed involving modification of body position, minimising errors in movement and strengthening the specific muscles engaged in the action. Similarly, contemporary systems used in testing permit the integration of several devices into an 'all in one' versatile unit for the simultaneous analysis of a wide range of performance variables. An appropriate example is the recent development of Global Positioning Systems for field sports (http://www.gpsports.com/ and http://www.microtechnologycrc.com/). These lightweight devices (see Figure 1.3) enable the collection and storage of data on movement (e.g. speed, time and distance) to be synchronised with the cardiac responses to exercise.

The processing, analysis and presentation of performance-related data within official competitive conditions via computer and high-quality digital video are now reality. Some sports practitioners exploit real-time data to implement instantaneously changes in the way players and teams are performing. An example is the

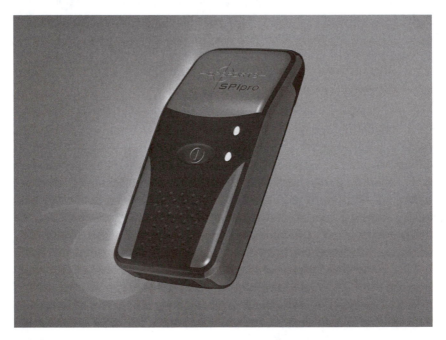

Figure 1.3 A GPS receiver commonly used in field sports to measure work rate and cardiac responses to exercise (courtesy of GPSports Ltd)

development and utilisation over the last decade of the computerised tracking and analysis of player performance from digital video during live competitive soccer play. These analysis systems provide coaches with real-time data on technical, tactical and physical performance, facilitating their choices and decision-making over the course of the game. For example, the live provision and evaluation of work rate data on high-intensity running can indicate whether a particular player is tiring towards the end of a match and may need replacing. In the past, obtaining information on work rate proved difficult due to the laborious collection and analysis of data when using manual motion-analysis techniques. Similarly, the rules of many field sports do not permit players to carry electronic devices for collecting data on movement during live competition, promoting instead the development of unobtrusive technologies such as the image processing of digital video.

Large computer databases of past performances are being developed to store, visualise and combine any form of data on demand, for any aspect of playing performance. This technology provides opportunities to create 'ideal' models of performance. Coaches can also access database technology to analyse trends in performance over any defined period of time. A strength and conditioning coach may be interested in examining match to match or periodic variations in high-intensity work rate of a hockey player over the course of the season. The analysis can easily be taken one step further by combining technical data with these work rate data to determine whether the player's technical performance (e.g. success rate in passing or controlling the ball) was simultaneously affected by variations in his or her work rate.

Finally, the role of the Internet within sports assessment briefly merits attention. This worldwide network has an important part to play as it facilitates the transfer and visualisation of different forms of information collected from the analysis of training and competition. A sports scientist can easily publish (at the touch of a button) assessment data on the Internet for visualisation and downloading via a remote secure access by coaching staff. Similarly, video teleconferencing technologies now permit live communication between coach, athlete and researcher from different points across the globe.

SOME CONSIDERATIONS WHEN ASSESSING PERFORMANCE

Before using any test, the reasons for assessing performance should be clearly defined from the outset. Whilst these have already been considered earlier in this chapter, it is clear that a needs analysis based on the requirements and views of the coach, science staff and players should precede any assessment. A plethora of tests has been developed to evaluate the performance of players representing a variety of field sports. The methods of assessment used depend greatly on the requirements of the individual sport or event, the availability of equipment and facilities, the practicality of assessment and the personal perspectives of the researcher (Maud, 2006). Similarly, it is recognised that to be effective, assessment procedures should be specific and valid and resulting measures should be reproducible and sensitive to changes in performance (Winter et al., 2007a). When testing sports performers, the single most important aim is quality control (Stratton et al., 2004).

The health and safety of the athlete and ethical considerations of the protocol must always be taken into account when designing and employing tests. The athlete should complete a voluntary consent form before undertaking the test protocol and prior approval for assessment is needed by the institution's human ethics committee. A participant information sheet should be provided giving full details of what the test entails. Research protocols should always ensure, even after obtaining written, voluntary and informed consent, that an athlete's physiological and psychological wellbeing are never compromised. There is a need for a strict risk assessment approach to health and safety management in both the field and laboratory setting. Although various considerations when assessing performance are covered below, a detailed review of every methodological issue is beyond the scope of this chapter. For further information the reader is referred to other sourcebooks such as those written by Maud and Foster (2006) and by Winter et al. (2007a, 2007b). For more information on the validity, reliability and sensitivity of measures of performance, see a recent review by Currell and Jeukendrup, (2008). Nevertheless, the main considerations when using tests to assess performance are briefly discussed below.

TEST CRITERIA

Once the reasons for assessing play in field sports have been clearly identified, an appropriate performance-related test must then be selected. A test should have discrete characteristics if it is to be adopted and yield useful information (Reilly, 2007). These characteristics refer to its specificity, reliability and validity. The chosen test protocol should be specific to the sport and mimic the form of exercise under scrutiny. The discrete characteristics of assessment protocols and equipment all play a part in determining the sensitivity with which measures explain changes in performance. A sensitive protocol is one that is able to detect small, but important changes in performance especially as the difference between finishing first and second in a sporting event can be 1% (Currell and Jeukendrup, 2008).

14

introduction

Specificity

The typical items usually covered in a fitness evaluation include a battery of tests measuring aerobic fitness, peak and mean anaerobic power, anthropometry and body composition, flexibility and muscular strength and endurance (Maud, 2006). Information gleaned from a test is of little or no benefit to the coach or player unless the recorded measurement can be applied to the sport. Therefore, an appropriate form of assessment for each sport must be selected. This is a key challenge for multiple-sprint activities such as field games in which speed and direction of movement predominate (Winter et al., 2007b). The experimenter must consider the intensity and duration of the sport in question as well as the muscle groups and the energy systems recruited during exercise. For example, if a sprint-training intervention is to be performed and then assessed, the corresponding test should mainly be anaerobic in nature.

The assessment of performance can be broken down into two main categories – laboratory and field testing. Laboratory testing provides sensitive measures of physiological function (in terms of detail and accuracy) within a controlled environment and can detect significant variations in physiological capacities. Such tests are often used to obtain a general rather than a sport-specific indication of a player's fitness due to the time-consuming nature of testing large population groups. In contrast, field tests are more suitable for investigating large population groups (e.g. a large squad of players can be tested simultaneously), require minimal equipment and have greater specificity to the sport. They also provide a familiar and less intimidating environment for players. Data obtained from field testing probably provide a better indication of the ability to perform in competition than a laboratory-based evaluation (Svensson and Drust, 2005). However, the identification of the relevant energy systems which contribute to how a player will perform are not always straightforward due to the limited amount of physiological data yielded from field testing in field sports. This restriction in interpreting associated physiological mechanisms may require complementary testing within a laboratory environment. A challenge for applied sports science researchers is to collect research data in the natural training and competition environment yet still maintain sufficient scientific control for the results to be accepted empirically (Williams and Kendall, 2007a).

Various tests have been designed for field sports either to be part of an overall assessment battery or to measure specific components of performance. All players should be subjected to a battery of tests designed to reflect the overall demands of their sport. Whilst a single test such as a progressive shuttle run test to exhaustion commonly used to evaluate soccer players (Edwards et al., 2003) can simultaneously provide information on exercise and recovery heart rate, blood lactate

15
introduction

concentration, average and peak sprinting speed and rate of fatigue, there is no single test that provides a concurrent assessment of all components of performance. Furthermore, various fitness tests used in soccer, for example, still appear to lack ecological validity with respect to the motion types, directions, turns and intensities of the physical demands as well as under-providing protocols for different positions (Bloomfield et al., 2007). An example of a battery of tests employed to evaluate the specific physical capacities of international Rugby Union players is presented in Table 1.3.

Reliability and validity

Equally important as the specificity of a test is the reliability of the test result. For data to be considered reliable and therefore meaningful, they must be reproducible if repeated soon after, at the same time of day and under the same conditions of testing. Also, to ensure a test is reliable, it should be free of any subjective bias on the part of the experimenter, thereby assuring its objectivity. In essence, variability in measures can be attributed to technical and biological sources (Winter et al., 2007b). The former concerns the administration procedures of the test such as the precision and accuracy of instruments and the skills of the operator. Exercise testing is a complex activity involving the academic knowledge, practical skills, experiential awareness and personal capacity of the team doing the assessments (Mahoney,

Table 1.3 The various components of performance and order of testing commonly employed in international Rugby Union (adapted from Tong and Wiltshire, 2007)

Measurement	Performance component	Order of test
Height	Stature	1
Weight	Body mass	2
Skinfold measures	Body composition	3
Countermovement jump	Leg power	4
Vertical jump	Leg power	5
2nd day		
10- & 40-m sprint	Speed	6
40-m multiple sprint	Anaerobic capacity	7
Bench press	Strength	8
Bench pull	Strength	9
Half-squat	Strength	10
Chin-ups	Strength	11
3-km timed run	Aerobic capacity	12

2007). The latter factor refers to the relative consistency with which a subject can perform as this may be affected by random or cyclic biological variation.

The conditions of testing (e.g. choice, quality and calibration of equipment) are essential and must be standardised each time a test is performed to ensure that the same conditions are accurately reproduced. Standardising an assessment protocol can prove more difficult for field-based tests where problems may arise due to variations in environmental conditions. The standardisation of test procedures also refers to the way in which the test is administered, for example, the order in which each player performs the test (Balsom, 1994). To ensure reliable and accurate test-retest comparisons of data, tests should always be completed in the same order. Such factors are closely linked to the overall feasibility of the assessment process where the amount of time needed compared to what is available and the availability of players, staff, facilities and equipment must always be accounted for by testing staff.

In addition, experimenters are required to take into consideration the time of day when conducting assessments in both the field and laboratory. There is irrefutable evidence that the body's circadian rhythms influence fitness and performance measures (Drust et al., 2005). Attention to planning and organisation is again essential. Similarly, familiarisation sessions should be undertaken to habituate players to various protocols. Players must be fully briefed prior to the test, undertake a standardised pre-test warm-up routine, be free of injury and well rested. Where tests require players to exercise at maximal levels, motivation is a key issue that can affect results, and mental preparation before testing and encouragement by personnel during the test are therefore important. It has also been shown that auditory feedback of performance during a field-based assessment of maximal aerobic power leads to superior performance levels being achieved (Metsios et al., 2006) indicating that motivation is a significant test-component in stimulating maximal performance.

Finally, all assessment protocols and equipment must have undergone checks for validity. For example, a fitness test is valid if it measures the component of fitness it purports to measure. An appropriate example is the Yo-Yo Intermittent Recovery Level 2 field test designed to evaluate the ability to perform intense intermittent exercise (Krustrup et al., 2006). The validity of this test for field sports such as soccer has been demonstrated as the physiological responses to the exercise showed that both aerobic and anaerobic systems were heavily stimulated and the test results were strongly related to the competitive level of the players. The validity of an instrument such as an automated metabolic gas analyser may be verified for example, by comparing data obtained from the system against those from a criterion or gold-standard apparatus such as the Douglas Bag. Another important example is the validity of psychometric instruments used for personality profiling of athletes. Whilst such methods have been widely employed across a range of sports, their validity and usage have been questioned in the scientific literature (Meyers, 2006) and therefore these are not covered in this book. For further information on examining test-retest reliability measurement and validity, see work by Atkinson and Nevill (1998, 2007), Hopkins (2000) and Drust et al. (2007). For information on the general design and analysis of sports performance research, see article by Atkinson and Nevill (2001).

As mentioned earlier, the choice and quality of equipment are essential factors in measuring and assessing key components of performance. According to Katz (2001), the criteria for success of the various applications and resources used to assess contemporary performance in sport should:

- be based on techniques that are currently being used and for which there is clear evidence of success;
- address clearly defined and measurable needs;
- be interactive and responsive, in real time, to client needs;
- be transferable yet customisable across sporting environments;
- result in positive changes which may impact on attitudes, performance and/or costs; and,
- integrate technology with easy-to-use interfaces that are reliable, effective, efficient and transparent to the user.

Other factors to be taken into account include cost and portability (weight and compactness) of equipment which can influence the effectiveness of the assessment process. The plethora of computerised match analysis systems currently used in field sports is an excellent example of how modern assessment technology can vary in terms of the above mentioned criteria. For instance, the cost of a system can range from several hundred pounds to purchase a computer software program up to one hundred thousand pounds for the analysis of a whole season of matches by a service provider. In addition, the time required to analyse performance can vary considerably between systems. Systematic observation and analysis should be perceived as a time-effective rather than a time-consuming activity (Robertson, 2002). Coaches generally require match-analysis information to be available within a 48-hour time delay after the completion of a match. The variety and quantity of information provided by a match analysis system must also be taken into account as this will determine the depth and range of factors that can be evaluated. The factors that should be evaluated when acquiring a match analysis system and which are often relevant to other sports assessment equipment are outlined in Figure 1.4.

18

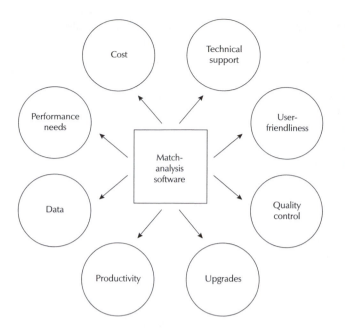

Figure 1.4
Outline of the major factors to be taken into account when acquiring a computerised match-analysis system (redrawn from Carling et al., 2005)

ANALYSIS, PRESENTATION, INTERPRETATION AND APPLICATION OF DATA

The assessment of performance involves the systematic collection of the evidence, assessment of quality, extraction of data from each source, compilation of data into tables or charts to facilitate comparison, appraisal of its overall strength and ultimately synthesis (Faulkner et al., 2006). The analysis and presentation of results are therefore important. Whilst the information provided from assessment should address the original research questions, more questions than answers can sometimes emerge from the analysis of data. Finding the right balance between quantity and relevance of results is essential with this process often depending on the analytic skills of the researcher and the time and tools available for analysis. Before dissemination and communication, results should always be presented in a concise and easy-to-read graphical format to ensure straightforward comparison and understanding. For more information on the different forms of presentation of performance assessment data, see Carling et al. (2005).

An integral part of any assessment programme is to interpret the results and give direct feedback to each player (Balsom, 1994). Whilst interpretation of results should involve coach, testing personnel and the player, interpretation may greatly depend on the personal knowledge, experience and subjective opinions of coaches and may therefore differ between coach and sports scientist. Such disagreements may be witnessed due to the apparent strength or lack of evidence or the inconsistency/consistency of results obtained from assessment. It may also be due to a lack of agreement between staff when interpreting changes in performance. The smallest worthwhile change in performance is important when assessing athletes with a performance test to make decisions about meaningful changes in an individual or to research strategies that might affect performance (Hopkins, 2004). In field sports, deciding on what is a meaningful change in performance can prove problematic. A coach may consider that an improvement of 5% in maximal aerobic capacity is not as critical as a 5% improvement in sprint performance.

Data should be interpreted according to the current coaching climate, goals and strategies as well as from the point of view of the personal capacity and responses of the individual. The genetic predisposition, physical and emotional maturity and training status of players may influence observations and result in a wide and inconsistent range of research findings. Finally, the correct interpretation of test results on an individual basis is linked to the reliability of the tests (Impellizzeri et al., 2005). Statistical analyses of results (such as coefficient of variation and typical error of measurement) must be provided on an ongoing basis during the interpretation of data in order to determine whether changes in performance are meaningful or merely an artefact of the test itself (Barnes, 2007).

The application of scientific research into practice is paramount to coaches (Williams and Kendall, 2007a). They may be unable to apply research findings unless this information is communicated in practical terms (i.e. in a language that is understood by the coach and athlete). Feedback given to coaches and then to athletes on performance must also be appropriate, constructive and accurate, and provided in the right amounts and at the correct time. The assessment of sports performance should aim to provide guidelines and recommendations either to bring about change in or to validate current coaching practices. There is a need to base the many aspects of coaching on a multi-disciplinary scientific evidence-base, yet the major challenge remains in integrating this research to impact on the way players perform. Research will only be taken up and used in prescribed coaching interventions if it has been proved to be plausible and practical as well as effective. Furthermore, scientific information and standards are constantly changing, serve only as guidelines and must be realistically adapted to the athlete's specific training environment (Meyers, 2006).

CONCLUSION

Over recent years, the multi-disciplinary field of sports science has influenced the traditional coaching process notably by optimising the practices used to assess the underlying and related mechanisms of elite sports performance. The adoption of technology combined with more refined and adapted procedures for assessing performance have and continue to be a hallmark of contemporary applied sports science. Elite practitioners within various field sports are progressively adopting the findings of scientific research as well as the technologies involved and are now formulating and planning their training and competition interventions and goals on the basis of this evidence. However, to ensure that this successful merger between science and sport continues well into the future, both sports scientists and coaches need to bear in mind the complexities when integrating performance assessment into their professional practices.

REFERENCES

Atkinson, G. and Nevill A.M. (1998) Statistical methods in assessing measurement error (reliability) in variables relevant to sports. *Sports Medicine*, 26: 217–238.

Atkinson, G. and Nevill A.M. (2001) Selected issues in the design analysis of sport performance research. *Journal of Sports Sciences*, 19: 811–827.

Atkinson, G. and Nevill A.M. (2007) Method agreement and measurement of error in the physiology of exercise. In E.M. Winter, A.M. Jones, R.C.R. Davison, P.D. Bromley and T.H. Mercer (eds), *Sport and Exercise Physiology Testing: Guidelines. Volume I Sport Testing* (pp. 41–48). The British Association of Sport and Exercise Sciences Guide. London: Routledge.

Balmer, N. and Franks, A. (2000) Normative values for 5 and 15 metre sprint times in young elite footballers. *Insight – The Football Association Coaches Journal*, 4(1): 25–27.

Balsom, P. (1994) Evaluation of physical performance. In B. Ekblom (ed.), *Football (Soccer)* (pp. 102–123). London: Blackwell Scientific Publications.

Barnes, C. (2007) Soccer. In E.M. Winter, A.M. Jones, R.C.R. Davison, P.D. Bromley and T.H. Mercer (eds), *Sport and Exercise Physiology Testing: Guidelines. Volume I Sport Testing* (pp. 241–248). The British Association of Sport and Exercise Sciences Guide. London: Routledge.

Bloomfield, J., Polman, R.C.J. and O'Donoghue, P.G. (2007) Physical demands of different positions in FA Premier League soccer. *Journal of Sports Science and Medicine*, 6: 63–70.

Campbell, S. (1993) The future of sports science in coaching. Cutting Edge Developments in Sports Science Conference. Canberra, Australia (video recording).

Carling, C. (2001) Sports science support at the French Football Federation. *Insight – The Football Association Coaches Journal*, 4(4): 34–35.

Carling, C., Williams, A.M. and Reilly, T. (2005) *The Handbook of Soccer Match Analysis*. London: Routledge.

Currell, K. and Jeukendrup, A.E. (2008) Validity, reliability and sensitivity of measures of sporting performance. *Sports Medicine*, 38: 297–316.

Drust, B., Atkinson, G. and Reilly, T. (2007) Future perspectives in the evaluation of the physiological demands of Soccer. *Sports Medicine*, 37: 783–805.

Drust, B., Waterhouse, J., Atkinson, G., Edwards, B. and Reilly. T. (2005) Circadian rhythms in sports performance: an update. *Chronobiology International*, 22: 21–44.

Edwards, A.M., Macfadyen, A.M. and Clark, N. (2003) Test performance indicators from a single soccer specific fitness test differentiate between highly trained and recreationally active soccer players. *Journal of Sports Medicine Physical Fitness*, 43: 14–20.

Faulkner, G., Taylor, A., Ferrence, R., Munro, S. and Selby, P. (2006) Exercise science and the development of evidence-based practice: A 'better practices' framework. *European Journal of Sport Science*, 6: 117–126.

Farrow, D. and Hewitt, A. (2002) Sports science support for the Australian Institute of Sport Football Programme. *Insight – The Football Association Coaches Journal*, 4(5): 49–51.

Foster, C., Daniels, J.T., deKoning, J.J. and Cotter, H.M. (2006) Field testing of athletes. In P.J. Maud and C. Foster (eds), *Physiological Assessment of Human Fitness*, 2nd edition (pp. 253–326). Champaign, IL: Human Kinetics.

Franks, I.M. (2004) The need for feedback. In M.D. Hughes and I. M. Franks (eds), *Notational Analysis of Sport: Systems for Better Coaching and Performance* (pp. 17–40). London: E & FN Spon.

Gilbourne, D. and Richardson, D. (2005) A practitioner-focused approach to the provision of psychological support in soccer: adopting action research themes and processes. *Journal of Sports Sciences*, 23: 651–658.

Goldsmith, W. (2000) Bridging the gap? Now there is a gap in the bridge! *ASCA Newsletter*, 3: 4.

Grantham, N. (2007) Netball. In E.M. Winter, A.M. Jones, R.C.R. Davison, P.D. Bromley and T.H. Mercer (eds), *Sport and Exercise Physiology Testing: Guidelines. Volume I Sport Testing* (pp. 249–255). The British Association of Sport and Exercise Sciences Guide. London: Routledge.

Hopkins, W.G. (2000) Measures of reliability in sports medicine and science. *Sports Medicine*, 30: 1–15.

Hopkins, W.G (2004) How to interpret changes in an athletic performance test. *Sportscience*, 8: 1–7.

Impellizzeri, F.M., Rampinini, E. and Marcora, S.M. (2005) Physiological assessment of aerobic training in soccer. *Journal of Sports Sciences*, 23: 583–592.

Katz, L. (2001) Innovations in sport technology: implications for the future. Proceedings of the 11th International Association for Sport Information (IASI) Congress, Lausanne, Switzerland.

Krustrup, P., Mohr, M., Nybo, L., Jensen, J.M., Nielsen, J.J. and Bangsbo J. (2006) The Yo-Yo IR2 test: physiological response, reliability, and application to elite soccer. *Medicine and Science in Sports and Exercise*, 38: 1666–1673.

Lawlor, J. (2003) Performance enhancement in football: the role of information technology. *Insight – The Football Association Coaches Journal*, 6(2): 46–48.

Lees, A. and Nolan, L. (1998) The biomechanics of soccer: a review. *Journal of Sports Sciences*, 3: 211–234.

Mahoney, C.A. (2007) Psychological issues in testing. In E.M. Winter, A.M. Jones, R.C.R. Davison, P.D. Bromley and T.H. Mercer (eds), *Sport and Exercise Physiology Testing: Guidelines. Volume I Sport Testing* (pp. 18–24). The British Association of Sport and Exercise Sciences Guide. London: Routledge.

Maud, P.J. (2006) Fitness assessment defined. In P.J. Maud and C. Foster (eds), *Physiological Assessment of Human Fitness*, 2nd edition (pp. 1–9). Champaign, IL: Human Kinetics.

Maud, P.J. and Foster, C. (eds) (2006) *Physiological Assessment of Human Fitness*, 2nd edition, Champaign, IL: Human Kinetics.

Metsios, G.S., Flouris, A.D., Koutedakisb, Y. and Theodorakis, Y. (2006) The effect of performance feedback on cardiorespiratory fitness field tests. *Journal of Science and Medicine in Sport*, 9: 263–266.

Meyers, M.C. (2006) Enhancing sport performance: Merging sports science with coaching. *International Journal of Sports Science and Coaching*, 1: 89–100.

Mujika, I. (2007) Challenges of team-sport research. *International Journal of Sports Physiology and Performance*, 2: 221–222

Reilly, T. (2001) Assessment of sports performance with particular reference to field games. *European Journal of Sport Science*, 1: 1–12.

Reilly, T. (2005) An ergonomics model of the soccer training process. *Journal of Sports Sciences*, 23: 561–572.

Reilly, T. (2007) *Science of Training: Soccer*. London: Routledge.

Reilly, T. and Gilbourne, D. (2003) Science and football: a review of applied research in the football codes. *Journal of Sports Sciences*, 21: 693–705.

Reilly, T. and Williams, A.M. (eds.) (2003) *Science and Soccer*, 2nd edition. London: Routledge.

Robertson, K. (2002) *Observation, Analysis and Video*. Leeds: The National Coaching Foundation.

Salci, Y., Coskun, O.O., Ozberk, Z.N., Yildirim, A., Akin, S. and Korkusuz, F. (2007) Physical features of American football players in post- and pre-season period. *Journal of Sports Science and Medicine*, Supplement 10: 22–25.

Stølen, T., Chamari, K., Castagna, C. et al. (2005) Physiology of soccer: an update. *Sports Medicine*, 35: 501–536.

Stratton, G., Reilly, T., Richardson, D.R. and Williams, A.M. (2004) *Science of Youth Soccer*. London: Routledge.

Svensson, M. and Drust, B. (2005) Testing soccer players. *Journal of Sports Sciences*, 23: 601–618.

Tong, R.J. and Wiltshire, H.W. (2007) Rugby Union. In E.M. Winter, A.M. Jones, R.C.R. Davison, P.D. Bromley and T.H. Mercer (eds), *Sport and Exercise Physiology Testing Guidelines: Volume I Sport Testing* (pp. 262–271). The British Association of Sport and Exercise Sciences Guide. London: Routledge.

Williams, A.M. and Hodges, N.J. (2005) Practice instruction and skill acquistion in soccer: challenging tradition. *Journal of Sports Sciences*, 23: 637–650.

Williams, A.M. and Reilly, T. (2004) Extending the boundaries of science: implications for the various codes of football. *Journal of Sports Sciences*, 22: 483.

Williams, S.J. and Kendall, L.R. (2007a) A profile of sports science research (1983–2003). *Journal of Science and Medicine in Sport*, 10: 193–200.

Williams, S.J. and Kendall, L.R. (2007b) Perceptions of elite coaches and sports scientists of the research needs for elite coaching practice. *Journal of Sports Sciences*, 25: 1–10.

Winter, E.M., Jones, A.M., Davison, R.C.R., Bromley, P.D. and Mercer, T.H. (eds) (2007a) *Sport and Exercise Physiology Testing Guidelines: Volume I Sport Testing*. The British Association of Sport and Exercise Sciences Guide. London: Routledge.

Winter, E.M., Jones, A.M., Davison, R.C.R., Bromley P.D. and Mercer, T.H. (eds) (2007b) *Sport and Exercise Physiology Testing Guidelines: Volume II Exercise and Clinical Testing*. The British Association of Sport and Exercise Sciences Guide. London: Routledge.

CHAPTER TWO

ASSESSING SKILL LEARNING AND PERFORMANCE

CHAPTER CONTENTS

INTRODUCTION

The ability to execute motor skills is an essential element of performance in the field sports. As spectators, we often marvel at the technical skills demonstrated by elite performers. For example, consider the sublime ball wizardry of Cristiano Ronaldo as he dribbles the ball past a string of helpless defenders on the soccer field or the amazing accuracy and reliability of Jonny Wilkinson as he kicks a rugby ball between the goal posts located at an angle some 40 metres away. The key features of such skills are they are goal oriented (performed with a specific aim in mind), effective and reliable (achieved with maximum certainty and consistency), efficient (employ no more effort than necessary), adaptable (can be used in a range of situations) and learned (developed with practice). While there remains considerable debate as to the type of practice and instruction that best facilitates the effective acquisition of motor skills (Williams and Hodges, 2004, 2005), an essential task for practitioners and scientists is to assess how well players execute such skills. The capacity to measure performance accurately is essential in determining the effectiveness of training and in identifying areas of weakness that players need to improve upon in future. It can also be useful in reducing the risk of injury through incorrect execution of motor skills.

In this chapter we provide an overview of the methods that may be employed to evaluate the learning and performance of motor skills. In the first instance, we define key terms such as learning and performance and explain why these two components need to be evaluated separately in order to ascertain whether players are developing the correct motor skills needed at the elite level in field sports. We present a range of qualitative and quantitative methods for evaluating human movement. Some of the methods presented may be employed fairly easily in the field setting, whereas others are more complex and require access to sophisticated measurement systems within the laboratory. We begin by outlining the important distinctions between learning and performance.

LEARNING AND PERFORMANCE

Learning is the process that underlies the acquisition and retention of motor skills. It is defined as a set of processes associated with practice or experience which leads to a relatively permanent change in the capability for skilled performance (Schmidt and Wrisberg, 2004; Schmidt and Lee, 2005). In contrast, *performance* simply refers to the behaviour that can be observed at any given moment. An important issue is that learning is not directly observable, since it involves changes in central nervous system function; rather it must be inferred by observing changes in performance over an extended period of time. Learning can only be deemed to have taken place if the improvement in performance is relatively permanent in nature. A difficulty is that temporary variations in performance can occur for reasons that may not be indicative of skill learning, such as changes in motivation, anxiety, injury and fatigue.

To measure learning accurately, it is therefore necessary to evaluate performance over time using an agreed measure such as the score obtained on a sports skills test. The score at each test session may be plotted onto a graph in order to portray a performance profile or curve. Some examples of typical performance curves are plotted in Figure 2.1 (for a detailed discussion on learning curves and their implications, see Schmidt and Lee, 2005; Magill, 2006). However, in order to assess learning accurately, a *retention* and/or *transfer* test must be used in association

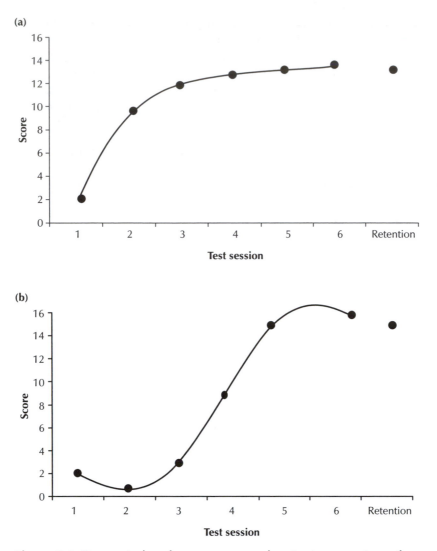

Figure 2.1 Two typical performance curves showing increases in performance on a soccer skills test for shooting. The first curve **(a)** is a negatively accelerated, gradually increasing learning curve showing a rapid improvement in performance at first followed by a general 'levelling off', during which improvements are relatively slow. The results of a retention test to assess learning are highlighted on the right-hand side. The second curve **(b)** is a sigmoid function learning curve showing a slow gradual increase followed by a sharp improvement in performance and then a gradual slowing down in performance gains

assessing skill learning and performance

with performance curves. A retention test is when the player is retested after a rest period when the transient effects of performance have subsided (usually a few days or weeks). Alternatively, a transfer test requires the learner either to perform the skill that has been practiced in a new situation or to perform a new variation of the practiced skill (i.e. passing a soccer ball over a different distance to that used in practice). The majority of skills in field sports are performed in an open environment with high variability (e.g. passing, shooting, tackling) and, consequently, are likely best evaluated using some measure of transfer of performance from practice to the playing field.

A key issue for coaches, practitioners and scientists to grasp is that in order to evaluate learning it is necessary to measure improvements in performance over an extended period of time. Although the level of performance observed provides an indication of whether or not learning has occurred, this type of inference should be made very cautiously since some variables affect learning and performance differently. For example, several instructional variables and the scheduling of practice affect practice and learning differently (for a detailed review, see Williams and Hodges, 2005). Low frequency of feedback, massed practice scheduling, variability of practice and high contextual interference (i.e. practising more than one skill in a session) conditions have sometimes been shown to affect performance negatively within the training session (as indicated by performance curves), whilst having no detrimental effect on skill learning (as indicated by retention or transfer tests). Perhaps more importantly, high frequency of feedback, distributed practice scheduling, specificity of practice and low contextual interference (i.e. practising only one skill per session) conditions have positive effects on performance during the session, while sometimes being detrimental to the skill-learning process (Williams and Hodges, 2005).

Variations in performance may also arise because of physiological, physical, tactical or psychological reasons (Marshall and Elliott, 1999). For instance, physiological factors such as fatigue, strength and power can impact on the manner in which players perform motor skills, as can psychological factors such as anxiety and self-confidence. Poor anticipation and decision-making skills can equally cause players to make the incorrect tactical decision or to select an inappropriate technique for the situation presented. Finally, maturational factors may also greatly influence the manner in which technical skills are performed (e.g. see Scott et al., 2003). A practitioner must therefore consider the impact of all of these factors when measuring performance and evaluating learning effects.

While the benefits of plotting performance improvements over time, and employing retention and transfer tests may be clearly apparent, and should be the cornerstone of any systematic skill evaluation or monitoring process, the issue of what tests or measures to record when evaluating performance is somewhat

27

problematic. A range of methods exists for evaluating performance. Some of these methods are subjective, relying almost exclusively on an acute eye and the qualitative opinion of the observer, whereas others are more objective and are based on quantitative evaluation of movement kinetics (i.e. forces generated) and kinematics (i.e. motion characteristics). We review a number of these methods, starting with the cheapest and most subjective method involving the use of models or templates of correct movement form and ending with much more sophisticated and costly measurement systems.

QUALITATIVE ANALYSIS OF PERFORMANCE

The qualitative analysis of movement has a long history in sport as well as in other fields such as physical therapy and dance instruction. The advantage of a qualitative analysis is that it can be used relatively easily by a wide range of people. Most coaches regularly use subjective evaluation techniques when working with players. For example, in rugby a coach may advise a player to increase range of motion at the hip or to strike the ball in a different spot based on purely visual inspection of the kicking technique. The disadvantage is that the accuracy of this approach is based on an individual's observation skills and subjective judgement. Although the process remains largely intuitive and based on extensive experience within the sport, there have been attempts to develop models to assist systematic observation (for a review, see Knudson and Morrison, 1997). Such models typically provide a framework for observing and modifying the technical execution of skills. The skill is typically broken down into phases (e.g. preparation, retraction, action and follow-through) and sub-phases, temporal durations or critical features (Lees, 2002, 2007).

Hay and Reid (1988) identified four key stages in undertaking effective qualitative analyses of skill: develop a model or template of the skill, observe practice and identify faults, prioritise the importance of these faults and provide instruction and opportunities for practice so that the faults may be rectified. In relation to the first stage, a model template is a representation of the ideal form of a movement in each phase which may be depicted in written, tabular or pictorial form. The model template or framework may be developed by drawing upon expert knowledge from coaches within the sport and through reference to existing research literature. A checklist or visual template that provides an overview of the key technical elements of the skill may help the observer identify the main faults, particularly when several individuals may be involved in the observation process. Such a framework may, for example, divide the movement into various phases and sub-phases along one continuum and highlight the main observational points relating to accurate execution of the skill on another. An example of a typical framework for a soccer kicking task based on the approach adopted by Lees (2007) is highlighted in Table 2.1.

28

Table 2.1 A template or framework that may be used to facilitate systematic qualiative analysis of the soccer kick

The FRAMEWORK approach

Event								
Phases								
Defining Moments								
Sub-phases								
Critical features								
Outcome / Function								
Movement Principle								
Limitations								

BREAKDOWN & DESCRIPTION

EVALUATION

Event	SOCCER KICK			
Phases	APPROACH	LEG RETRACTION	FORWARD SWING AND CONTACT	FOLLOW– THROUGH
Defining Moments				
Sub-Phases	• Initial few strides • Preparation for kick and foot plant	• Knee flexion • Hip extension • Hip rotation backwards	• Hip rotation towards ball • Hip flexion • Knee extension	• Follow-through

SOCCER KICK

	APPROACH	LEG RETRACTION	FORWARD SWING AND CONTACT	FOLLOW–THROUGH
Critical features	• Last stride length	• Kicking leg hip extension and opposite arm backwards	• Maximum flexion of kicking leg knee • Body posture at impact	• Fully extended kicking leg knee and opposite arm backwards • Flexed knee
Outcome / Function	• Develop initial speed into the kick • Improve contact with good foot placement	• Increase ROM in which to accelerate the limb and foot towards the ball	• Develop foot speed and make sound contact with the ball • Transfer foot speed onto ball	• Decelerate limb and reduce risk of injury
Movement principle	• Controlled whole-body speed • Speed–accuracy trade–off	• Range of motion • Action–reaction	• Sequential movements • End point speed (P–D) • Impact stationary object	• Action • Reaction

Knudson and Morrison (1997) provided a comprehensive integrated model of qualitative analysis. The authors identified four important tasks when analysing skill: preparation, observation, evaluation/diagnosis and intervention. The model and some of the important issues for each task are presented in Figure 2.2. The model may be adapted for use in all field sports, with the main source of variation being the technical model for the skill being evaluated (for a detailed overview of how to apply such a model in practice, see Knudson and Morrison, 1997). This chapter focuses mainly on the process of performance evaluation. However, it is important to note that when designing any programme of intervention, practitioners should ensure that they adhere to the principles of effective instruction highlighted in the literature (see Schmidt and Wrisberg, 2004; Williams and Hodges, 2004, 2005; Magill, 2006).

An increasingly used method of qualitative analyses involves the use of digital video replay such that the skill may be viewed repeatedly and often from different viewpoints (Marshall and Elliott, 1999). In relation to the latter issue, most video-based analysis software packages now allow multiple viewpoints of the action to be observed simultaneously on the same screen provided more than one camera is employed. Moreover, the use of slow-motion replay and still-frame elements can help capture elements of movement that are not observable via the human eye (for a more detailed overview of the role of video in performance analysis, see Knudson and Morrison, 1997; Carling et al., 2005; and Chapter 4 in this book). The effective use of video in such situations would adhere to the same principles as outlined in Figure 2.2.

QUANTITATIVE ANALYSIS OF PERFORMANCE

A number of quantitative methods exist for evaluating skill performance. Some of these methods evaluate the performer's ability to achieve a specific outcome (e.g. the distance and accuracy of the kick or throw), whereas others focus more on the processes or procedures that contribute to performance outcome (e.g. coordination pattern employed). In this section we provide a brief overview of the most common methods for evaluating outcome and process measures of performance. These range from simple and cost-effective methods involving testing of sports skills to expensive and highly sensitive measurement systems involving an assessment of the kinetic (i.e. force) and kinematic (i.e. motion) characteristics of the movement.

Before progressing, it is important to note that while changes in performance outcome are often accompanied by causal changes in the underlying process measures it is conceivable that these measures may function independently. For

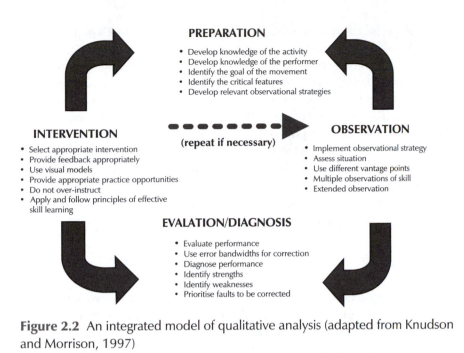

PREPARATION
- Develop knowledge of the activity
- Develop knowledge of the performer
- Identify the goal of the movement
- Identify the critical features
- Develop relevant observational strategies

INTERVENTION
- Select appropriate intervention
- Provide feedback appropriately
- Use visual models
- Provide appropriate practice opportunities
- Do not over-instruct
- Apply and follow principles of effective skill learning

(repeat if necessary)

OBSERVATION
- Implement observational strategy
- Assess situation
- Use different vantage points
- Multiple observations of skill
- Extended observation

EVALATION/DIAGNOSIS
- Evaluate performance
- Use error bandwidths for correction
- Diagnose performance
- Identify strengths
- Identify weaknesses
- Prioritise faults to be corrected

Figure 2.2 An integrated model of qualitative analysis (adapted from Knudson and Morrison, 1997)

example, a young child may learn to kick a stationary ball very accurately towards a target using a straight leg and a 'toe-poke' action, but it is unlikely that such a technique will enable the child to apply this skill in the more variable conditions that occur during match-play. In light of this potential differentiation between outcome and process measures, a more accurate assessment of skill progression may be obtained by recording both types of measures simultaneously (Horn, Williams, and Scott, 2002; Horn, Williams, Scott, and Hodges, 2005).

OUTCOME MEASURES OF PERFORMANCE

Sport skills tests

Several sports skills tests have been developed for field sports over the years (for a detailed overview, see Collins and Hodges, 2001). These skills tests provide valid, objective and reliable measures of performance on a range of skills such as passing, shooting, heading and dribbling. Collins and Hodges (2001) suggested that the scores derived from these tests may be used for a number of reasons, such as, evaluating student progress and achievement, class grading or marking, classifying learners into ability groups for individualised instruction, motivation and competition, detecting weaknesses/faults on certain skills and instructor and programme evaluation.

The use of sports skills tests was widespread in the 1960s and 1970s, particularly in North America where their use was endorsed by the dominant body in physical education at that time – the American Association for Health, Physical Education and Recreation. During this period established tests were developed for several field sports such as field-hockey, American football, lacrosse and soccer (for a description of these tests, see Collins and Hodges, 2001). Moreover, there have been attempts to design tests that combine physiological and technical measures (see Lemmink et al., 2004; and Chapter 6 in this book), to integrate a number of technical skills (Reilly and Holmes, 1983) and to develop skills tests for disabled field sports athletes (Yilla and Sherrill, 1998). Several National Governing Bodies of sport have also developed skills tests and these are now routinely employed in the grassroots development of skills (see http://www.fa-soccerstar.com/).

PRACTICAL EXAMPLE 1

A nice example of how sports skills tests may be used to evaluate the effectiveness of various practice schedules in soccer is provided by Williams and Wells (2001). In this study three groups of 12–14-year-old children were initially tested using separate sports skills tests for passing, shooting and dribbling in soccer. The children were then divided into three matched-ability groups based on their initial scores on these tests and allocated to one of three different practice structure groups. One group practised a single skill (i.e. passing, shooting or dribbling) in a blocked manner during each 60-min practice session, whereas another group practised all three skills in the same practice session for the same duration. A total of three practice sessions per week was completed over a 4-week period. The amount of practice did not differ across skills or groups, only the nature of the practice scheduling differed across practice sessions. Another group acted as controls and merely completed the pre- and post-tests. The post-test required the children to complete the same sports skills tests as administered in the pre-test. The players who practised a number of different skills in each session showed a greater relative (pre- to post-test) improvement in performance on the sports skills tests when compared to those who practised only one skill each session and the control group who did not engage in systematic practice. These results supported previous researchers in highlighting the benefits of more random practice conditions when compared to blocked practice scheduling in the learning of sports skills.

assessing skill learning and performance

Although these types of skills tests can provide valuable information, particularly when attempting to track the development of technical skills in young children, their use in older age groups and as a global measure of performance may be limited. A difficulty is that the field sports performance is multifaceted, with weaknesses in one area being compensated for by strengths in another (Williams and Ericsson, 2005). It is likely therefore that as players progress the proportion of the variance in attainment level accounted for by these skills tests reduces, implying that the predictive utility of such measures decrease over time. Nonetheless, such measures may be particularly helpful in tracking the development of skills during the early stages of skill development.

Match analysis

Contemporary match analysis systems, whether based on conventional video coding of matches or player tracking technology, provide a rich source of quantitative data on how well skills are performed during competition (see Carling et al., 2005; and Chapter 4 in this book). The collection of such data enables key performance indicators for a single player or the team as a whole to be identified. The performance indicators may relate to biomechanical, technical, tactical or behavioural measures of performance. For example, measures such as passing success rate, numbers of shots/kicks on target, proportion of tackles won and lost and the number of fouls committed may be derived from the quantitative match analysis process, and each provides some indication of technical proficiency. These measures can be derived for a single match or over a series of matches in order to provide measures of performance and learning respectively. Hughes and Bartlett (2002) provided an overview of the types of performance indicators that may be employed in field sports.

PROCESS MEASURES OF PERFORMANCE

Biomechanical measures

The field of biomechanics has grown markedly since the early published work on human locomotion in the late nineteenth century (Muybridge, 1887). The main biomechanical measures of performance describe the kinematics (i.e. motion characteristics) or kinetics (i.e. force characteristics) of movement behaviour. Kinematic measures describe the location and movements (i.e. displacement) of the limbs while a person is performing a skill. Higher order variables such as velocity (rate of change of position) and acceleration (rate of change of velocity)

33

may be derived if the time relations between the movement of one joint and another are recorded (Schmidt and Lee, 2005). The measures of displacement, velocity and acceleration can refer to either linear or angular motion. Linear motion refers to motion in a straight line as in the case of walking or running, whereas angular or rotary motion relates to motion about an axis of rotation (e.g. movement at the knee or ankle joint). Some typical angular velocity data for a soccer kick are presented in Figure 2.3.

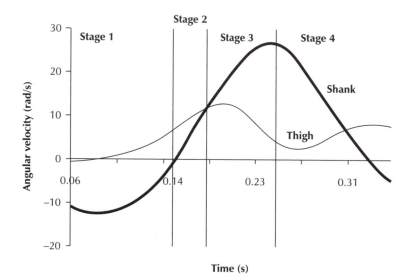

Figure 2.3 Some typical angular velocity data for the thigh and shank during a soccer kick. The four stages of the kick are marked on the graph with ball–foot contact occurring at the end of Stage 3 just as the shank reaches peak angular velocity (from Lees, 2003)

PRACTICAL EXAMPLE 2

Anderson and Sidaway (1994) provided an example of how quantitative and qualitative measures of coordination may be combined to evaluate how the kicking action changes with practice. Kinematic data were gathered from six novice soccer players as they kicked a ball towards a defined target area with maximum velocity before and after 20 regular practice sessions. A control group of three skilled participants was also employed. The two-dimensional data were captured using a video camera sampling at 60 frames per second and then digitised in order to analyse movement at the hip, knee and ankle joints. Changes in coordination were assessed qualitatively by examining topological characteristics of the relative motions of the knee and hip using angle–angle diagrams, whereas quantitative measures were derived to evaluate pre- to post-test differences in phase durations, peak linear and angular velocities at the foot, knee and hip, and changes in joint range of motion at the hip and knee. The results showed that the novice players fundamentally altered their pattern of coordination as a result of extended practice. Changes were observed in individual measures as well as in the topological characteristics of the movement such that the pattern observed was more comparable with that of the expert soccer players. Unfortunately, no attempts were made to assess more global characteristics of the movement pattern using, for example, Principal Component Analysis or cross correlation techniques.

Although this quantitative approach is ideal for detailed analysis of single elements of technique, it is less suitable for examining characteristics of the movement as a whole (Lees, 2002). However, in recent years scientists have attempted to develop techniques that evaluate global changes in movement coordination as a function of learning. When evaluating movement coordination it is necessary to examine the relationships within a single limb (e.g. intra-limb coordination involving the knee and ankle) or between two or more limbs (e.g. inter-limb coordination involving the right and left leg). A measure of coordination may describe the positional orientation between two body parts and/or their temporal phasing. At an introductory level, such relationships may be presented pictorially using angle–angle diagrams. For example, Figure 2.4 demonstrates changes in range of motion at the hip, knee and ankle after two sessions of practice a day over a 9-day period when learning a soccer chipping task (see Hodges et al., 2005).

The quantification of coordination has generally been achieved using a cross-correlation technique where, for example, the angular orientation of one joint is correlated with that of another joint. A positive correlation indicates that the two joints or limbs are 'in phase', whereas a negative correlation suggests that they are 'out of phase'. This approach has been used to describe the coordination pattern employed in soccer kicking (see Anderson and Sidaway, 1994) and the volley-ball serve (see Temprado et al., 1997). Conjugate cross-correlations may also be calculated between two data sets over several positive and negative time lags (see Amblard et al., 1994). These data may be used to calculate the relative phase between two segments which can be a valuable measure of coordination that may be tracked as the skill develops with practice (Lees, 2002). An alternative approach

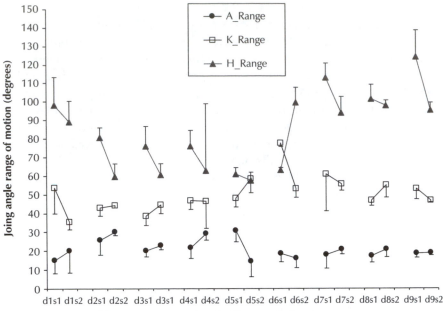

Figure 2.4 Angle–angle diagrams showing changes in range of motion at the hip, knee and ankle following successive practice sessions designed to improve kicking performance in soccer (from Hodges et al., 2005)

to using cross-correlation techniques is the normalised root mean square difference method (NoRM-D) proposed by Horn and colleagues (2005).

There are more sophisticated techniques that allow scientists to examine global rather than localised changes in motor coordination over time. Such techniques include principal component analysis (PCA, see Daffertshofer et al., 2004), cluster analysis (see Schorer et al., 2007) and artificial neural networks or Kohonen nets (see Barton, 1999). These methods require specialist knowledge and expertise and, consequently, are unlikely to be used routinely in the field setting.

Although there are various techniques available commercially for analysing movement kinematics (e.g. accelerometry, electrogoniometry), not all of these are available for general use due to the financial cost or need for detailed biomechanical knowledge. The most commonly used methods are video or optoelectronic motion detection. These systems differ in relation to cost, accuracy and ease of use with the most appropriate system largely being determined by type of data to be gathered and the manner in which they are to be integrated into the instruction process. Several digital video-based analysis systems exist on the market. These are relatively inexpensive, have a sampling rate of 25–30 frames-per-second

assessing skill learning and performance

(depending on whether the system is PAL [European] or NTSC [North American]), and provide fairly accurate, two-dimensional analysis of movement. The systems are generally very user-friendly, requiring only a limited amount of technical knowledge and training, and the user-interface software is typically very attractive and 'easy-on-the-eye', enabling coaches and analysts to feed back quantitative and qualitative information quickly and efficiently. Some of the most popular systems include Dartfish (www.dartfish.com), Silicone Coach (www.silicon coach.com) and Quintic (www.quintic.com).

High-speed film two- and three-dimensional analysis of movement skills is also possible using cinematographic techniques (see Nunome et al., 2006). Single- or multi-camera systems may be used with sampling rates varying from 100–1000 frames per second. These systems may require that key markers be digitised on a frame-by-frame basis or using 'pseudo' real-time video-based motion tracking systems (see www.simi.com). An example of a typical frame of data captured via the Simi system is shown in Figure 2.5. Although these high-speed sampling systems offer added measurement capability and sensitivity, and may be essential for a

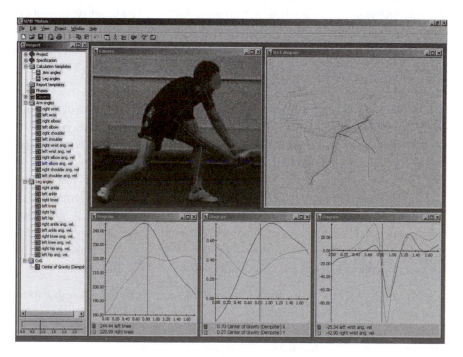

Figure 2.5 A typical frame of data involving a rugby passing action captured using the Simi Motion analysis software (image created using the Simi Motion system)

detailed analysis of rapid ballistic actions, there are potential disadvantages in relation to an increase in financial cost and need for greater technical 'know-how' and training.

Alternatives to video-based analysis software include passive and active marker systems. Passive marker systems use retro-reflective markers (spherical or hemi-spherical reflective markers) that allow for very accurate measurement of movement using multiple cameras (typically between four and eight are employed simultaneously, although more may be used for greater accuracy and to reduce the likelihood of missing markers). The cameras send out infrared light signals and detect the reflection from markers placed on the body. The angle and time delay between the original and reflected signal triangulation of the marker in space are used to calculate the x, y and z coordinates of the marker. Such systems enable three-dimensional data to be captured at sampling frequencies up to 1000 frames per second, greatly increasing the accuracy of data collection particularly when analysing rapid ballistic actions. Some examples of such systems include ProReflex produced by Qualisys (see www.qualisys.se), Vicon developed by Vicon Motion Systems/Peak Performance Technologies (see www.vicon.com) and MotionAnalysis by Motion Analysis Corp (see www.motionanalysis.com). The latest systems such as Oqus (see www.qualisys.se) can combine high-speed motion and video analysis (at 500 frames per second) and can sample at 10,000 frames per second at a reduced resolution.

Active marker systems are similar to the passive marker system, but use 'active' markers. These markers are triggered by the incoming infrared signal and respond by sending out a corresponding signal of their own. This signal is then used to triangulate the location of the marker in similar vein to passive marker systems. The advantage of this system over the passive one is that individual markers work at predefined frequencies and, therefore, have their own 'identity'. This means that no post-processing of marker locations is required. However, the systems tend to be less forgiving for 'out-of-view' markers than the passive systems; some active systems cannot be used outdoors and the markers need an external power that has to be strapped to the body. An example is the Coda motion system developed by Charnwood Dynamics (see www.codamotion.com).

The term kinetics refers to the forces produced during movement behaviour. Kinetic measures are more difficult to obtain outside the laboratory context and specialist advice is typically necessary. The most common method of measuring force is via a floor-mounted force platform (Marshall and Elliott, 1999). A piezoelectric force platform (see www.kistler.com) or strain gauge-based systems (e.g. www.amtiweb.com) may be used to record the slightest deviations in the body's centre of gravity and exact measurement of the centre of pressure (COP)

38

and ground reaction forces. As in most areas of science, technology is improving all the time and a number of platforms can now be used outside the laboratory. At a more local level, the electrical activity generated by a particular muscle can be measured by means of surface electromyography (EMG), providing a very precise measure of the timing of muscle contraction and a moderately accurate indication of the force produced. Surface electrodes are attached to the skin adjacent to the muscle and the signal generated by the muscle during contraction is amplified and recorded on a polygraph or computer for later analysis (see www.biometricsltd.com). The EMG signals may be gathered from several muscles simultaneously, providing some information on the temporal phasing or co-ordination pattern between muscle groups during motor skill performance. The data may also be used as an indication of muscle fatigue in field sports (see Rahnama et al., 2006). On the negative side, there is considerable variability in signals between individuals, making comparison difficult, and the approach is very specialised and requires considerable training and processing skills.

Psycho-physiological measures

A number of psycho-physiological measures may be used to evaluate changes in performance and learning over time. These include the recording of eye move-ments (see Chapter 3) and brain activity measures such as electroencephalography (EEG), magnetoencephalography (MEG), event-related potentials (ERP) and functional magnetic resonance imaging (fMRI). The latter neural imaging techniques are useful in identifying those parts of the brain that are active during performance and how these change with learning. These techniques were initially used in clinical and hospital settings for diagnostic purposes, but recent years have seen an increase in the number of scientists who study learning and performance at a neuro-physiological as opposed to a purely behavioural level (for a recent review, see Janelle et al., 2004).

With the exception of eye movement recording, access to such techniques remains limited and their use requires specialist training and resources. Moreover, the inherent movement requirements of most sports introduces artifacts, rendering the recording of brain activity impractical or at best necessitating that participants remain stationary throughout data collection. The difficulty is that since these measures can only be employed under very restrictive laboratory conditions there is an inherent danger in having to modify the task to such an extent that it no longer adequately captures the essence of performance (Williams and Ericsson, 2005).

CONCLUSION

In summary, the aim in this chapter was to overview some of the methods that are available for evaluating the learning and performance of motor skills in field sports. We began by highlighting the important distinction between learning and performance, and emphasising the need to partition out short-term performance effects from more permanent changes in skilled behaviour. An evaluation of the effectiveness of any instructional programme necessitates that changes in performance be accurately monitored and evaluated over time. We highlighted existing qualitative and quantitative methods for evaluating performance and identified the key differences between outcome and process measures of learning. Although most quantitative techniques often require access to sophisticated measurement technology, qualitative methods may be employed in a systematic manner by all those involved in the assessment of learning and performance. Finally, the need to rely on both outcome and process measures of performance in order to provide a thorough evaluation of learning effects was highlighted.

REFERENCES

Amblard, B., Assaiante, C., Lekhel, H. and Marchand, A.R. (1994) A statistical approach to sensorimotor strategies: conjugate cross-correlations. *Journal of Motor Behavior*, 26(2): 103–112.

Anderson, D.I. and Sidaway, B. (1994) Coordination changes associated with practice of soccer kick. *Research Quarterly for Exercise and Sport*, 65: 93–99.

Barton, G. (1999) Interpretation of gait data using Kohonen neural networks. *Gait and Posture*, 10: 85–86.

Carling, C., Williams, A.M. and Reilly, T. (2005) *The Handbook of Soccer Match Analysis: A Systematic Approach to Performance Enhancement*. London: Routledge.

Collins, D.R. and Hodges, P.B. (2001) *A Comprehensive Guide to Sports Skills Tests and Measurement*. Lanham, MD: The Scarecrow Press Inc.

Daffertshofer, A., Lamoth, C.J.C., Meijer, O.G. and Beek, P.J. (2004) PCA in studying coordination and variability: a tutorial. *Journal of Clinical Biomechanics*, 19(4): 415–428.

Hay, J.G. and Reid, G. (1988) *Anatomy, Mechanics and Human Motion*. Englewood Cliffs, NJ: Prentice-Hall.

Hodges, N.J., Hayes, S., Horn, R. and Williams, A.M. (2005) Changes in coordination, control and outcome as a result of extended practice with the non-dominant foot on a soccer skill. *Ergonomics*, 48: 1672–1685.

Horn, R.R., Williams, A.M. and Scott, M.A. (2002) Learning from demonstrations: the role of visual search during observational learning from video and point-light models. *Journal of Sports Sciences*, 20: 253–269.

Horn, R.R., Williams, A.M., Scott, M.A. and Hodges, N.J. (2005) The role of feedback and demonstrations in skill acquisition. *Journal of Motor Behavior*, 37 (4): 265–279.

Hughes, M.D. and Bartlett, R.M. (2002) The use of performance indicators in performance analysis. *Journal of Sports Sciences*, 20: 739–754.

Janelle, C.J., Duley, A.A. and Coombes, S.A. (2004) Psychophysiological and related indices of attention during motor skill acquisition. In A.M. Williams and N.J. Hodges (eds), *Skill Acquisition in Sport: Research, Theory and Practice* (pp. 282–308). London: Routledge.

Knudson, D.V. and Morrison, C.S. (1997) *Qualitative Analysis of Human Movement*. Champaign, IL: Human Kinetics.

Lees, A. (2002) Technique analysis in sports: a critical review. *Journal of Sports Sciences*, 20: 813–828.

Lees, A. (2003) Biomechanics applied to soccer skills. In T. Reilly and A.M. Williams (eds) *Science and Soccer* (pp. 109–119). London: Routledge.

Lees, A. (2007) Qualitative biomechanical assessment of performance. In M. Hughes and I. Franks (eds), *The Essentials of Performance Analysis* (pp. 162–179). London: Taylor & Francis.

Lemmink, K.A.P.M., Elferink-Gemser, M.T. and Visscher, C. (2004) Evaluation of the reliability of two field hockey specific sprint and dribble tests in young field hockey players. *British Journal of Sports Medicine*, 38: 138–142.

Magill, R.A. (2006) *Motor Learning and Control: Concept and Applications*, 8th edition. Boston, MA: McGraw-Hill.

Marshall, R.N. and Elliott, B.C. (1999) The analysis and development of technique in sport. In B.C. Elliott (ed.), *Training in Sport: Applying Sports Science* (pp. 118–144). Chichester: John Wiley & Sons.

Muybridge, E. (1887) *Animal Locomotion: An Electro-photographic Investigation of Consecutive Phases of Animal Movements*. Philadelphia: J.B. Lippincott.

Nunome, H., Lake, M., Georgakis, A. and Stergioulas, L.K. (2006) Impact phase kinematics of instep kicking in soccer. *Journal of Sports Science*, 24: 11–22.

Rahnama, N., Lees, A. and Reilly, T.P. (2006) Electromyography of selected lower-limb muscles fatigued by exercise at the intensity of soccer match-play. *Journal of Electromyography and Kinesiology*, 16: 257–263.

Reilly, T. and Holmes, M. (1983) A preliminary analysis of selected soccer skills. *Physical Education Review*, 6: 64–71.

Schmidt, R.A. and Lee, T.D. (2005) *Motor Control and Learning: A Behavioral Emphasis*, 4th edition. Champaign, Il: Human Kinetics.

Schmidt, R.A. and Wrisberg, C. (2004) *Motor Learning and Performance: A Problem-based Learning Approach*, 4th edition. Champaign, IL: Human Kinetics.

Schorer, J., Baker, J., Fath, F. and Jaitner, T. (2007) Identification of interindividual and intraindividual movement patterns in handball players of varying expertise levels. *Journal of Motor Behavior*, 39(5): 409–422.

Scott, M.A., Williams, A.M. and Horn, R.R. (2003) The co-ordination of kicking techniques in children. In G. Savelsbergh, K. Davids, J. van der Kamp and S.J. Bennett (eds), *Development of Movement Co-ordination in Children* (pp. 241–250). London: Routledge.

Temprado, J.J., Della-Grasta, M., Farrell, M. and Laurent, M. (1997) A novice-expert comparison of (intra-limb) coordination subserving the volleyball serve. *Human Movement Science*, 16: 653–676.

Williams, A.M. and Ericsson, K.A. (2005) Some considerations when applying the expert performance approach in sport. *Human Movement Science*, 24: 283–307.

41

Williams, A.M. and Hodges, N.J. (eds) (2004) *Skill Acquisition in Sport: Research, Theory and Practice*. London: Routledge.

Williams, A.M. and Hodges, N.J. (2005) Practice, instruction and skill acquisition: challenging tradition. *Journal of Sports Sciences*, 23: 637–650.

Williams, A.M. and Wells, M. (2001) Further evidence for contextual interference effects in skill acquisition. *Insight, The Football Association Coaches Journal*, 5(1): 46–47.

Yilla, A.B. and Sherrill, C. (1998) Validating the Beck Battery of quad rugby skill tests. *Adapated Physical Activity Quarterly*, 15: 155–167.

CHAPTER THREE

ANTICIPATION AND DECISION-MAKING SKILLS

INTRODUCTION

Anticipation and decision-making skills are essential to performance in all field sports. It is reported that the ability to 'read the game' and to formulate appropriate decisions under time pressure are likely to discriminate elite and sub-elite field sports athletes better than physiological and anthropometric characteristics (Williams and Reilly, 2000). The perceived importance of 'game intelligence' skills such as anticipation and decision-making to elite-level performance has led to a significant growth in empirical research focusing on these topics over the last two decades. Sports scientists have attempted to develop methods that enable these skills to be captured under controlled conditions both in the laboratory and field setting. Process-tracing measures have been employed in order to try and identify the mechanisms underpinning effective performance. Finally, researchers have attempted to examine whether the acquisition of these skills can be facilitated through relevant training programmes (see Williams and Ericsson, 2005).

In this chapter we present a brief overview of recent research on this topic in order to provide an understanding of the skills that contribute to superior anticipation and decision-making in field sports. We discuss how these component skills can be assessed in laboratory and field settings, and some of the measures that may be used to examine the strategies governing successful performance are highlighted. Finally, we provide some examples to illustrate how technology may be used to help develop these skills in field sports.

SOME KEY PERCEPTUAL–COGNITIVE SKILLS AND METHODS OF CAPTURING PERFORMANCE

Several researchers have examined whether skilled and less skilled performers in field sports may be differentiated based on standardised tests that measure aspects of visual function, such as acuity, depth perception and peripheral visual field (for a review, see Williams et al., 1999; Ward et al., 2000). This body of work has been inconclusive and there remains no strong evidence to support the claim that such measures reliably discriminate skill groups, or that attempting to enhance aspects of visual function beyond average levels would benefit sports performance (see Williams and Ward, 2003). In contrast, over recent years scientists have been successful in identifying a number of component skills that reliably contribute to superior anticipation and decision-making in field sports. These components are typically referred to as perceptual–cognitive skills, illustrating the integral role played by both perceptual and cognitive processes. These component skills are closely interrelated during expert performance with the relative importance of each varying

44

as a function of the task and situation presented (Williams and Ward, 2007). Some of these skills and the manner in which they may be assessed are reviewed in the following sections.

ADVANCE CUE UTILISATION

Skilled performers are able to anticipate opponents' intentions by picking up information from their postural orientation ahead of a key event such as foot– or stick–ball contact. For example, skilled soccer goalkeepers are able to anticipate penalty takers' intentions accurately by processing information from their run up and bodily movements just before ball contact (see Williams and Burwitz, 1993; Savelsbergh et al., 2002), whereas in a similar vein skilled field-hockey goalkeepers are able to make use of advance visual information cues when attempting to save the penalty flick (see Williams et al., 2003). The skilled performer's ability to process advance visual cues has been demonstrated in outfield players as well as goal-keepers in soccer (see Williams and Davids, 1998) and rugby (Jackson et al., 2006).

Temporal occlusion

The performer's ability to utilise advance postural cues can be assessed using a film-based temporal occlusion approach. In this approach, the action is captured on film by placing a video camera in the position normally occupied by the performer such as, for example, the goalkeeper in soccer or field-hockey. A number of opponents are then filmed from the same perspective as a goalkeeper facing the penalty in an actual match. These clips are then selectively edited to present varying extents of advance and ball flight information. For example, the film sequences may be occluded 120 ms before ball contact, 80 ms before, at ball–foot contact and 120 ms after ball contact. The goalkeepers are required typically to indicate either verbally or using a pen-and-paper response to which area of the goal the penalty kick is likely to be directed. In order to make the task as realistic as possible, the filmed images of the penalty takers may be back projected onto a large screen (e.g. 2.5 m × 3.0 m) to create a life-size viewing perspective, and goalkeepers may be asked to move physically in response to the clips (see Williams and Davids, 1998). An illustration of some temporal occlusion conditions is provided in Figure 3.1.

Skilled goalkeepers or outfield players are more accurate in their judgements than their less skilled counterparts only at the earliest occlusion conditions. Moreover, these players record response accuracy scores above chance levels even in the

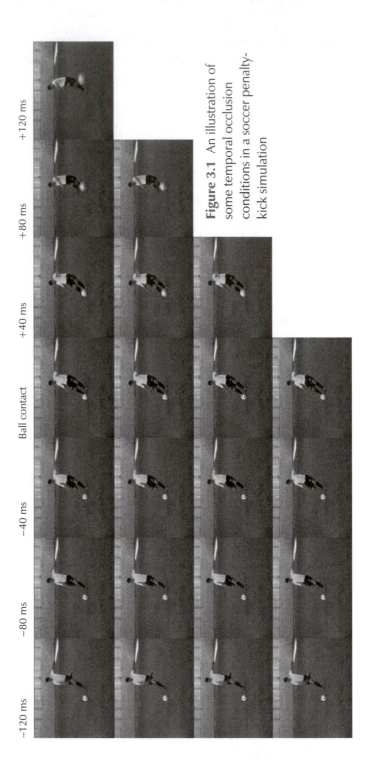

Figure 3.1 An illustration of some temporal occlusion conditions in a soccer penalty-kick simulation

pre-ball contact conditions, illustrating their ability to process advance information from the penalty taker's movements and postural orientation. The type of errors made may also be examined. Players tend to accurately predict the lateral placement of the kick at levels above chance prior to foot–ball contact, whereas errors in judging the height of the kick only reduce significantly after viewing the first portion of ball flight (Williams and Burwitz, 1993). Table 3.1 presents a breakdown of the types of errors reported across occlusion conditions in a study involving soccer penalty kicks.

This type of film-based simulation may be routinely developed and used in field sports to test anticipation skills with goalkeepers and with defensive and offensive outfield players (see Starkes, 1987; Lyle and Cook, 1984; Williams et al., 2008). Moreover, most clubs now have access to video cameras and digital editing systems that enable such test footage to be easily created and administered to large groups of players.

A field-based alternative to the film occlusion technique is provided by liquid crystal occlusion glasses (see Farrow and Abernethy, 2003). These glasses may be triggered to occlude at varying time periods relative to the key event so as to occlude vision *in situ*. The glasses may be triggered using a range of electronic devices such as infrared beams, pressure-sensitive pads and optoelectronic motion analysis systems (see Starkes et al., 1995; Oudejans and Coolen, 2003; Müller and Abernethy, 2006). Although there are some potential health and safety issues to consider when using these glasses, they are relatively simple to use and not overly expensive (see http://pages.ca.inter.net/~milgram/). The main difficulty when using field-based methods to capture anticipation skills is that there are problems in relation to test reliability, particularly when attempting to compare performance between players or groups. The repeatability of the stimuli may be improved by using trained individuals to act out the action sequences in a consistent manner.

Table 3.1 Variations in error made across the four temporal occlusion conditions as a proportion of the total errors (in %) (from Williams and Burwitz (1993)

Error category	Condition 1 120 ms prior impact	Condition 2 40 ms prior impact	Condition 3 at foot-ball impact	Condition 4 40 ms after impact
Incorrect height	71.2	67.0	68.4	40.6
Incorrect side	17.4	26.9	25.6	32.9
Height and side incorrect	11.2	6.1	6.4	26.3

47

Spatial occlusion

The spatial or event occlusion technique may be used to identify the specific information cues that players use to anticipate an opponent's intentions. This approach is similar to the temporal occlusion technique, but while the time of occluding the footage usually remains constant (e.g. ball–foot contact) different areas of the display may be occluded for the entire duration of the clip. For example, the penalty taker's hips may be occluded or the non-kicking leg. Some examples of event occlusion conditions are presented in Figure 3.2. If there is a decrement in performance when a particular area of the display is occluded the assumption is that this area provides an important source of information for the performer (see Williams and Davids, 1998; Müller et al., 2006). A repeated-measures design is employed, with participants being shown the same set of clips under different temporal occlusion conditions. It is customary to include a control condition involving the occlusion of an irrelevant display area. The same variety of presentation and response modes as illustrated with the temporal occlusion approach may be employed.

A difficulty with this approach is that the editing work involved is fairly extensive and time-consuming (Williams et al., 1999). This editing work was initially undertaken manually by overlaying opaque mats directly on to the film, but new digital editing software now enables the foreground to be replaced with the background, allowing more subtle and refined manipulations (see Commotion Pro by Pinnacle Systems – http://www.pinnaclesys.com/). Despite recent advancements in technology, the time required to produce the edited sequences remains somewhat prohibitive, at least for routine testing work, and such testing is only valuable if the practitioner or scientist is interested in determining the specific sources of information that players are using when making anticipatory judgements.

Response time paradigm

The film footage and response methods employed with the temporal occlusion approach may also be used with the response time paradigm. In this approach, the viewing duration is controlled by the participant rather than the tester. In other words, participants initiate a response as soon as they feel that they can make an accurate decision. Response time and response accuracy are recorded as dependent measures. A variety of methods can be used to measure response characteristics including pressure-sensitive floor-mounted pads, pressure switches, infrared beams and optoelectronic motion analysis systems (for a more detailed review, see Williams and Ericsson, 2005).

48

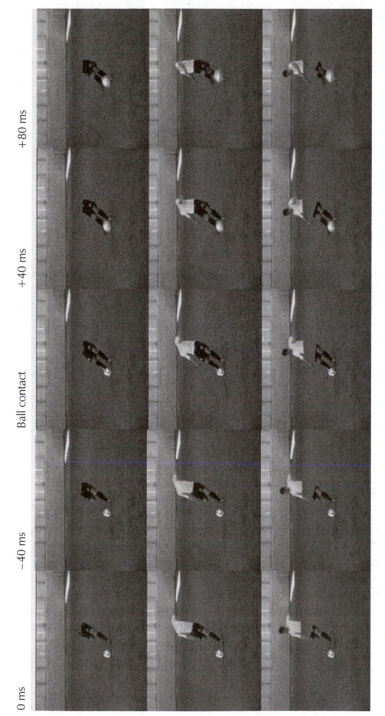

Figure 3.2 The types of spatial occlusion conditions that may be employed in soccer penalty-kick simulations

This type of paradigm has been successfully used to assess anticipation and decision-making skills during various offensive (see Helsen and Starkes, 1999) and defensive scenarios (see Williams and Davids, 1998; Williams et al., 1994) in soccer and during the penalty flick in field-hockey (see Williams et al., 2003). Skilled players typically respond more quickly than less skilled players while maintaining the same level of accuracy. A major limitation with this approach is that it is difficult to isolate the key moment when information is extracted from the display; a player may be reasonably confident of the correct decision but may wait a few moments longer to be certain that the intended response is correct. Subtle trade-offs between speed and accuracy can therefore make analysis and interpretation of findings difficult.

IDENTIFYING SEQUENCES OF PLAY

In field sports the ability to recognise an evolving pattern of play early in its development is presumed to be an important component of anticipation skill (Williams and Davids, 1995). If players can recognise a pattern of play early on then they can accurately predict how the sequence may end. This skill is usually examined using either the recall or recognition paradigm, although it should be acknowledged that neither provides a direct measure of pattern recognition (North et al., submitted).

Recognition paradigm

In the recognition paradigm, players are presented with filmed sequences of play taken directly from actual matches and involving either structured (i.e. footage involving a typical offensive move) or unstructured sequences (e.g. players warming up before a match). The level of structure presented by each sequence may be determined using an independent panel of expert coaches. These sequences typically last between 3 and 10 seconds. In a subsequent recognition phase, players are presented with a similar sample of clips, some of which have been presented in the earlier viewing phase and some of which are novel. Players are required to indicate either verbally or using a pen-and-paper response which sequences are new and which have been presented earlier. The accuracy with which players are able to recognise previously viewed clips is taken as the dependent variable.

The skilled players are more accurate than the less skilled players in recognising the structured sequences only. The proposal is that experts are able to combine low- and high-level cognitive processes. Performers are thought to extract motion information and temporal relationships between features (e.g. team-mates,

anticipation and decision-making skills

opponents, the ball) initially, before matching this stimulus representation with internal semantic concepts or templates stored in memory (Dittrich, 1999). In contrast, novices are unable to pick up important relational information and have fewer semantic concepts or templates, constraining them to employ more distinctive surface features when making such judgements (see North and Williams, 2008). The unstructured sequences are intended only as a basic measure of visual short-term memory. This approach has been used successfully in soccer (see Ward and Williams, 2003; Williams and Davids, 1995; Williams et al., 1994) and field-hockey (see Smeeton et al., 2004). The typical viewing perspective employed during this test is presented in Figure 3.3.

A novel variation to the film-based approach has been to present action sequences as point-light displays. An example of such a point-light display is presented in Figure 3.4. In this approach the players' positions and movements are presented as points of light against a black background that includes the pitch markings and position of the ball. Such sequences may be used to examine the relative importance of isolated display features and the relational information between players, the ball and pitch markings. The superiority of skilled players over novices is maintained even under the point-light conditions, implying that the crucial information is conveyed by the relative motions between players and the higher order strategic information conveyed by this information (see Williams et al., 2006). Moreover, this information emerges at relatively discrete moments as the pattern of play unfolds and is not continuously available throughout each action sequence (North and Williams, 2008).

Figure 3.3
The viewing perspective most often employed in the recognition paradigm

Figure 3.4
An attacking sequence of play in soccer presented as a point-light display (from Williams et al., 2006)

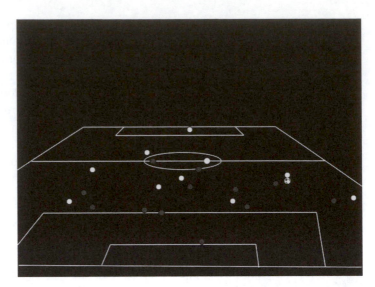

Garland and Barry (1991) examined the ability of expert and non-expert players to recall, recognise and semantically classify stimuli in American football. Following a 5-second presentation of schematic football slides, experts recalled significantly larger perceptual structures containing more elements of information than did non-experts. These differences were evident on structured trials only. In a second study using a recognition paradigm, players were presented with 56 football slides, 28 of which had been displayed previously and 28 that were new. The expert players were significantly more accurate than non-experts in recognising structured slides only. In a final study, players were instructed to separate 30 new diagrams into categories based on their own criteria. The diagrams represented various aspects of football, such as defensive, offensive and kicking situations. The experts sorted the pictures into significantly more categories than did non-experts, suggesting that they were using more discriminative sorting criteria. Non-experts adopted fairly superficial criteria such as the number of players on each diagram. In contrast, the experts used a more discriminating classification strategy containing a clear hierarchical structure. This structure included defensive techniques, offensive pass plays, offensive running plays and kicking techniques. The experts organised the diagrams in terms of their associative elements and the strategic factors evident in the picture. The results of these studies suggest that experts possess a highly refined network

anticipation and decision-making skills

of task-specific information that enables them to more accurately recall, recognise and semantically classify information in their memory than novice performers. These enhanced knowledge and more sophisticated processing strategies are assumed to contribute to the expert's superior anticipation and decision-making skills.

Recall paradigm

An alternative approach to assessing pattern recognition ability is provided by the recall paradigm. Participants are presented with structured and unstructured sequences of play lasting 3–10 seconds and are required to recall each player's position at the end of each sequence. The players' positions are entered onto a blank representation of the field of play using either a pen-and-paper response or computer-generated images of the players. The radial, vertical and horizontal error scores are computed by comparing each player's actual position with that recalled by participants. A skill effect is usually observed on the structured sequences only. The skilled players' superior knowledge of related sequences of play enables them to recall more accurately the positions of players when compared with less skilled players. This skill effect has been demonstrated in soccer (Williams et al., 1993; Williams and Davids, 1995; Ward and Williams, 2003), Rugby Union (Nakagawa, 1982), American football (Garland and Barry, 1991) and field-hockey (Starkes, 1987).

SITUATIONAL PROBABILITIES

Skilled players develop accurate expectations as to what their opponents are likely to do in advance of the actual event. The proposal is that experts are able to assign accurate probabilities to each event that may or may not occur such that they are able to allocate attention judiciously to the most important sources of information, thereby facilitating the anticipation process. The experts' superior ability to 'hedge their bets' in relation to likely event probability has been demonstrated empirically in soccer. Ward and Williams (2003) presented skilled and less skilled players with filmed action sequences from live matches. At the end of each 10-second action sequence, the filmed footage was paused and the player in possession of the ball highlighted. Participants were required to highlight the potential offensive passing options facing the player in possession of the ball and to rank these in order of their likelihood of occurrence. The final frame of action from a typical film sequence is

Figure 3.5 The final frame of action typically used in the situational probabilities paradigm (from Williams and Ward, 2007)

presented in Figure 3.5. The players' ratings were then compared to that of a panel of expert coaches. The skilled players were more accurate than the less skilled players in highlighting and ranking players most likely to receive a pass from a team-mate.

STRATEGIC DECISION-MAKING

In comparison to the number of published reports focusing on anticipation, relatively few researchers have focused on decision-making. Moreover, most of these have tended merely to measure decision-making outcomes rather than to identify the mechanisms underpinning skilled performance (see Starkes and Deakin, 1984; McMorris and Graydon, 1996). Helsen and Starkes (1999) did attempt to examine the visual search behaviours employed by expert and non-expert players when attempting to decide whether to shoot, pass or dribble the ball in a number of open and set-play situations in soccer. The decision-making scenarios were simulated by actors on the actual field of play and then captured on film so as to provide controlled and repeatable stimuli. An eye-movement registration technique was employed to analyse the visual behaviours adopted by the soccer players. Skill-based differences were reported for decision time and accuracy and systematic differences in visual behaviour were observed, with the skilled players employing fewer fixations of longer duration and focusing their gaze for a longer period of time on areas of 'free space' that could be exploited or exposed when compared to the non-experts.

Vaeyens and colleagues (2007a) reported similar results when they tested elite, sub-elite, regional and non-players using 2 vs. 1, 3 vs. 1, 3 vs. 2, 4 vs. 3 and 5 vs. 3 offensive simulations in soccer. The differences in visual search behaviours between groups were more pronounced when participants were stratified into groups based on a within-task criterion (i.e. actual performance on the decision-making test) rather than their level of attainment within the sport (see Vaeyens et al., 2007b). The experimental set-up used by Vaeyens et al. (2007a, 2007b) is illustrated in Figure 3.6.

An alternative method that may be used to evaluate decision-making skills in situ is the use of Likert-type rating scales where a panel of coaches is asked to rate players based on various components of decision-making skills (Elferink-Gemser et al., 2004). Split-screen video assessments of decision-making behaviours (Jordet, 2005) as well as high-speed film analysis of behaviour have also been used in an effort to evaluate anticipation and decision-making in actual field settings (James et al., 2006).

CHOOSING THE RIGHT PERCEPTUAL–COGNITIVE TEST AND SOME ADDITIONAL PRACTICAL CONSIDERATIONS

The difficulty for practitioners and applied sports scientists is deciding which test to administer to players. It is likely that the relative importance of each of these

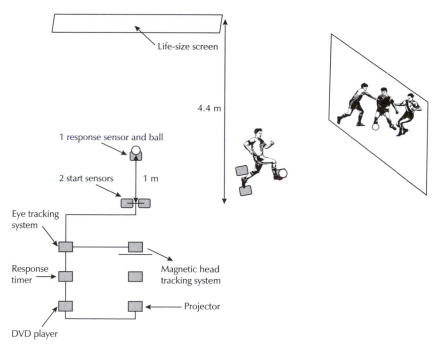

Figure 3.6 The experimental set-up used by Vaeyens et al. (2007a, 2007b) to assess decision-making skills in soccer

perceptual–cognitive skills varies from one sport to another and from one moment to the next. As illustrated in Figure 3.7, these skills are likely to be seamlessly integrated and tightly interwoven as the action unfolds on the field of play (Williams and Ward, 2007). For example, players may develop initial expectations as to likely event probabilities, and then this *a priori* judgement is confirmed or rejected through the processing of contextual information within the display, based on the relational information between players and/or the postural information arising from the player in possession of the ball. This intricate relationship is likely to be dynamic with the contextual information present within the display continuously altering the probabilities associated with every conceivable event.

One approach to solving this problem would be to adopt initially a multitask approach by administering a large battery of tests. The relative importance of these tests to performance in the sport can then be determined statistically using multivariate statistical analysis techniques (see Ward and Williams, 2003). The amount of variance between each skill group accounted for by the different perceptual–cognitive tests can be identified and their relative importance ranked. This approach provides a parsimonious method when attempting to decide which tests should be administered to players in each of the field sports.

A number of other practical considerations should be taken into account by those interested in undertaking routine testing in this area. What skill level and age of performer(s) should be employed when creating the test film? How many different

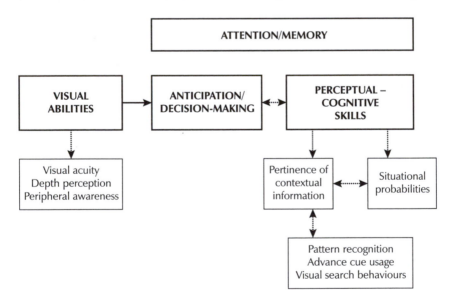

Figure 3.7 The different perceptual–cognitive skills and how they relate to anticipation and decision-making skills (from Williams and Ward, 2007)

actors should be employed? How frequently should this type of testing take place? Can the results of such tests be used for talent identification? Providing answers to such questions is not easy, particularly given that several factors can influence the advice provided. Ideally, the skill level and age of the performer(s) used to create the test footage should not differ greatly from that of the sample group to be tested. As many actors as possible should be used to create the test footage, but certainly more than one so as to eliminate the potential impact of idiosyncrasies in technique. It would seem prudent to test at least annually so as to monitor appropriately the longitudinal development of such skills. It is unclear whether such tests may be used for talent identification, mainly because there have been no longitudinal studies in this area. Although there is evidence to suggest that perceptual–cognitive skills develop at an early age (see Ward and Williams, 2003), we have no data to suggest that a player who scores well on these tests at an early age (e.g. 10–12 years) will continue to perform above average at an older age (e.g. 15–16 years). The predictive value of these tests has yet to be established. We would counsel practitioners interested in developing systematic test programmes in this area to seek advice from a suitably qualified skill-acquisition specialist prior to progressing.

IDENTIFYING THE UNDERLYING MECHANISMS: PROCESS-MEASURES OF PERFORMANCE

The discussion in the preceding sections has mainly focused on the issue of how best to capture and measure anticipation and decision-making skills. It is also important for scientists and, perhaps to a lesser extent, practitioners to identify the strategies and processes that are employed by performers when attempting to anticipate and make appropriate decisions. The measures most commonly employed by scientists include the collection of eye-movement data and verbal reports.

Eye-movement recording

An eye-movement recording system may be used to evaluate the visual search behaviours employed by participants during anticipation and decision-making tasks (for a review of this literature, see Williams et al., 2004). The head-mounted corneal reflection system is the favoured approached in the sport and exercise sciences. Perhaps the most popular system currently is the Mobile Eye System which is produced by Applied Science Laboratories (see http://www.a-s-l.com/). The Mobile Eye System is highlighted in Figure 3.8. The system is a video-based monocular system that works by detecting the position of the pupil and the

Figure 3.8
The Mobile Eye
System being
employed to
collect data in
soccer

reflection of a light source from the surface of the cornea in a video image of the eye. The relative position of these two signals is used to compute eye point-of-gaze with respect to the optics. This system is a significant advance on previous generations since it is a truly tetherless eye-tracking system for use when total freedom of movement is required and video with overlaid cursor is the desired output. This system is designed to be easily worn by an active participant. The eye-tracking optics are extremely lightweight and unobtrusive and the recording device is small enough to be worn on a belt. The eye and scene image are interleaved and saved on a DVCR tape. A recent extension enables the eye-movement data to be analysed concurrently with the athlete's physical actions using a vision-in-action paradigm (see Vickers, 2007).

The taped data are analysed to ascertain several measures of search behaviour, most notably, fixation duration, frequency of fixations, fixation areas and search

anticipation and decision-making skills

order (for a more detailed review of this technology, see Williams et al., 1999). The system is designed for indoor or outdoor use and is compact and rugged enough to be used in many sports applications. The only real disadvantage with the system is that the sampling rate is relatively low at 25 frames per second, making its use potentially unreliable when looking at interceptive actions involving catching and striking.

Verbal reports

Verbal reports can provide a valid method for identifying the processing strategies underlying performance (see Ericsson and Simon, 1993; Nisbett and Wilson, 1977). Ericsson and Simon (1993) described the conditions under which participants are able to report accurately on their mediating thought processes either concurrently during task performance, using think-aloud protocols, or retrospectively immediately after completing the task. The key factor is to ensure that individuals are properly instructed to give verbal expression to their thoughts rather than to explain their solution for the task to the experimenter or to provide a summary of the general strategy adopted. For example, rather than being instructed to report verbally the number of players considered when attempting to anticipate an opponent's intentions in field-hockey, participants should be instructed to report the thought process that comes to mind as they react to a presented representative situation. Participants normally require only 15 minutes of instruction and warm-up to give such reports, but in some dynamic situations longer periods of experience with non-domain specific tasks are necessary to become sufficiently familiar with this procedure prior to data collection. Additional effort is required to undertake a detailed task analysis of each situation prior to data collection and to transcribe, collate and analyse verbal protocols. Ward and colleagues (2003) have provided an example of how this type of approach may be used to explore perceptual–cognitive expertise in soccer.

TRAINING PERCEPTUAL–COGNITIVE EXPERTISE IN FIELD SPORTS

In recent years an increasing number of scientists have started to explore the practical utility of developing training programmes to facilitate the acquisition of perceptual–cognitive skills (for a detailed review of this literature, see Williams and Ward, 2003; Williams et al., 2005a). Several applied sports scientists have also been implementing these types of interventions with elite-level athletes, particularly within the Australian Institute of Sport system (see www.ais.org.au/psychology/stafffarrow.asp). The most often used approach has been to combine film-based simulations, with instruction as to the key sources of information underpinning successful performance, practice and feedback in relation to task performance. For example, this type of approach has been used successfully to improve the ability to pick up advance visual cues in field-hockey (see Williams et al., 2003) and soccer goalkeepers (see Williams and Burwitz, 1993). Significant improvements in anticipation may be evident following fairly short periods of practice (e.g. 60–90 minutes), with researchers recently demonstrating that the improvements observed in the laboratory also transfer to the field setting (Williams and Ward, 2003). A summary of the published studies involving the use of field sports is presented in Table 3.2.

PRACTICAL EXAMPLE 2

Williams, Ward and Chapman (2003) examined the value of perceptual–cognitive training in field-hockey goalkeepers. Twenty-four novice goalkeepers were separated into three groups of equal ability. A training group was exposed to 45 minutes of video simulation training where the key information cues underlying anticipation of the penalty flick were highlighted under normal viewing and using a 'freeze-frame' facility, and an opportunity was provided to practice under progressively shorter viewing conditions. A control group completed the pre- and post-tests, as did a placebo group that also viewed a 45-minute instructional video focusing on the technical skills involved in goalkeeping. A laboratory-based anticipation test required participants to respond to near 'life size' images of the hockey flick presented on film, whereas a measure of transfer was obtained by requiring the goalkeepers to respond to actual penalty flicks in the field taken by the same players as employed in the test film. Only participants who received perceptual–cognitive training significantly improved their response times on laboratory and field-based tests of anticipation. No differences in response accuracy were observed across groups. The anticipation skills of field-hockey goalkeepers can be improved following only 45 minutes of instruction, practice and feedback, and this improvement represents a meaningful training effect rather than the result of increased familiarity with the test environment. The training effect transferred from the laboratory to the field, highlighting the practical utility of video-based training programs in enhancing anticipation skills in field sports.

Video-based training may also be combined with instruction and practice in the field setting (see Williams et al., 2002), whereas others have reported that field-based instruction may be sufficient to elicit a training effect on its own (see Williams et al., 2004). A few researchers have explored the value of using virtual

60

Table 3.2 A summary of the published research examining the training of anticipation and decision-making skills in field sports

Authors	Year	Sport	Participants	Groups — Experimental	Control	Placebo	Laboratory test	Transfer test	Conclusions
Damron	1955	American Football	52 high-school players	■ 18 × 20-min sessions ■ 2D or 3D tachistoscopic slide presentation ■ Verbal instruction			■ Slide recognition test ■ Verbal response	■ Simulated field-based recognition test ■ Verbal response	■ No pre-test measure ■ Superior performance by 2D training group on the lab test ■ Similar performance by 2D and 3D on field
Londerlee	1967	American Football	28 high-school players	■ 9 × 10-min, 1 × 20-min sessions over 3 weeks ■ Film-based or flashcard training ■ Manual progressive temporal occlusion training ■ Low and high IQ groups				■ Simulated field-based recognition test ■ Verbal response timed using a stopwatch	■ No pre-test measure ■ Significantly quicker response times for film-based training compared to flashcard group ■ No difference in response accuracy ■ No differences between IQ groups

Table 3.2 Continued

Authors	Year	Sport	Participants	Groups			Laboratory test	Transfer test	Conclusions
				Experimental	Control	Placebo			
Christina Baressi Shaffner	1990	American Football	1 experienced player	■ 4-week training programme ■ Film-based simulation ■ Question-and-answer sessions ■ Feedback provided			■ Film-based test ■ Joystick response		■ No change in response time as a result of training ■ Significant improvement in response accuracy
Williams Burwitz	1993	Soccer penalty kick	10 novice players	■ 90 min of video simulation training ■ Key cues highlighted ■ Feedback every trial			■ Video-based anticipation test ■ Pen-and-paper response		■ Significant improvement observed on the post-test
Grant Williams	1996	Soccer 'open play'	16 novice players	■ 3 × 2-hr training sessions ■ Skills practices ■ Small-sided games ■ Key cues highlighted ■ Feedback provided	■ 3 × 2-hr training sessions ■ Skills practices ■ Small-sided games			■ Simulated small-sided 'freeze' play situations	■ Significant pre- to post-test improvement in accuracy for the experimental group only

Authors	Year	Task	Participants	Intervention	Control	Test	Results
Franks Harvey	1997	Soccer penalty kick	18 experienced players	■ Key cues highlighted ■ Video-based simulation	■ Observation of video-based simulation only	■ Video-based anticipation test ■ Press button response	■ Significant increase in accuracy for the experimental group only
McMorris Hauxwell	1997	Soccer penalty kick	30 novice players	■ Video-based simulation training (250 or 500 trials) ■ Written instructions to look for certain pre-contact cues	■ Completed pre- and post-tests only	■ Video-based anticipation test ■ Pen-and-paper response	■ Significant improvement in performance on the anticipation test for the experimental group only ■ No difference between experimental groups that viewed 250 or 500 practice trials
Williams Ward Chapman	2003	Field hockey penalty flick	24 novice goalkeepers (experienced outfield players)	■ 1 × 45 min session ■ Video-based simulation training ■ Key cues highlighted ■ Progressive temporal occlusion training and feedback	■ Completed pre- and post-tests only ■ 1 × 45-min instructional video field hockey goal-keeping skills	■ Video-based anticipation test ■ Pen-and-paper response ■ Field assessment using video analysis	■ Significant pre-post improvements in response time by experimental group

reality technology as a method of creating a suitable immersive environment for training (for a discussion, see Ward et al., 2006). Although there has been no published empirical literature focusing on the use of virtual reality technology in field sports, computer scientists based at the University of Michigan have developed an innovative system for training American football players using such technology (www-VRL.umich.edu/project/football/). Virtual reality may offer practitioners many exciting opportunities to develop realistic training stimuli in the future, but at present there are some technical difficulties, mainly related to the reduction in image quality, and practical constraints based on the financial cost, which ensure that video remains the preferred method of capturing performance.

The majority of researchers have attempted to improve the ability of players to pick up advance visual cues and very few researchers have focused on trying to improve other perceptual–cognitive skills such as the ability to recognise patterns of play or to predict likely event probabilities accurately. Only a few exceptions exist. Christina et al. (1990) used video training to successfully develop pattern-recognition and decision-making skills in American football. Williams et al. (2005a) attempted to improve players' abilities to use situational probabilities when attempting to predict pass destination in soccer. Many field sport teams use video to review recent performances and to scout on forthcoming opponents. Although this process is often rather informal, relying mainly on the observation of edited match footage access, there is scope to include more quantitative information regarding the probabilities associated with the moves and actions typically performed by forthcoming opponents. For example, analysis may reveal that the opposition typically plays to a certain pattern or that attackers are consistent (i.e. predictable) in their movement patterns. Awareness of such points markedly improves players' abilities to make accurate predictions regarding their opponents' actions. This information can be built upon in training using specific coaching practices or drills.

The lack of research focusing on whether the processes associated with identifying patterns of play and using situational probabilities can be trained may be because there is limited knowledge as to the mechanism underpinning effective perform-ance of these skills. Several questions remain unanswered. What are the essential information sources that facilitate the identifying patterns of play? Are all the players important or is it merely a small cluster of players that gives each pattern its unique perceptual signature? In the case of situational probabilities, what information should be conveyed to the learner? Which probabilities are important and which ones should be ignored? Systematic programmes of research are required to determine the key sources of information underlying the effective performance of these skills in field sports.

64

Another question for scientists and practitioners is how should the effectiveness of this type of training be evaluated? The best solution to this problem can perhaps best be achieved through collaboration between scientists and practitioners. The opinions of coaches could be gleaned before and after training by developing behavioural assessment scales (see Elferink-Gemser et al., 2004; Oslin et al., 1998), whereas a panel of expert coaches could be used to assess anticipation and decision-making skills over a number of matches to improve objectivity and reliability, respectively. The validity of these assessment scales could be substantiated by identifying behavioural indicators of anticipation and decision-making coupled with qualitative and quantitative video analysis. Also, many sports keep seasonal records on various aspects of performance such as the proportion of penalty kicks saved, number of pass interceptions per match or successful pass completion rates. Although it may be difficult to apportion improvements directly to the intervention employed, data obtained using these types of records may help substantiate the validity of the training protocol. It may prove much easier to assess training improvements in more 'closed skill' situations such as the penalty kick or flick in soccer and field-hockey, respectively. In the latter situations, quantitative data on success rates usually exist and components of performance may be examined in situ using modern measurement technology such as high-speed film analysis (see Williams et al., 2003).

Although there is evidence to demonstrate the benefits of employing perceptual–cognitive training to facilitate the development of anticipation and decision-making skills in field sports, there remains a paucity of researchers working in this area. Undoubtedly, more questions than answers remain. At what age and skill level should players engage in this type of instruction? What types of simulation training and instruction are likely to be most beneficial for performance enhancement? How should this type of training be structured and implemented for effective training? Answers to these questions have to some extent been presented elsewhere in the literature (see Williams and Ward, 2003; Williams et al., 2005b; Ward et al., 2006), yet a lack of clear consensus highlights the need for further empirical research. Moreover, scientists and practitioners need to work more closely together to promote understanding and develop effective training interventions that may be routinely used with elite athletes in field sports.

CONCLUSION

In summary, the aim in this chapter was to examine how anticipation and decision-making skills may be assessed in field sports. Initially, we reviewed some of the key perceptual–cognitive skills that contribute to effective anticipation and decision-making. We then highlighted the range of methods and measures that may be employed to evaluate these skills in laboratory and field settings. Finally, we briefly illustrated how the development of perceptual–cognitive skills may be facilitated through relevant training interventions. Although empirical research on anticipation and decision-making in sport remains limited, certainly in comparison to more established areas of study such as body composition and strength/power training, it is ironic that at the elite level factors related to 'game intelligence' are more likely to discriminate successful from less successful field sport athletes.

REFERENCES

Christina, R.W., Barresi, J.V. and Shaffner, P. (1990) The development of response selection accuracy in a football linebacker using video training. *The Sport Psychologist*, 4: 11–17.

Damron, C.F. (1955) Two and three dimensional slide images using tachistiscope training techniques in instructing high school football players defenses. *Research Quarterly*, 26: 26–43.

Dittrich, W.H. (1999) Seeing biological motion: Is there a role for cognitive strategies? In A. Braffort, R. Gherbi, S. Gibet, J. Richardson and D. Teil (eds), *Gesture-Based Communication in Human-Computer Interaction* (pp. 3–22). Berlin, Heidelberg: Springer-Verlag.

Elferink-Gemser, M.T., Visscher, C., Richart, H. and Lemmink, K.A.P.M. (2004) Development of the tactical skills inventory for sports. *Perceptual and Motor Skills*, 99: 883–895.

Ericsson, K.A. and Simon, H.A. (1993) *Protocol Analysis: Verbal Reports as Data* (Rev. edition). Cambridge, MA: Bradford Books/MIT Press.

Farrow, D. and Abernethy, A.B. (2003) Do expertise and the degree of perception-action coupling affect natural anticipatory performance? *Perception*, 32: 1127–1139.

Franks, I.M. and Harvey, T. (1997) Cues for goalkeepers: high-tech methods used to measure penalty shot response. *Soccer Journal* (May/June), 30–38.

Garland, D.J. and Barry, J.R. (1991) Cognitive advantage in sport: the nature of perceptual structures. *The American Journal of Psychology*, 104: 211–228.

Grant, A. and Williams, A.M. (1996) Training cognitive decision making in intermediate youth soccer players. Unpublished manuscript, Liverpool John Moores University.

Helsen, W.F. and Starkes, J.L. (1999) A multidimensional approach to skilled perception and performance in sport. *Applied Cognitive Psychology*, 13: 1–27.

Jackson, R.C., Warren, S. and Abernethy, B. (2006) Anticipation skill and susceptibility to deceptive movement. *Acta Psychologica*, 123(3): 355–371.

James, N., Caudrelier, T. and Murray, S. (2006) The use of anticipation by elite squash players. *Journal of Sports Sciences*, 23: 1249–1250.

Jordet, G. (2005) Applied cognitive sport psychology (ACSP) in team ball sports: an ideological approach. In R. Stelter and K.K. Roessler (eds) *New Approaches to Sport and Exercise Psychology* (pp. 147–174). Oxford: Meyer and Meyer Sports Books.

66

Londerlee, B.R. (1967). Effect of training with motion pictures versus flash cards upon football play recognition. *Research Quarterly*, 38(2): 202–207.

Lyle, J. and Cook, M. (1984) Non-verbal cues and decision-making in games. *Momentum*, 9: 20–25.

McMorris, T. and Graydon, J. (1996) Effect of exercise on the decision-making performance of experienced and inexperienced soccer players. *Research Quarterly for Exercise and Sport*, 67: 109–114.

McMorris, T. and Hauxwell, B. (1997) Improving anticipation of soccer goalkeepers using video observation. In T. Reilly, J. Bangsbo and M. Hughes (eds), *Science and football III* (pp. 290–294). London: E & FN Spon.

Müller, S. and Abernethy, B. (2006) Batting with occluded vision: an in situ examination of the information pick-up and interceptive skills of high- and low-skilled cricket batsmen. *Journal of Science and Medicine in Sport*, 9: 446–458.

Müller, S., Abernethy, B. and Farrow, D. (2006) How do world-class cricket batsmen anticipate a bowler's intention? *The Quarterly Journal of Experimental Psychology*, 59(12): 2162–2186.

Nakagawa, A. (1982) A field experiment on recognition of game situations in ball games: in the case of static situations in rugby football. *Japanese Journal of Physical Education*, 27: 17–26.

Nisbett, R.E. and Wilson, T.D. (1977) Telling more than we can know: verbal reports on mental processes. *Psychological Review*, 84, 231–259.

North, J.S. and Williams, A.M. (2008) The critical time period for information extraction when identifying patterns of play in soccer. *Research Quarterly for Exercise and Sport*, 79: 268–273.

North, J.S., Williams, A.M, Hodges, N.J., Ward, P. and Ericsson, K.A. (submitted) Perceiving patterns in dynamic action sequences: investigating the processes underpinning stimulus recognition and anticipation skill.

Oslin, J., Mitchell, M. and Griffin, L. (1998) Game performance assessment instrument (GPAI): development and preliminary validation. *Journal of Teaching in Physical Education*, 17: 231–243.

Oudejans, R.R.D. and Coolen, H. (2003) Human kinematics and event control: on-line movement registration as a means for experimental manipulation. *Journal of Sports Sciences*, 21: 567–576.

Savelsbergh, G.J.P., Williams, A.M., van der Kamp, J. and Ward, P. (2002) Visual search, anticipation and expertise in soccer goalkeepers. *Journal of Sports Sciences*, 20: 279–287.

Smeeton, N., Ward, P. and Williams, A.M. (2004) Transfer of perceptual skill in sport. *Journal of Sports Sciences*, 19: 3–9.

Starkes, J.L. (1987) Skill in field hockey: the nature of the cognitive advantage. *Journal of Sport Psychology*, 9: 146–160.

Starkes, J. L. and Deakin, J. (1984) Perception in sport: a cognitive approach to skilled performance. In W.F. Straub and J.M. Williams (eds), *Cognitive Sport Psychology* (pp. 115–128). Lansing, NY: Sport Science Associates.

Starkes, J. L., Edwards, P., Dissanayake, P. and Dunn, T. (1995) A new technology and field test of advance cue usage in volleyball. *Research Quarterly for Exercise and Sport*, 66: 162–167.

Vaeyens, R., Lenoir, M., Williams, A.M., Mazyn, L. and Phillippaerts, R.M. (2007a) The effects of task constraints on visual search behaviour and decision-making skill in youth soccer players. *Journal of Sport and Exercise Psychology*, 29: 147–169.

Vaeyens, R., Lenoir, M., Williams, A.M., Mazyn, L. and Philippaerts, R.M. (2007b) Visual search behavior and decision-making skill in soccer. *Journal of Motor Behavior*, 39(5): 395–408.

Vickers, J.N. (2007) *Perception, Cognition, and Decision Training: The Quiet Eye in Action*. Champaign, IL: Human Kinetics.

Ward, P. and Williams, A.M. (2007) Perceptual and cognitive skill development in soccer: the multidimensional nature of expert performance. *Journal of Sport and Exercise Psychology*, 25(1): 93–111.

Ward, P., Williams, A.M. and Ericsson, K.A. (2003) Underlying mechanisms of perceptual-cognitive expertise in soccer. *Journal of Sport and Exercise Psychology*, 25: S136.

Ward, P., Williams, A.M. and Hancock P. (2006) Simulation for performance and training. In K.A. Ericsson, P. Hoffman, N. Charness and P. Feltovich (eds), *Handbook of Expertise and Expert Performance* (pp. 243–262). Cambridge: Cambridge University Press.

Ward, P., Hodges, N.J., Williams, A.M. and Starkes, J. (2007) The role of deliberate practice in the development of expert performers. *High Ability Studies*, 18: 119–153.

Ward, P., Williams, A.M. and Loran, D. (2000) The development of visual function in elite and sub-elite soccer players. *International Journal of Sports Vision*, 6: 1–11.

Williams, A.M. and Burwitz, K. (1993) Advance cue utilization in soccer. In T.P. Reilly, J. Clarys and A. Stibbe (eds), *Science and Football II* (pp. 239–244). London: E & FN Spon.

Williams, A.M. and Davids, K. (1995) Declarative knowledge in sport: a byproduct of experience or a characteristic of expertise? *Journal of Sport and Exercise Psychology*, 7(3): 259–275.

Williams, A.M. and Davids, K. (1998) Visual search strategy, selective attention, and expertise in soccer. *Research Quarterly for Exercise and Sport*, 69: 111–128.

Williams, A.M. and Ericsson, K.A. (2005) Some considerations when applying the expert performance approach in sport. *Human Movement Science*, 24: 283–307.

Williams, A.M. and Reilly, T. (2000) Talent identification and development in soccer. *Journal of Sports Sciences*, 18: 657–667.

Williams, A.M. and Ward, P. (2003) Perceptual expertise: development in sport. In J. L. Starkes and K.A. Ericsson (eds), *Expert Performance in Sports: Advances in Research on Sport Expertise* (pp. 220–249). Champaign, IL: Human Kinetics.

Williams, A.M. and Ward, P. (2007) Perceptual-cognitive expertise in sport: exploring new horizons. In G. Tenenabum and R. Eklund (eds), *Handbook of Sport Psychology*, 3rd edition (pp. 203–223). New York: John Wiley and Sons.

Williams, A.M., Davids, K., Burwitz, L. and Williams, J.G. (1993) Cognitive knowledge and soccer performance. *Perceptual and Motor Skills*, 76: 579–593.

Williams, A.M., Davids, K., Burwitz, L. and Williams, J.G. (1994) Visual search strategies of experienced and inexperienced soccer players. *Research Quarterly for Exercise and Sport*, 5: 127–135.

Williams, A.M., Davids, K. and Williams, J.G. (1999) *Visual Perception and Action in sport*. London: E & FN Spon.

Williams, A.M., Heron, K., Ward, P. and Smeeton, N.J. (2005a) Using situational probabilities to train perceptual and cognitive skill in novice soccer players. In T. Reilly, J. Cabri and D. Arajuo (eds), *Science and Football V* (pp. 337–340). London: Taylor & Francis.

Williams, A.M., Hodges, N.J., North, J. and Barton, G. (2006) Perceiving patterns of play in dynamic sport tasks: investigating the essential information underlying skilled performance. *Perception*, 35: 317–332.

Williams, A.M., Janelle, C.M. and Davids, K. (2004) Constraints on the search for visual information in sport. *International Journal of Sport and Exercise Psychology*, 2: 301–318.

Williams, A.M., Ward, P. and Chapman, C. (2003) Training perceptual skill in field hockey: Is there transfer from the laboratory to the field? *Research Quarterly for Exercise and Sport*, 74: 98–103.

Williams, A.M., Ward, P., Allen, D. and Smeeton, N. (2004) Training perceptual skill using on court instruction in tennis: perception versus perception and action. *Journal of Applied Sport Psychology*, 16(4): 1–11.

Williams, A.M., Ward, P. and Smeeton, N.J. (2005b) Perceptual and cognitive expertise in sport: implications for skill acquisition and performance enhancement. In A.M. Williams and N.J. Hodges (eds), *Skill Acquisition in Sport: Research, Theory and Practice* (pp. 328–348). London: Routledge.

Williams, A.M., Ward, P., Knowles, J.M. and Smeeton, N.J. (2002) Perceptual skill in a real-world task: training, instruction, and transfer in tennis. *Journal of Experimental Psychology: Applied*, 8(4): 259–270.

Williams, A.M., Ward, P., Smeeton, N.J. and Ward, J. (2008) Task specificity, role, and anticipation skill in soccer. *Research Quarterly for Exercise and Sport*, 79: 429–433.

CHAPTER FOUR

MATCH ANALYSIS

INTRODUCTION

A key task for any coach is to analyse performance and provide players with the feedback necessary for skill learning and performance enhancement. The primary function of match analysis is to provide information about team and/or individual playing performance. Information on performance is obtained through the use of notational analysis which is a technique for producing a permanent record of the events being analysed (James, 2006). Notational analysis involves categorising what actions have occurred within a game, enabling coaches to create an objective statistical account of the match to use when giving feedback. The coaching process generally comprises a number of steps or cycles and the importance of analysing play is highlighted in Figure 4.1. Initial observation and analysis of play, then interpretation of the information obtained on match performance, are necessary before feedback can be given to players. Subsequent practices may then be planned and organised with the aim of providing supporting preparation for competition.

Over the last 10 years, the increased use of match analysis in elite sport has led to the formation of numerous companies selling specialist software and services. This period has also witnessed acceptance of the need within clubs and institutions for specialised sports science staff known as performance analysts who are trained to study match-play. Similarly, dedicated education schemes are now allowing coaches to understand and make use of match-analysis software. At elite levels of sport, the use of digital video and computer technology in training and competition to collect data and provide feedback on play has become prominent in recent years. Innovations in technology are now providing coaches with fast, accurate, objective and relevant information allowing them to dissect each and every aspect of the game. Modern computerised systems facilitate the technical, tactical and physical analysis of performance and have enhanced the scientific approach to field sports. Data acquired through match analysis are used to help coaches make informed judgements about playing performance and avoid incomplete or

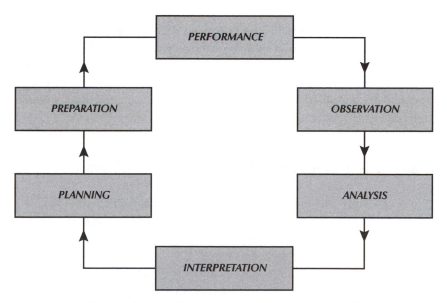

Figure 4.1 The coaching cycle highlighting the importance of observation and analysis (adapted from Carling et al., 2005)

inaccurate recollection of various aspects of game-play. The dynamic nature of field sports means that coaches may only observe critical aspects of play (commonly referred to as 'highlighting') and can miss key events in other areas of the pitch. Match analysis data may also help avoid personal bias and reduce the effect of emotions which may distort a coach's impression of the match.

One of the main uses of match analysis by coaches for their own team purposes is to provide information to identify weaknesses in various areas of performance. Gathering large amounts of data allows the identification of strengths and weaknesses of the team and/or individual (Nevill et al., 2008). However, effective employment of match analysis is dependant on selecting what information is important and how it can be used to improve performance (Carling et al., 2005). On the basis of the information selected, the subsequent aim would be to iron out these problems by applying and integrating the results into specific training drills and programmes. Information on positive aspects of play, such as a pre-planned set-play which was successful, can also be underlined by coaches as this feedback will have a reinforcing effect and increase player self-confidence. Many coaches also use data from competition to analyse the play of opposition teams and their players in order to try and counter their strengths and exploit their weaknesses. Early identification of the strategies and tactics of a future opponent may allow teams to gain an advantage as they will have a good idea of what to expect when the contest takes place. Relevant training drills can then be put into practice with the aim of offsetting the opponent's strengths and exploiting any weaknesses.

The very latest developments in computerised video analysis technologies employed in field sports to assess performance are reviewed in this chapter. A brief section on using hand-based match analysis is also provided. Some examples of data on physical, technical and tactical performance that can be obtained through match analysis are presented. Finally, relevant examples taken from the literature on match analysis are provided.

HAND-BASED MATCH ANALYSIS SYSTEMS

Whilst computerised match-analysis systems can potentially reduce the workload involved in analysing matches and enable information to be stored in databases, often with accompanying video footage, such systems are nonetheless expensive and only remain an option for clubs at the elite level. Fortunately, however, manual hand-based notation systems can be developed very easily, providing answers to questions posed by the majority of coaches, particularly at lower levels of the game. Such notation systems are very cheap (pen and paper), adaptable (easily personalised for own requirements) and simple data sets are readily available for dissemination. These systems tend to concentrate on tactical and technical aspects of performance as analysing physical performance on paper by tracing a player's movement pathway is too prone to error and does not yield any useful information.

The match analysis process (whether manual or computerised) is based on using a notation system that enables the observer to record four key factors: these are the performer involved, the action itself, the location (position) of the action and the time at which the action took place (Robertson, 2002). Information on the player simply involves recording his or her name or shirt number. Notating the position of actions can be straightforward, for example, these can be recorded according to the half of the pitch (own half) or in more detail (opposition penalty area). Graphical pitch representations divided into zones are often used for more accurate marking of positional information. Action time can be recorded as the exact time of each action or simply counted and summed for separate segments (e.g. every 10 minutes for a rugby match). Finally, action types can be provided at different levels, from the input of a simple number (total) of one-on-one contests to the categorisation of this total figure into numbers of headers, tackles and pressings.

There are typically four stages involved when using a hand-based notation system. These are deciding the quantity and type of information needed and why, designing the hand-based notation system, checking on the accuracy of this data and collating and presenting the findings. The basic components in almost every hand-based match-analysis system are player, action and position. More sophisticated systems may also measure time and sequence of events. A simple notation system may employ a tally sheet to record match actions as seen in Table 4.1. Positional data can be notated by breaking down the pitch into numbered zones or cells as highlighted in Figure 4.2. Such systems can be created using pen and paper or via a basic word-processing or graphics software package.

In determining the most appropriate method for recording data, coaches must consider the attention required to make an entry onto the analysis sheet, the speed

Table 4.1 A simple tally sheet to record frequency counts of successful and unsuccessful actions

	Successful actions	Unsuccessful actions
Tackle	✓✓✓✓✓	✓✓
Header	✓✓✓	✓✓
Interception	✓	
Free-kick (won/conceded)	✓✓	✓✓✓
Total	11	7

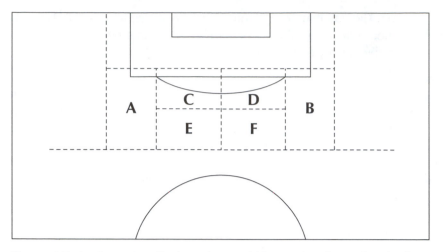

Figure 4.2 A schematic tally sheet that could be used to determine the frequency count of passes from central areas into the penalty area or shots on goal

with which data can be entered and the ease of collating the information at the end of the analysis. There is a clear trade-off between the level of detail required and the speed with which such information can be provided. The more complex the data the longer it takes to collect and process, so observers should record only what is needed. Coaches should resist the temptation to code every aspect of the game. Simple notation systems that focus on a small number of actions that are relevant to coaches are of greater value than those that produce reams of data – more is not always better as far as match analysis is concerned.

Coaches often decide on what information is useful according to their personal philosophy, previously defined objectives and previous performances of the team (Franks et al., 1983). It may be wise to analyse performance initially at a general level, before focusing on any one specific aspect of the game. For example, analysing performance on a team scale can give indicators of successful or unsuccessful key match events which may then be examined further to determine which team unit and which individual players were responsible. These main areas are often called Key Performance Indicators (KPI). Primary analysis may simply involve looking at the total time spent in possession by a team and the number of shooting opportunities it created. Secondary analysis may break this information down further to see which player(s) lost possession, how and where it was lost and the subsequent route taken to goal. For further information on creating and using hand-notation systems, see Hughes and Franks (2004) and Carling et al. (2005).

The main barriers to adopting these manual methods of performance analysis are the perceived complexity and the significant investment of time needed to code, analyse and interpret the data (James, 2006). Hand-notation systems are also often combined with analogue video-cassette recordings of game performance. These combined methods for collecting data tend to be both time-consuming and tedious. Manual searching (rewinding and fast forwarding) through video cassettes and analysing data takes time. Similarly, efficient archiving of data is difficult as these records are often written on sheets of paper. Furthermore, some of the data-collection methods are subject to inaccuracies, notably when recording positional information.

The ultimate problem facing the analyst is how best to transform oceans of data into meaningful interpretations (Hughes and Franks, 2004). Once the data have been collected, these need to be collated and presented in a simple, easy to understand format (such as in graphical format or summary tables). The processing and presenting of data obtained from hand-based analysis can be extremely time-consuming. For detailed advice on how to present data from match analysis, the reader is referred to Carling et al. (2005). These disadvantages have led to the development of match-analysis systems using computers and digital video footage.

MATCH ANALYSIS USING COMPUTER AND DIGITAL VIDEO TECHNOLOGY

Video provides a powerful medium for obtaining, evaluating and presenting information on sports performance. It offers coaches an opportunity to observe situations more closely and analyse why and how decisions were made (Robertson, 2002). Video is both an appealing and familiar means of communication between players and coaches during team talks. Footage of competition and training allows the movements and actions of players to be recorded, observed, analysed and evaluated and provides both qualitative and quantitative information on playing performance.

Contemporary digital video analysis systems used by coaches have streamlined the entire match-analysis process and improved the accuracy of performance data. Advances in the power of computer technology, its user-friendliness and the quality of audio-visual equipment combined with a major reduction in cost have allowed match analysis to play a bigger role in the contemporary coaching process. Combining the playback of high-quality video footage obtained from digital cameras with the input of selected match actions through a dedicated computer interface has eased the process of data collection. Methods of entering data have vastly improved over the years thanks to user-friendly interfaces combined with advanced inputting technology such as voice recognition and touch screens. Electronic event indexing through a digital time code also eases the workload as the precise time is automatically recorded for each inputted action as the analyst works through the video.

Real-time analysis of live match performance is now a reality and coaches can access specific information at any time during the game (e.g. during the half-time period or immediately after the final whistle, while the performance is still fresh in their mind). Contemporary systems automatically provide various forms of easy-to-understand data presentation such as graphs or tables. A list of the various commercial systems currently used to analyse performance in field sports is presented in Table 4.2.

The advent of digital video has taken the analysis process a step further as it enables video footage of performance to be recorded directly onto a computer and analysed in real time. The footage can then be accessed, observed, replayed, edited, re-edited and archived at the simple touch of a button. For example, important match actions can be immediately accessed and played back to highlight and break down the points in question. The positional, technical and behavioural performances of players may then be analysed image by image, in slow motion and/or freeze-framed to highlight problematic areas. Slow-motion playback in high quality combined with special effects such as synchronised split-screen visualisation or image blending can be used to compare two actions. Similarly, graphical information such as text or drawing tools may be added to video sequences to help coaches and players to pinpoint areas requiring improvement.

Digital video has also helped to streamline and optimise coach/player team talks. For example, selected sequences of game highlights on any particular theme can now easily be edited and put together so that coaches can directly access and highlight the most important actions. For example, through a search logic facility (using information on factors such as time, position, player or action), the coach can interrogate the software to generate a list of every time a hockey team won back possession in the opposition's half. A short edited sequence of these particular actions can easily be generated and viewed by players. These actions can be complemented at any time with corresponding statistical information such as the frequency of the actions used to win possession (interceptions, tackles). Some contemporary video analysis systems also have a built-in database to store and provide statistical information on previous performance automatically. In addition, such databases provide the possibility of trend analysis to enable comparison of performances over a particular course of time such as over an intense period of matches or over the whole season.

One example of a modern system is the Sportscode digital video analysis system (see http://www.sportstecinternational.com/) developed by the Australian company Sportstecinternational (Figure 4.3). This powerful cutting-edge system has been

Table 4.2 Some of the computerised video analysis systems used in field sports currently available on the market

Company	Country	Software	Website
Digital video-based statistical analysis			
Dartfish	Switzerland	DartTrainer	http://www.dartfish.com/
Digital Soccer Project	Italy	Digital Soccer	http://www.digitalsoccer.it/
Elite Sports Analysis	UK	Focus X2	http://www.elitesportsanalysis.com/
MasterCoach Int. GmbH	Germany	Mastercoach	http://www.mastercoach.de/
Pinnacle Systems	USA	SportsEdit	http://www.pinnacleteamsports.com/
PosiCom AS	Norway	Posicom	http://www.posicom.no/
REM Informatique	France	StadeXpert	http://www.af-d.com/
Scanball	France	Scanfoot	http://www.scanball.com/
SoftSport Inc	USA	SecondLook	http://www.softsport.com/
Sportstec	Australia	SportsCode	http://www.sportstecinternational.com/
Sport-Universal SA	France	Videopro	http://www.sport-universal.com/
Touch-Line Data Systems Ltd	UK	SoccerScout	http://www.touch-line.co.uk/
Videocoach	UK	Ascensio system	http://www.thevideocoach.com/
Wige Media AG	Germany	Wige data	http://www.wige-mic.de/

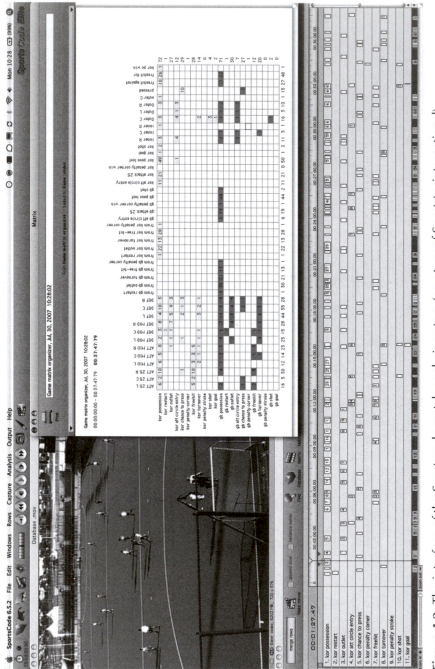

Figure 4.3 The interface of the Sportscode match-analysis system (courtesy of Sportstecinternational)

adopted by many elite clubs worldwide due to its capacity to obtain, analyse and present technical and tactical performance data thanks to a high level of portability, flexibility and user-friendliness. One of the major advantages of the Sportscode system is that it can be tailored or personalised for the specific needs of different sports and individual coaches. For example, a coach may prefer to concentrate on defensive actions and can therefore customise the interface to include specific, more detailed coding keys on the desired areas of performance. The company Sportstecinternational has recognised that one size does not fit all and as a result has developed a suite of sports video analysis software options that cover a wide range of needs and budgets. This flexibility is important as not all clubs (even at elite levels) have the financial capacity to access computerised video analysis.

However, computerised digital video-based analysis does have certain limitations. For example, pitch positions of match events are often determined by guesswork and clicking the position on a schematic pitch representing the playing area. This procedure will to a certain extent lead to the production of inaccurate positional data. Furthermore, as the video used is often restricted to a single camera viewpoint, the performance analysis is limited to only the player in possession and those around the ball. Valuable 'off the ball' information such as player marking may be missed due to footage concentrating on the player in possession. This lack of 'off the ball' information is particularly important as players are often in possession of the ball for only a small part of the match duration (e.g. 2–3% in soccer). At any time, traditional video footage may at best allow visualisation of only half the players on the pitch. There may be further problems if footage obtained from television is used due to the occurrence of action replays. Whilst the replay is being shown, the viewer cannot analyse the ongoing match-play and may miss several actions.

The apparent lack of precision and 'missed' tactical and technical data has led to the development of high-tech analysis systems for tracking players and reconstructing match-play. The Viewer™ software developed by Sport-Universal Process is used by many top soccer and Rugby Union teams to dissect play through digital recordings obtained from a multiple-camera system. The overhead two-dimensional animated representation software (see Figure 4.4) is especially useful for examining tactical play such as team shape or playing style and can be combined with video from any of the multi-camera viewpoints. The graphical line seen in Figure 4.4 helps the coach to visualise and evaluate team shape. The coach can examine what every player is (or is not!) doing for the entire duration of the match, whatever his or her position on the pitch.

Figure 4.4 The AMISCO Pro Match Viewer software (courtesy of Sport-Universal Process)

VIDEO AND STATISTICAL ANALYSIS OF TACTICAL AND TECHNICAL PERFORMANCE

Team sports involve many strategic, tactical and technical dimensions which give rise to many different coaching questions. Success is dependant on these dimensions and it is only by their analysis and evaluation that a complete picture and understanding of performance can be achieved. Tactical and technical performance can be analysed quantitatively (frequencies, percentages) or qualitatively (edited video recordings, animated game reconstructions). Quantitative match analysis is invaluable to the coach in that it can help create an objective unbiased view of events and provide a solid platform upon which to make informed decisions as to successful strategy and tactics. However, some form of qualitative analysis from video footage or match reconstructions may be needed as pure statistical information may not always paint a true picture of a player's performance or effort. For example, a midfield player may have a high percentage failure rate when making forward passes, yet when the coach examines the video recording, he or she may decide that the quality of the forward runs of the attacking players may be partly to blame for the low success rate.

Qualitative analysis of defensive performance may simply involve observing and evaluating technical aspects of play such as a defender's heading ability, tactical aspects such as team organisation during set-plays or behavioural aspects such as the confidence of a goalkeeper when dealing with crosses. Although this type of analysis is subjective in nature, coaches at elite levels use their experience and know-how to observe and judge players' technical and tactical performance from video. Information provided by the video footage may, if necessary, be backed up by relevant statistical information to confirm the coach's interpretation of the performance. The same qualitative analysis of defensive performance mentioned above can also be notated and examined up to a certain extent from a quantitative point of view by evaluating the number of headers won or lost by the defender, goals conceded by the team at set-plays and crosses successfully or unsuccessfully dealt with by the goalkeeper.

In field sports, quantitative analyses of performance may look at KPI such as set-plays as significant proportions of goals and points are scored from corner, line out, free-kick or penalty situations. Breen et al. (2006) reported that set-plays accounted for 36.1% of goals scored in the last soccer World Cup (Table 4.3). Van Rooyen et al. (2006a) presented data showing that the winning team in the 2003 Rugby World Cup (England) scored more points from penalties obtained than any other team. Successful soccer teams are generally far more efficient than their opponents at scoring from set-plays. A recent study on the 2006 World Cup reported a set-play to goal ratio of 1:7.5 for successful teams (semi-finalists) compared to 1:14 for unsuccessful opponents (Bell-Walker et al., 2006).

Statistical information on where teams obtained possession can have important tactical implications for creating chances and scoring goals. In professional soccer, goals are generally created from winning back possession (mainly through tackles and interceptions) in one's own defensive and midfield areas although up to one third may originate from attacking areas. In elite field-hockey, goals were more likely to be scored if the ball was repossessed in the attacking 25-yard (22.9-m) area compared with the other areas of the pitch (Sunderland et al., 2006).

Over the years, match analysis has also concentrated on examining the effectiveness of differing styles of play in creating chances and scoring points/goals. Recent research on soccer has shown that the most successful teams are generally the ones who can vary their style of play between a short- and long-ball type of game. Nevertheless, whatever the playing style of teams, the majority of goals are scored

Table 4.3 Source of goals in 2006 Soccer World Cup (Breen et al., 2006)

	Total	%
Open play	90	61.2
Set play	40	27.3
Penalty	13	8.8
Own goals	4	2.7
Total	147	100

following sequences of play involving between one and four passes. In the English Premier League, the vast majority of goals result from a build-up of less than 5 seconds. In contrast, the results from a study of international Rugby Union suggested that the ability to keep possession by constructing movements that lasted longer than 80 seconds was a key influence on scoring points and the final result (van Rooyen et al., 2006b). These discrepancies between sports demonstrate the specificity of attacking play of each field sport.

The pitch diagram (Figure 4.5) presents the build-up play and the number of movements before three individual try-scoring actions. This information is useful for identifying which 'channels' were used and the patterns of actions in the build-up. Unsuccessful (e.g. possession lost quickly) and successful attacking sequences (e.g. entries into attacking third, penalties won, tries or goals scored) can be compared to identify reasons for success and failure. In American Football, an analysis of playing styles has shown that from plays which started within 10–20 yards of the defensive 'end zone', a significantly higher proportion of passing plays resulted in touchdowns compared to running plays (Hughes and Charlish, 1988).

Many coaches are interested in statistical information on the key (or final) actions before a goal or try is scored. In soccer, the majority of goals are preceded by actions

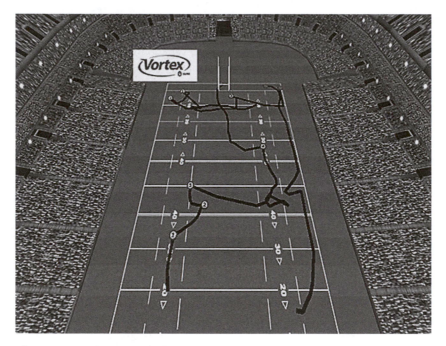

Figure 4.5 Schematic pitch representation of attacking routes and number of actions used by a team prior to three tries (data courtesy of Virtual Spectator)

such as passes and crosses. These actions accounted for around 70% of goals scored in the 2006 soccer World Cup (Breen et al., 2006). In Rugby Union, the final action before a try is scored mainly involves a pass. However, analysis of one particular team may show the use of kicks through behind the defensive lines as a common and decisive tactic in scoring points. Research on elite field-hockey by Sunderland et al. (2006) showed that the majority of the goals were scored from hits (24%), deflections (25%) or pushes (22%). Recent research on soccer demonstrated an upward trend across World Cup winners in the importance of dribbling as a key event preceding goal attempts and goals scored (Yates et al., 2006).

Whilst a coach may judge the performance of his or her team on the percentage of possession or number of goals scored and chances created, analysis of other match-related KPI can provide helpful information on individual and team performance. For example, the number of duels won or lost, successful or unsuccessful passes and dribbles, interceptions or turnovers made and free-kicks won or conceded can give a good impression of team performance and/or the contributions of individual players. Combining the total number of actions with the corresponding percentage of success and failure for each action provides a simple way of evaluating performance.

PRACTICAL EXAMPLE 1

A simple yet practical example of the use of match analysis in professional soccer has been presented by James (2006). The author examined four key performance indicators: shots, corners, ball entries into the critical scoring area and regains of possession in the opponents' half. Data were obtained over six consecutive matches for a professional team as well as for its opponents. Performance indicators were coded using manual analysis combined with the Noldus 'Observer Video Pro' behavioural measurement software package and 'MatchInsight' developed by ProZone. Statistical analysis of data showed that the team analysed generally outperformed all its opponents on all the performance indicators. However, the results of the team did not correspond to these data (1 win, 2 draws and 2 defeats) so the match statistics were used as a motivational tool to demonstrate to the players that their performance remained good even though this was not necessarily reflected by the result. The analysed team scored notably well on the number of entries into the critical scoring area, suggesting that it was successful in getting into dangerous attacking positions. However, more of these chances needed to be converted into goals and increasing the relatively low percentage of shots on target was necessary (42.7%). Such results could be translated by coaches into the design and application of relevant training drills to improve future attacking performance.

Analysing pitch coverage in terms of the number of actions played or percentage of time spent in the individual zones of the pitch is particularly useful. Schematic representations of the pitch (Figures 4.6 and 4.7) allow coaches to identify the areas covered by and the actions made by players. A coach may want to evaluate whether a player respected his or her wishes by restricting their movements to one part of the pitch. For example, did the player tend to stay in defensive areas and contribute little to attacking play, thereby respecting the coach's advice? This information can be broken down into more detail by comparing the pitch coverage according to ball possession. Coaches can visualise the percentage of time spent in various zones by players when both defending and attacking.

Some coaches may use statistics from match analysis to identify specific technical weaknesses in a player's game, for example low success rates in forward passing by defenders. Subsequent tactics may also involve targeting a 'one-footed' opposition player and forcing him or her into using their weaker foot. Maps such as Figure 4.8 can allow coaches to evaluate success rates in areas such as passing, especially when frequency counts are supplied. In field sports, the ability to score when presented with an opportunity to do so is important. Coaches are often

Figure 4.6 Schematic pitch representation of various match actions (courtesy of Virtual Spectator) of an elite soccer player

match analysis

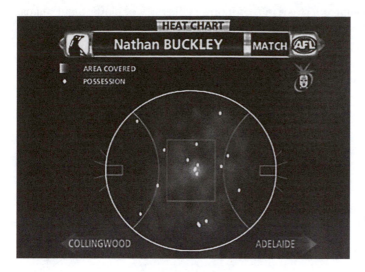

Figure 4.7 Schematic pitch representation of zone coverage of an elite Australian Rules footballer (courtesy of Virtual Spectator)

Figure 4.8 Schematic pitch representation of pass distribution of an elite soccer player (courtesy of Virtual Spectator)

interested in calculating the strike rate or scoring efficiency of players and teams, that is the ratio of shots to goals. Comparative research on successful and unsuccessful netball teams has shown winning teams to record significantly better shooting statistics than when losing (Borrie and Worrall, 2001). Successful teams in various field sports generally have a higher 'goal scored' to 'attempt on goal' ratio, highlighting the importance of having technically proficient players who can take full advantage of goal-scoring opportunities. Bell-Walker and co-workers (2006) showed that successful teams in recent soccer World Cup finals demonstrated greater efficiency at converting attempts into goals scored compared to unsuccessful teams (Table 4.4).

Table 4.4 Ratios for the number of attempts at goal to goals scored from open play and set plays at soccer World Cup 2002 and 2006 (Bell-Walker et al., 2006)

Successful Teams: Open play	Ratio	%
World Cup 2006	11:1	9.0
World Cup 2002	7:1	15.3
Unsuccessful Teams: Open play	Ratio	%
World Cup 2002	22:1	4.6
Successful Teams: Set plays	Ratio	%
World Cup 2006	7.5:1	13.0
World Cup 2002	10:1	10.4
Unsuccessful Teams: Set plays	Ratio	%
World Cup 2002	14:1	7.2

MOTION ANALYSIS TECHNIQUES

Fitness in any field sport refers to a number of characteristics that are essential in assisting a team and players to compete for possession of the ball, maintain high work rate levels throughout the duration of the match and react quickly to continually changing game situations. Strength and conditioning coaches aim to design programmes to equip players with the optimal physical attributes required for their sport. A primary step in this process is the monitoring of exercise intensity during competition to quantify the exact physical requirements and performance demands of the sport (Reilly, 2007). The process of classifying and coding match activities using notation techniques according to the intensity of different movements is known as motion analysis. Data obtained on match performance are translated into distances or velocities of movements or the time spent in different movement activities. This information can then help to identify the performance

86

demands and fitness requirements for play for different sports and playing positions. Moreover, it can then be used to make objective decisions for structuring the conditioning elements of training and subsequent match preparation.

Video-based motion analysis

The classical method of measuring physical performance or work rates employed a subjective assessment of distance and exercise intensity recorded manually or onto an audiotape recorder. Coded commentaries of activities onto a tape recorder by a trained observer have also been correlated with measurements taken from video recordings. The latter method entails stride characteristics to be established for each player according to the different exercise intensities. The data were then translated into distances or velocities of movement (see Reilly, 2003). However, these notational methods were not able to function in real-time, may have been subject to visual errors due to gait changes during game movements and were restricted to the analysis of a single player at a time. Limiting the analysis of the activity profile to one player per game does not permit relationships between the concomitant work rate profiles of team-mates or opposing players to be evaluated and can limit full understanding of the tactical importance of work rate (Drust et al., 2007). Importantly, manual methods are extremely labour-intensive in terms of the recording and analysis of data and cannot be efficiently employed in the busy schedules of elite teams. In 2002, Liebermann and co-workers reported that very few systems had the ability to analyse all the players in a team throughout a whole match, tracking each player both on and off the ball. In Table 4.5, we can see a list of the numerous contemporary tracking systems used in field sports of which several now allow the actions of every player to be tracked both on and off the ball.

The AMISCO Pro system initially developed in 1996 by the French company Sport-Universal Process (http://www.sport-universal.com/) in collaboration with the French Football Federation was the pioneer player-tracking system based on state-of-the-art video and computer technology and is used by numerous top European football clubs and international Rugby Union teams. This system analyses the movements of all players, referee and the ball, from 10 to 25 times a second during the whole game. This process leads to the collection of around 4.5 million positions as well as over 2000 ball touches for an average soccer match. A major advantage of video-based tracking systems such as AMISCO is that they have been designed so that players do not have to be equipped with an electronic transmitter and are therefore unobtrusive. Carrying such material is strictly forbidden by various (but not all) sporting institutions around the world.

Video-based systems for tracking players generally require the installation of multiple cameras optimally fixed and positioned to cover the whole pitch so that

Table 4.5 A list of the commercial player tracking systems used in field sports currently available on the market

Video-based Player Tracking Systems	Country	Software	Website
Feedback Sport	UK	Feedback Football	http://www.feedbacksport.com/
Orad	Israel	CyberSet	http://www.orad.co.il/
PGI	UK	DatatraX	http://www.datatrax.tv/
ProZone Holdings Ltd	UK	ProZone	http://www.pzfootball.co.uk/
Red Bee Media	UK	Piero	http://www.redbeemedia.com/
Symah Vision	France	EPSIS Locator	http://www.epsis.com/
Sport-Universal SA	France	AMISCO	http://www.sport-universal.com/
Tracab	Sweden	Tracab	http://www.tracab.com/
Trackmen	Germany	Trackmen	http://www.trackmen.de/

Electronic Player Tracking Systems

	Country	Software	Website
Abatec Electronic GmbH	Austria	LPM	http://www.abatec-ag.com/
Catapult Innovations	Australia	minimaxx	http://www.catapultinnovations.com/
Cairos Technologies AG	Germany	Cairos	http://www.cairos/
GPSports	Australia	SPI Elite	http://www.gpsports.com/
Trakus Inc	USA	Digital Sports Information	http://www.trakus.com/

Other Player Tracking Systems

	Country	Software	Website
Manapps	France	Stadmaster	http://www.manapps.tm.fr/
Sportstec	Australia	TrakPerformance	http://www.sportstecinternational.com/

all players are always captured on video, whatever their position on the pitch and the moment in time. The number and positioning of the cameras depend on factors such as the size of the pitch and the layout of the stadium. The stadium and pitch are calibrated (height, length, width) and transformed into a two-dimensional model to allow the calculation of player positions (x, y coordinates) from the camera viewpoints. Using complex trigonometry, mathematical algorithms and digital video/image processing techniques (Figure 4.9), each player's position and movement can be calculated and tracked on the videos, at every single moment of the game. Systems may also use supportive information such as shirt-colour identification, optical-character recognition of shirt numbers and prediction of running patterns to help maintain accurate identification and tracking of players. Some of these systems still require manual input from a performance analyst, for example when tracking becomes difficult during set-pieces such as corners (due to occlusions from the sheer number of players in a small area). For example, the Dvideo system designed at the University of Campinus, Brazil, has reported a 95% automatic tracking rate (Barros et al., 2007). All tracking systems require the separate notating of various match actions which cannot be automatically calculated by the computer software (e.g. red cards, off-sides, tackles).

At this moment in time, the original systems used in contemporary elite soccer (AMISCO Pro, PROZONE – http://www.pzfootball.co.uk/) do not provide real-time

Figure 4.9 An example of player tracking using the Dvideo match-analysis system (reprinted with permission from the *Journal of Sports Science and Medicine*, 2007)

match analysis, the results being available within 24 hours of the game. However, current top-level coaches using these systems seem satisfied with this time delay. The very latest video-based tracking systems such as DatatraX (http://www. datatrax.tv/) and TRACAB (http://www.tracab.com/) now provide real-time analysis through new and improved video image-processing techniques. The tracking processes recently developed by the Swedish company TRACAB are based on 'state-of-the-art' image-processing technology and enhanced mathematical algorithms for guiding missiles in the military industry. According to information available on the Internet, the DatatraX system uses pixel recognition to track the players automatically and voice recognition to code the match-specific events. Three manual operators are required to manage the process, two people to correct tracking mistakes real-time for each team and one to perform the voice-recognition coding procedure. The possibility of obtaining and evaluating live data allows coaches to assess performance and, consequently, to make split-second tactical changes during a game. The improved portability of these latter systems has also apparently solved the problem of this type of system being restricted to usage by teams in their own stadium (although some teams may share data) by using portable cameras from the stadium gantry. Some mathematical corrections for errors created are needed when players are further away from the camera lens. A good example of portable video tracking is the Feedback Sport System currently used in professional soccer (see http://www.feedbacksport.com/).

It is important to mention that the methodologies used in the match analysis process must comply with strict quality-control specifications; these include reliability, accuracy and objectivity (Drust et al., 2007). Up to now, the measurement precision and reliability of many commercial tracking systems via independent empirical analyses have not always been satisfactorily demonstrated (Carling et al., 2008). It is imperative that there is more research on the scientific legitimacy of these systems so that applied practitioners and the academic community can be assured of their accuracy when employing these methods.

Motion analysis through electronic tracking

Electronic tracking systems have previously been described as the future of computerised analysis of sport and are taking match analysis one step further in terms of time and accuracy (Carling et al., 2005). These systems allow real-time data acquisition and analysis and can record performance factors (movements and positions of every player and the ball) up to several hundred times per second. Before the advent of a real-time version of video tracking systems, electronic tracking systems presented several major advantages. First, analysis and processing of performance data are always carried out in real-time, meaning statistical information is available instantaneously during the game. Second, the data are possibly more precise than those obtained through video tracking methods (up to several centimetres). Third, player movements and positions may be analysed over a hundred times per second, leading to the production of highly detailed and previously unavailable information on player accelerations, decelerations and changes in direction.

This approach requires tagging individual players electronically and tracking their movements by means of satellites or radio transmitters and receivers positioned around a pitch. A small lightweight microchip transmitter is integrated into the shirts of the players or worn in a strap around the back. The identification signal of the transmitter is registered by several antennae in a fraction of a second (the reception time of the signal to the recipient is synchronised and as a result the position is determined). These antennae are optimally positioned around and outside the playing field at various heights. The positional data of the player and of the ball are ascertained and evaluated three-dimensionally at the same time and hundreds of times per second within the centimetre range. These data are relayed to the central computer and processed for immediate analysis. Constraints of such systems include potential electronic interference, the strength of the electronic signals from players due to the size of playing surfaces and the energy source need to accomplish this effect (Edgecomb and Norton, 2006).

These commercial systems developed by companies for the European soccer market require players to be equipped with electronic material which, as mentioned earlier, is still forbidden by various international football institutions. However, the LPM Soccer 3D® system developed by the Dutch company INMOTIO (http://www.inmotio.nl/) in collaboration with PSV Eindhoven Football Club is the first dedicated system for analysing player work rates during training sessions. Relatively easy to set up (see Figure 4.10), this field laboratory combines simultaneous heart-rate monitoring (built into the transmitter) and measurement of players' movements along with simultaneous video footage to provide a global picture of the daily, weekly and monthly workloads experienced in training. The data complement those which may be obtained from players during competition through the use of other motion-analysis technologies. It is important to monitor work rate in both training and competition in order to assess the degree to which training activities match the actual demands of the game (Dawson et al., 2004).

Global Positioning Technology (GPS) has begun to impact on the analysis of performance in various field sports. The GPS receivers worn by players (Figure 4.11) in training and competition draw on signals sent from at least four of the earth orbiting satellites to determine positional information and subsequently calculate movement speeds, distances and pathways as well as altitude. These data are stored in the GPS before being downloaded onto a computer for analysis by

Figure 4.10 A strategically placed antennae receiver of the LPM Soccer 3D® system placed above the goal area (courtesy of Inmotio)

Figure 4.11 GPS receivers worn in a training session by English Premier League team Middlesbrough Football Club (courtesy of GPSports)

means of dedicated software. The SPI Elite GPS receiver designed by the Australian company GPSports (http://www.gpsports.com/) has been designed specifically for professional team sports and is currently used by teams competing in English Premier League Football, Professional Rugby Union, Super 14 Rugby, Australian Rules Football League and the Australian National Rugby League. Similarly, in Spain a company known as RealTrack Football (http://www.realtrackfutbol.com/) has made team GPS systems specifically for soccer commercially available.

The SPI Elite GPS is capable of storing data on heart rate and records information on the frequency and intensity of impacts such as tackles and collisions that is important in impact field sports such as lacrosse and the various codes of football. The accuracy and reliability of these systems have also improved greatly as have their size and weight (now around 75 grams). However, GPS receivers are subject to problems such as receiving signals from satellites because the quality of the signal can be influenced by land configuration. The magnitude of error depends on the number of satellite connections. Furthermore, information on workrates must be complemented by tactical and technical performance data obtained separately through other video-analysis software in order to give a holistic idea of the level of performance. In addition, analysis is generally restricted to only one measurement per second (although this sampling frequency is increasing – see http://www. catapultinnovations.com/) which is insufficient for measuring detailed variations in speed and direction, and purchasing enough GPS units for use by the whole squad may be beyond all but the wealthiest clubs.

Other motion-analysis technologies

The Stadmaster system (http://www.manapps.tm.fr/stadmasterv2/gb_home.htm) has been developed from military hardware and software based on optronic technology (observation, detection, recognition and location of military objectives). It is portable and is apparently easy to set up and operate. A pair of binoculars mounted on a tripod is operated by the performance analyst to track in real-time the exact movements, five times per second, of a single player (more players can be simultaneously followed by other dedicated analysts and binoculars). The data are immediately transferred to a laptop computer connected to the binoculars for processing and presentation. This system is portable and easy to set up and operate although analysis is restricted to measuring one single player per operator and no information is available on precision, reliability and validity.

Trakperformance software developed by Sportstecinternational allows one player to be mechanically followed using a computer pen and tablet on a scaled-down version of the specific playing field. Ground markings around the pitch are used as reference points for tracking the players. The miniaturised playing field is calibrated so that a given movement of the mouse or mouse-pen corresponds to the linear distance travelled by the player. This system is relatively accurate although operator skill needs to be very high (Edgecomb and Norton, 2006), apparently cheaper than other tracking systems and allows real-time analysis, although only one player can be tracked at one time.

ANALYSIS OF PHYSICAL PERFORMANCE USING MOTION-ANALYSIS TECHNIQUES

The total distance covered during match-play provides a global representation of the intensity of the exercise and the individual contribution towards the total team effort (Reilly, 2007). Distance run varies between the differing field sports at elite levels. For example, elite junior male Australian Rules footballers can run up to 17 km (Veale et al., 2007), whereas elite senior field-hockey players can cover around 7 km (Edgecomb and Norton, 2006). Outfield male professional soccer players run on average 9–13 km though some players may run around 14 km (Reilly, 2007). A coach may simply want to compare the overall distance run by his or her players compared to opposition players to identify who is (or isn't!) working the hardest. However, this distance may not be a fair reflection of a player's performance as playing style, formations and tactics will determine overall work rate (Carling et al., 2008). Furthermore, regional differences (Rienzi et al., 2000), scoreline (O'Donoghue and Tenga, 2001) and quality of the opposition (Rampinini et al., 2007b) will affect physical performance. A more pertinent coaching question may be to measure the total distance run when defending (opposition in possession) compared to attacking (own team in possession). This comparison may help determine whether players are working as much in a defensive role as they are in attack.

The effect of positional role on distance run must be taken into account when evaluating work-rate data. For example, distances run by elite Junior Australian Rules football players ranged from 10,419 m to 16,691 m according to playing position (Veale et al., 2007). In netball, centres have been shown to run significantly greater distances than all other positions, covering around 6 km per match compared to distances ranging from 2–4.6 km for defenders and attackers (O'Donoghue and Loughran, 1998). In professional Rugby Union players, backs spend more time in free running, allowing them to cover greater distances notably in sprinting (Duthie et al., 2003, 2005). Di Salvo and co-workers (2007) reported that the number of sprints made per player in professional European soccer ranged greatly from 3–40 and was highly dependent upon playing position. A report on work rate in Super 12 players suggested that rugby training and fitness testing should be tailored specifically to positional groups (e.g. front row and back row forwards) rather than simply differentiating between forwards and backs as each positional group has its own unique physical demands (Deutsch et al., 2007).

The distance run can be broken down into discrete actions for each player across the whole game. The actions can then be classified according to intensity, duration and frequency. The activity may be placed on a time-base so that the average exercise to rest ratios or low- to high-intensity exercise ratios can be calculated. These ratios can then be used in physiological studies designed to represent the demands of the sport and provide objective advice on conditioning elements of the training programmes of players. Work-rate profiles can also be complemented by monitoring physiological responses such as heart rate or blood lactate concentration where possible to provide a more complete picture of performance for the fitness coach. The combination of the results from physiological testing and their strong relationship with work-rate data from analysis of competition is useful when evaluating performance (see Rampinini et al., 2007a). For example, the work rate of players depends strongly on physiological indicators of aerobic fitness. In Rugby Union, the aerobic system provides energy during repeated efforts and for recovery (Duthie et al., 2003) and its role is paramount in elite field-hockey as 95% of the recovery during repeated high-intensity efforts is of an active nature (Spencer et al., 2004).

The main categories of movement in field sports are classed as standing, walking, jogging, cruising (striding) and sprinting. These have recently been extended to include other activities such as skipping and shuffling for soccer (Bloomfield et al., 2004). There are many other game-related activities which must also be taken into account such as alterations in pace, changes in direction, impacts (see Table 4.6), unorthodox movements, execution of specific game skills and tracking opponents as these actions increase energy expenditure. The analysis of deceleration and turning movements in contemporary professional soccer suggests that these actions are a common and extremely important part of the modern game and there is a particular need for developing specific deceleration and turning exercises in sessions for strength and conditioning training (Bloomfield, 2007a, 2007b).

Spencer et al. (2004) showed that international field-hockey players spent the majority of total game time in the low-intensity motions of walking, jogging and standing (46.5±8.1, 40.5±7.0 and 7.4±0.9%, respectively). In comparison, the proportions of time spent in striding and sprinting were 4.1±1.1 and 1.5±0.6%, respectively. This work-rate profile in field-hockey is relatively comparable to profiles observed across other field sports. An example of the physical effort during competition of an elite Rugby Union player is presented in Figure 4.12. In soccer, players have to run with effort (cruise) or sprint every 30 s and sprint all-out once every 90 s on average, indicating exercise of an intermittent type (Reilly, 2007). In

Figure 4.12
Relative distances covered by an elite Rugby Union player according to categories of activity divided according to speed (in metres per second) (data courtesy of GPSports)

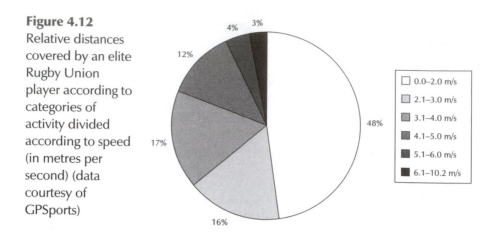

4% 3%
12%
48%
17%
16%

☐ 0.0–2.0 m/s
☐ 2.1–3.0 m/s
■ 3.1–4.0 m/s
■ 4.1–5.0 m/s
■ 5.1–6.0 m/s
■ 6.1–10.2 m/s

the endurance context of the game, each player performs 1000–1400 mainly short activities changing every 4–6 seconds (Stølen et al., 2005). Across all field sports, the majority of sprints are short in distance (between 10–25 m) and duration (2–3 seconds) (Spencer et al., 2005a). Due to the intermittent nature of field sports, performance can be enhanced through improving players' ability to perform high-intensity work repeatedly. The timing of anaerobic efforts, their quality (distance, duration) and the capacity to repeat these efforts, whether in possession of the ball or without, is crucial since the success of their deployment plays a critical role in the outcome of games (Carling et al., 2005).

The performance profile of a player can highlight individual weaknesses, such as a susceptibility to fatigue, shown up as a drop-off in work rate towards the end of the first or second half of a game or a need for a long recovery period after a sprint (Mohr et al., 2005). Simple comparisons of the overall work rate between first and second halves of matches can also indicate the occurrence of fatigue although it may also be more closely identified if activities during the game are broken up into 15-min or 5-min segments. An average difference of –3.1% in the total distance run between halves (range –9.4% to +0.8%) can be observed across all recent motion-analysis studies on elite soccer (Carling et al., 2008). Activity profiles of elite-level female field-hockey players during competition have shown that players undertake significantly less high-intensity exercise in the second half of the game despite the continual substitution rule (MacLeod et al., 2007). Mohr et al. (2003) demonstrated that the amount of high-intensity running was lower (35–45%) in the last than in the first 15 min of elite soccer games. There are implications for training so that any weaknesses exposed by the analysis can be remedied.

A recent development in the match-analysis field is the capacity to measure and assess the frequency and intensity of impacts such as tackles and collisions via GPS (see Table 4.6). The latest version of these systems has a built-in tri-axial accelerometer which registers force in three planes (www.gpsports.com). The extent of each impact is determined by the actual activity (e.g. tackle, fall) which dictates the impact intensity zones it falls into. These measurements, when combined with other movement data, allow a true insight into the physical demands and stresses of impact sports such as the Rugby codes and American football. 'Player Body Load' is a score developed by GPSports by collating the amount and extent of force placed on the body of a player during a session or game. This index provides a portrayal of the amount of stress placed upon a player from accelerations, decelerations, changes of direction and impacts. 'Body load' allows a detailed insight into the musculoskeletal demands of a player, permitting exercise and recovery programmes to be individualised. Implications of data on the frequency and intensity of impacts such as tackles are many for field sports. For example, the real demands according to playing position can be determined (e.g. comparison of average number and impact of tackles made and received per rugby game between centres and back-row forwards) and optimal individual conditioning programmes can then be designed. This index also has implications for the prediction of player injury risk and development of recovery training programmes as it can provide data on how well or otherwise players are coping with impacts. For example, in mid-season, is a player shoved back more often on impact at the beginning compared to the end of the season?

In an intense period of training or competitive fixtures, work-rate profiles may give objective confirmation of the coach's diagnosis that some players are coping well and others are failing to do so. There may be implications to aid both physiological and psychological recovery between matches. For example, if incomplete recovery has seemingly occurred, energy expenditure in training through measurements of heart rate and nutritional intake may be monitored by the coach. Teams may be required to play several games within a short time frame and there is potential for residual fatigue and incomplete recovery which may affect the movement patterns of players during subsequent games. Research focusing on elite field-hockey (Spencer et al., 2005b) and professional soccer players (Odetoyinbo et al., 2007) has shown significant changes in motion analysis data during an intense period of competitive matches. The frequency of repeated-sprint performance decreased in

Table 4.6 Impact intensity zone data for a professional Australian Rugby Union player (data supplied courtesy of GPSports)

Impact intensity zones	1st Half	2nd Half	Total
4.5–6G: Accelerations, Decelerations and Rapid Changes of Direction	38	54	92
5–6G: Light Impact, Very Hard Acceleration/ Deceleration/Change of Direction	22	32	54
6–6.5G: Moderate Impact (Player Collison, Contact with the Ground)	24	29	53
6.5–7G: Heavy Impact (Tackle)	3	1	4
7–8G: Heavy Impact (Tackle)	2	0	2
8–10G: Very Heavy Impact (Tackle)	0	0	0

the hockey players and recovery time between high-intensity efforts also increased in the soccer players in the latter game (see Figure 4.13). These results illustrate how motion analysis can play an important role in the approach to training and preparation before and during intense playing schedules.

Substituting players before the onset of fatigue can restore the imbalances in work rate. Mohr et al. (2003) showed that substitute soccer players covered 25% more ground during the final 15 min of high-intensity running than the other players. The

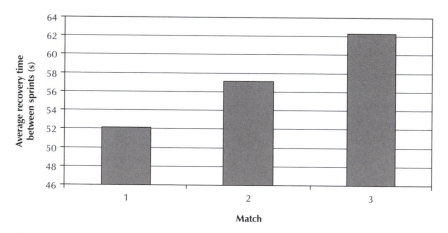

Figure 4.13 Analysis of recovery time between high-intensity actions during a period of three matches in five days in English professional soccer teams (data adapted from Odetoyinbo et al., 2007)

match analysis

latest tracking systems now allow coaches to analyse work rates in real-time and make split-second objective decisions when trying to identify players who are tiring and who may need replacing at certain moments of the game.

PRACTICAL EXAMPLE 3

A recent study by Impellizzeri and co-workers (2006) demonstrated how work-rate data can be used to examine and compare the effects on match performance of different modes of aerobic training in soccer players. Forty junior players divided equally into two groups, undertook either 12 weeks of generic (simple running exercises at 90–95% of maximum heart rate) or specific (small-sided games during which intensity was controlled by heart-rate monitoring) aerobic-interval training. Work rate was analysed via video-based motion analysis techniques during matches played pre-, mid- and post-training interventions. Results for both groups showed a significant overall gain of 14 and 18% in the time spent in low- and high-intensity activities respectively. Similarly, the total distance covered improved by 6% on average. However, no significant differences in work rate were reported between the two groups undertaking the different types of training. The authors suggested that these results demonstrate that the choice of aerobic training mode can mainly be based on practical necessity as both training types are effective. Nevertheless, small-sided games as an effective means to improve aerobic fitness and match performance have the added advantage of concurrently training tactical-technical components which would be particularly beneficial for younger players.

CONCLUSION

One of the main tasks of coaches is to analyse play so that objective feedback on performance can be given to players. This task is based on the utilisation of techniques to notate and record the different events occurring in games. Coaches must then meaningfully interpret, evaluate and transform information obtained from the analysis of performance into preparing and executing relevant practice sessions. In various field sports, match analysis has grown in popularity over recent years due to a recognition by elite coaches of its benefits in supplying objective information on playing performance. This recognition is partly due to major advances in computer and video technology, providing coaches with more efficient ways of obtaining and analysing data. Unfortunately, the current cost of many systems is often prohibitive to all but the most wealthy sports and clubs. However, an increasing number of scientific investigations are providing coaches at all levels with essential information on the physical, technical and tactical demands of field sports and with indications on how best to cope with these demands.

REFERENCES

Barros, R.M.L., Misuta, M.S., Menezes, R.P., Figueroa, P.J., Moura, F.A., Cunha, S.A., Anido, R. and Leite, N.J. (2007) Analysis of the distances covered by first division Brazilian soccer players obtained with an automatic tracking method. *Journal of Sports Science and Medicine*, 6: 233–242.

Bell-Walker, J., McRobert, A., Ford, P. and Williams, M.A. (2006) Quantitative analysis of successful teams at the 2006 World Cup Finals. *Insight – The F.A. Coaches Association Journal*, Autumn/Winter, 6: 37–43.

Bloomfield, J., Polman, R.C.J. and O'Donoghue, P.G. (2004) The 'Bloomfield Movement Classification': motion analysis of individuals in team sports. *International Journal of Performance Analysis of Sport*-e, 4: 20–31.

Bloomfield, J., Polman, R.C.J. and O'Donoghue, P.G. (2007a) Deceleration movements performed during FA Premier League soccer matches. In *VIth World Congress on Science and Football, Book of Abstracts* (p. 6). Antalya, Turkey.

Bloomfield, J., Polman, R.C.J. and O'Donoghue, P.G. (2007b) Turning movements performed during FA Premier League soccer matches. In *VIth World Congress on Science and Football, Book of Abstracts* (p. 7). Antalya, Turkey.

Borrie, A. and Worrall, P. (2001) Frequency analysis of netball teams when winning: Does the analysis aid understanding of performance? In *Proceedings of the Performance Analysis Sport Science (PASS), 5th World Congress*. Cardiff, Wales.

Breen, A., Iga, J., Ford, P. and Williams, M. (2006) World Cup 2006 – Germany. A quantitative analysis of goals scored. *Insight – The F.A. Coaches Association Journal*, Autumn/Winter, 6: 45–53.

Carling, C., Bloomfield, J., Nelsen. L. and Reilly, T. (2008) The role of motion analysis in elite soccer: Contemporary performance measurement techniques and work-rate data. *Sports Medicine*, 38: 839–862.

Carling, C., Williams, A.M. and Reilly, T. (2005) *The Handbook of Soccer Match Analysis*. London: Routledge.

Dawson, B., Hopkinson, R., Appleby, B., Stewart, G. and Roberts, C. (2004) Comparison of training activities and game demands in the Australian Football League. *Journal of Science and Medicine in Sport*, 7: 292–301.

Deutsch M.U., Kearney, G.A. and Rehrer, N.J. (2007) Time-motion analysis of professional rugby union players during match-play. *Journal of Sports Sciences*, 25: 461–72.

Di Salvo, V., Baron, R., Tschan, H., Calderon Montero, F.J., Bachl, N. and Pigozzi, F. (2007) Performance characteristics according to playing position in elite soccer. *International Journal of Sports Medicine*, 28: 222–227.

Drust, B., Atkinson, G. and Reilly, T. (2007) Future perspectives in the evaluation of the physiological demands of soccer. *Sports Medicine,* 37: 783–805.

Duthie, G., Pyne, D. and Hooper, S. (2003) Applied physiology and game analysis of rugby union. *Sports Medicine*, 33: 973–991.

Duthie, G., Pyne, D. and Hooper, S. (2005) Time motion analysis of 2001 and 2002 super 12 rugby. *Journal of Sports Sciences*, 23: 523–530.

Edgecomb, S.J. and Norton, K.I. (2006) Comparison of global positioning and computer-based tracking systems for measuring player movement distance during Australian Football. *Journal of Science and Medicine in Sport*, 9: 25–32.

Franks, I.M., Goodman, D. and Miller, G. (1983) Analysis of performance: quantitative or qualitative? *SPORTS*, March.

Hughes, M.D. and Charlish, P. (1988) The development and validation of a computerised notation system for American Football. *Journal of Sports Sciences*, 6: 253–254.

Hughes M.D. and Franks I M. (2004) Sports analysis. In M.D. Hughes and I.M. Franks (eds), *Notational Analysis of Sport: Systems for Better Coaching and Performance* (pp. 107–117). London: Routledge.

Impellizzeri, F.M., Marcora, S.M., Castagna, C., Reilly, T., Sassi, A., Iaia, F.M. and Rampinini, E. (2006) Physiological and performance effects of generic versus specific aerobic training in soccer players. *International Journal of Sports Medicine*, 27: 483–492.

James, N. (2006) The role of notational analysis in soccer coaching. *International Journal of Sports Science and Coaching*, 1: 185–198.

Liebermann, D.G., Katz, L., Hughes, M.D, Bartlett, R.M., McClements, J. and Franks, I.M. (2002) Advances in the application of information technology to sport performance. *Journal of Sports Sciences*, 20: 755–769.

MacLeod, H., Bussell, C. and Sunderland, C. (2007) Time-motion analysis of elite women's field hockey, with particular reference to maximum intensity movement patterns. *International Journal of Performance Analysis in Sport-e*, 7: 1–12.

Mohr, M., Krustrup, P. and Bangsbo, J. (2003) Match performance of high-standard soccer players with special reference to development of fatigue. *Journal of Sports Sciences*, 21: 519–528.

Mohr, M., Krustrup, P. and Bangsbo, J. (2005) Fatigue in soccer: a brief review. *Journal of Sports Sciences*, 23: 593–599.

Nevill, A., Atkinson, G. and Hughes, M. (2008) Twenty-five years of sport performance research in the Journal of Sports Sciences. *Journal of Sports Sciences*, 26: 413–426.

Odetoyinbo, K., Wooster, B. and Lane, A. (2007) The effect of a succession of matches on the activity profiles of professional soccer players. In *VIth World Congress on Science and Football, Book of Abstracts* (pp. 16–17). Antalya, Turkey.

O'Donoghue, P.G. and Loughran, B. (1998) Analysis of distance covered during intervarsity netball competition. *Proceedings of the IV World Congress of Notational Analysis of Sport*, University of Porto, Porto, Portugal.

O'Donoghue, P.G., Tenga, A. (2001) The effect of score-line on work rate in elite soccer. *Journal of Sports Sciences*, 19: 25–26.

Rampinini, E., Bishop, D., Marcora, S.M, Ferrari Bravo D., Sassi, R. and Impellizzeri, F.M. (2007a) Validity of simple field tests as indicators of match-related physical performance in top-level professional soccer players. *International Journal of Sports Medicine*, 28: 228–235.

Rampinini, E., Coutts, A.J., Castagna, C., Sassi, R., Impellizzeri, F.M. (2007b) Variation in top level soccer match performance. *International Journal of Sports Medicine*, 28: 1018–1024.

Reilly, T. (2003) Motion analysis and physiological demands. In T. Reilly and A.M. Williams (eds), *Science and Soccer*, 2nd edition (pp. 59–72). London: Routledge.

Reilly, T. (2007) *Science of Training: Soccer*. London: Routledge.

Rienzi E., Drust B., Reilly T., Carter, J.E.L. and Martin, A. (2000) Investigation of anthropometric and work-rate profiles of elite South American international soccer players. *Journal of Sports Medicine and Physical Fitness*, 40: 162–169.

Robertson, K. (2002) *Observation, Analysis and Video*. Leeds: The National Coaching Foundation.

Spencer, M., Bishop, D., Dawson, B. and Goodman, C. (2005a) Physiological and metabolic responses of repeated-sprint activities: specific to field-based team sports. *Sports Medicine*, 35: 1025–1044.

Spencer, M., Lawrence, S., Rechichi, C., Bishop, D., Dawson, B. and Goodman, C. (2004) Time-motion analysis of elite field hockey, with special reference to repeated-sprint activity. *Journal of Sports Sciences*, 22: 843–850.

Spencer, M., Rechichi, C., Lawrence, S., Dawson, B., Bishop, D. and Goodman, C. (2005b) Time-motion analysis of elite field hockey during several games in succession: a tournament scenario. *Journal of Science and Medicine in Sport*, 8: 382–391.

Stølen, T., Chamari, K., Castagna, C. and Wisløff, U. (2005) Physiology of soccer: an update. *Sports Medicine*, 35: 501–536.

Sunderland, C., Bussell, C., Atkinson, G., Alltree, R. and Kates, M. (2006) Patterns of play and goals scored in international standard women's field hockey. *International Journal of Performance Analysis in Sport-e*, 6: 13–29.

van Rooyen, M.K., Lambert, M.I., Lambert, Mike I. and Noakes, T.D. (2006a) A retrospective analysis of the IRB statistics and video analysis of match play to explain the performance of four teams in the 2003 Rugby World Cup. *International Journal of Performance Analysis in Sport-e*, 6: 57–72.

van Rooyen, M.K., Michele, K. and Noakes, T.D. (2006b) Movement time as a predictor of success in the 2003 Rugby World Cup Tournament. *International Journal of Performance Analysis in Sport-e*, 6: 30–39.

Veale, J.P., Pearce, A.J. and John, S. (2007) Profile of position movement demands in elite junior Australian Rules Football. In *VIth World Congress on Science and Football, Book of Abstracts* (p. 12). Antalya, Turkey.

Yates, I., North, J., Ford, P, and Williams. M. (2006) A quantitative analysis of Italy's World Cup performances. A comparison of World Cup winners. *Insight – The F.A. Coaches Association Journal*, Autumn/Winter, 55–59.

CHAPTER FIVE

AEROBIC PERFORMANCE

INTRODUCTION

Aerobic performance is dependent on the effective functioning of the oxygen transport system. The lungs, the heart, the oxygen-carrying capacity of the blood, and the capability of the active tissues to utilise the oxygen supplied to them are all implicated. Aerobic performance therefore has both central and peripheral aspects, reliant on cardiac output and circulation of the blood on the one hand and on the other the ability of skeletal muscle to take up and consume the oxygen that is offered.

Aerobic fitness is influenced by both aerobic power and aerobic capacity. Aerobic power is reflected in the maximal oxygen uptake or $\dot{V}O_{2\,max}$. Maximal oxygen uptake represents the highest level at which oxygen can be consumed by the individual and is determined by means of analysing respiratory gas exchange during a progressive exercise test to voluntary exhaustion. Aerobic capacity refers to the ability to sustain endurance exercise, for example the highest proportion of $\dot{V}O_{2\,max}$ that can be sustained in long-lasting conditions. Muscle endurance constitutes a local factor reflected in the ability of a specific muscle group to contract repeatedly under prescribed conditions (see Figure 5.1).

In field sports, a high level of aerobic fitness helps to sustain the work rates associated with team play, supporting team mates, running off the ball, and chasing opponents to regain possession. In soccer, for example, elite players cover about 9–13 km during a competitive match at an average intensity of around 75% of their maximal oxygen uptake ($\dot{V}O_{2max}$) and the aerobic system contributes approximately 90% of the total energy cost of match-play (Stølen et al., 2005). Whilst the aerobic contribution to a single short-duration sprint is small, there is an increasing aerobic contribution during repeated sprint activities observed in field sports (Spencer et al., 2005); therefore aerobic fitness will aid recovery in the intermissions between the high-intensity exercise bouts. A good aerobic conditioning base provides a platform of fitness for tolerating the strain of sport-specific training and playing matches. Its importance is further underlined by the findings that improved aerobic fitness in junior soccer players led to a significant increase in match work rate (Impellizzeri et al., 2006).

In this chapter aerobic metabolism is first explained and its relevance in games contexts is outlined. The various ways in which aerobic fitness can be determined in laboratory conditions at both maximal and submaximal exercise intensities are

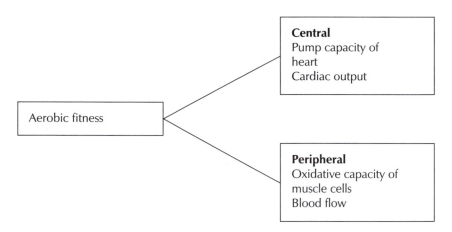

Figure 5.1 The factors influencing endurance capability of games players are both central and peripheral

then considered. There are adjustments made with respect to the exercise protocol and the ergometry used in order to satisfy sports specificity requirements. The analytical equipment used in these assessments has become increasingly automated, although conventional approaches are still employed in many laboratories. In recent years there has been increased emphasis on the use of field tests for practical convenience and some of the more established performance tests are highlighted. Despite the large number of recent studies on fitness in various field sports at all levels of play, there is no nationally or internationally adopted test nor are there associated standards for measuring aerobic performance.

AEROBIC METABOLISM

Aerobic energy is produced within the muscle mitochondria from the use of oxygen, which is supplied in the blood. The substrate for this reaction may be formed through glycolysis, by means of the utilisation of carbohydrates. Substrates may also be derived by catabolism of fat and, to a small extent, amino acids. The net reaction of carbohydrate utilisation is:

glycogen (glucose) + 39(38)ADP + 39(38)P_i + 39(38)H^+ + $6O_2 \rightarrow$
39(38) ATP + $6CO_2$ + $6H_2O$

Three of the 39 ATP molecules produced are formed anaerobically (i.e. without oxygen). Glycogen stored within the exercising muscles is the primary form of carbohydrate provision for glycolysis, but glucose taken up in the blood from the liver also can be used. Glucose is formed in the liver when glycogen is broken down by means of a process known as glycogenolysis. It may also be formed from precursors such as glycerol, pyruvate, lactate and amino acids through gluco-neogenesis.

Triglycerides (triacylglycerol) are lipids which are stored in the body's adipose tissue cells and also within the skeletal muscles. They form the substrates for fat oxidation and are broken down by lipase enzymes into glycerol and free fatty acids. The free fatty acids are mobilised in the bloodstream and enter the muscle fibres by diffusion where they are catabolised by the mitochondria. Fat (lipids) provides about twice as much energy per gram as does carbohydrate, and so is a good means of storing energy reserves. The oxidation of carbohydrate requires less energy than does fat and consequently, the latter is the preferred fuel when exercise is at high intensity. In contrast, fat is the preferred substrate for prolonged exercise and when the intensity is relatively low.

The relative contribution to the energy produced from oxidation of carbohydrates is increased at higher exercise intensities. Glycolysis leading to formation of lactate contributes significantly to the production of energy only when exercise intensities exceed about 60% of maximum oxygen uptake ($\dot{V}O_{2\,max}$). As exercise continues, the glycogen concentration in the exercising muscles becomes progressively reduced, which leads to increased uptake of glucose from the blood and a greater reliance on oxidation of fat. The change to fat as a source of fuel for exercise is reflected in a lowered respiratory exchange ratio, i.e. the relative proportions of CO_2 and O_2 in the expired air.

The main purpose of ventilation ($\dot{V}E$) during aerobic exercise is to maintain constant and favourable concentrations of $\dot{V}O_2$ and CO_2 in the alveolar chambers. An effective exchange of gases is thereby ensured before the oxygenated blood leaves the lungs for distribution throughout the body. Performance of aerobic exercise is not normally limited by lung capacity except under certain circumstances. Pulmonary function may be restricted in asthmatic individuals. This restriction is usually indicated by a subnormal value for the forced expiratory volume (FEV_1) which is measured in a single breath of forceful exhalation and reflects the power of the lungs. Values are reduced in players suffering from asthma or exercise-induced bronchospasm. Exercise-induced asthma is generally triggered in the post-exercise period and recovery may take 30–50 min unless bronchodilators are used to ease breathing difficulties.

Ventilatory responses to exercise may be altered as a result of aerobic training. As maximal oxygen uptake ($\dot{V}O_{2\,max}$) is improved with training, there is a corresponding increase in the maximal minute ventilation ($\dot{V}E_{max}$). There is a reduction in the ventilation equivalent of oxygen ($\dot{V}E/\dot{V}O_2$) at submaximal exercise such that less air is inhaled at a given oxygen uptake. The expired air of trained athletes contains less oxygen than that of untrained individuals for a given $\dot{V}O_2$. This difference reflects the capacity of trained muscle to extract more of the oxygen passing through the tissues in the local circulation. Endurance training also causes a rise in the ventilation threshold (T_{vent}) which represents the exercise intensity at which $\dot{V}E$ starts to increase disproportionately to rises in $\dot{V}O_2$ in response to a progressive exercise test. This effect may be related to metabolic alterations, but is specific to the type of exercise used in training (Reilly and Bangsbo, 1998).

The cardiac output indicates the amount of blood pumped from the heart and is a function of both stroke volume and heart rate. Cardiac output may increase from $5\,l\,min^{-1}$ at rest to $30\,l\,min^{-1}$ at maximal oxygen uptake, depending upon the capacity of the individual. The cardiac output of Olympic endurance athletes may exceed this upper level. Endurance training causes an increase in left ventricular chamber size and a consequent decrease in resting and submaximal heart rate, an increase in maximal cardiac output, a rise in maximal oxygen uptake and an increase in total blood volume. The maximal oxygen uptake tends to be limited by central factors (cardiac output) rather than peripheral factors (including oxidative capacity of skeletal muscle) in elite athletes who are adapted physiologically to endurance training. Both of these limitations may apply to games players (see Figure 5.1).

The oxygen-carrying capacity of the blood is dependent on the total amount of haemoglobin it contains. Oxygen is transported bound to haemoglobin within the red blood cells and unloaded when blood reaches the active tissues. The red blood cell population is renewed by the actions of the hormone erythropoietin, secreted by the kidneys and targeted at the bone marrow. A decrease in haemoglobin concentration is characteristic of anaemia and this condition causes aerobic performance to deteriorate. A diet low in iron intake or in vitamins facilitating iron absorption may compromise red blood cell production. Deficiencies in serum ferritin and low haemoglobin concentration can be identified in games players by means of routine blood sampling.

The ability of skeletal muscle to consume oxygen is influenced by blood flow, the network of capillaries around the muscle cells, the number and content of mitochondria and the type of muscle fibres. Enzymes of the metabolic pathways engaged in aerobic performance are enhanced due to endurance training and the number and size of the mitochondria are increased. The twitch characteristics and histochemical properties of muscle fibres also influence performance. Individuals specialising in endurance sports tend to have a predominance of slow-twitch fibre types, whereas sprinters are characterised by their high proportion of fast-twitch or Type II fibres. Games players are generally somewhere in between these extremes of fibre types. Endurance training increases the oxidative enzymes and myoglobin content of the intermediate Type IIa fibres, without altering their twitch properties. Muscle biopsies of games players demonstrate a balanced combination of muscle fibre types, reflecting the multiple requirements of the sport and variability between positional roles (Reilly and Doran, 2003).

MAXIMAL OXYGEN UPTAKE

Assessment protocols

The maximal ability to consume oxygen is established in a laboratory protocol whereby the exercise intensity is gradually increased until the individual reaches voluntary exhaustion. Respiratory gases are analysed during the test, the volume of air is recorded and the utilisation of oxygen and production of CO_2 are calculated. The maximal oxygen uptake is the highest value of $\dot{V}O_2$ attained during exercise, usually over a 20- to 30-s period. As evidence that a maximal value has been reached, the assessment is subjected to the following criteria; two out of these three criteria are normally accepted as fulfilling test requirements:

i)   a plateau in $\dot{V}O_2$ despite an increase in the exercise intensity;
ii) a blood lactate concentration in excess of 8 mmol l^{-1};
iii) a maximal heart rate within 95% or 10 beats.min^{-1} of the age-predicted maximal value (220 – age);
iv) a final respiratory exchange ratio of 1.15 or higher;
v)   a rating of perceived exertion of 19 or 20 on Borg's 6–20 scale.

For further information on criteria (terminologies and methodologies) used to quantify maximal effort, see work by Howley et al. (1995), Cooke (2003) and Svensson and Drust (2005).

The exercise protocol may be continuous or discontinuous. A common protocol is for 2-min stages after a warm-up, the velocity being increased by 2 km.h^{-1} until a speed of 16 km.h^{-1} is reached, after which an increase in incline by 2.5° every 2 min is implemented until the individual can no longer maintain the exercise intensity. The advantage of this protocol is that exhaustion is reached relatively quickly, within 10–16 min. The discontinuous protocol can be comprised of 3 or 4-min stages with a brief intermission in between. Blood samples may be obtained in this interval, as the likelihood is that the athlete will have displayed a steady-state response to exercise by this time. A disadvantage of this protocol is the length of time it takes to reach a maximal response. Often the two methods are combined with three to four stages to determine submaximal responses, followed by a more progressive advance to voluntary exhaustion in steps of shorter duration.

As locomotion is an important feature of games play, a running treadmill is the most appropriate ergometer for the assessment of participants. A motor-driven treadmill is preferable since the velocities and inclines can be controlled with great precision. The belt speed should be checked regularly for correct calibration and the gradient compared against the values shown using an inclinometer. Contemporary treadmills have programmable functions and the exercise protocol may be pre-set rather than regulated manually as the assessment is being conducted. Non-motorised treadmills are more suitable for training rather than assessment purposes, but have been used for anaerobic assessments and tests of repeated-sprint ability (Hughes et al., 2006).

A selection of mean values for maximal oxygen uptake of soccer teams is shown in Table 5.1. In all cases the measurements were made directly in laboratory assessments. The average values tend to exceed 60.ml.kg^{-1}.min^{-1} for the elite professional team but the variability is noticeable. This variation is due to positional differences, playing style, stage of fitness or age of individual players and tactical roles assigned to them. A significant difference in aerobic fitness of amateur Rugby League players, compared with that of professional Rugby League players has been reported (Gabbett, 2000). Although differences in findings between playing levels

108

Table 5.1 Maximal oxygen uptake of elite soccer players (from Reilly and Doran, 2003; Svensson and Drust, 2005; Stølen et al., 2005; Gil et al., 2007)

Original source	Team/level	VO_{2MAX} $(ml.kg^{-1}.min^{-1})$
Europe		
Wisløff et al. (1998)	Norway – Champions	67.6 ± 4.0
Casajús (2001)	Spain – Division 1 (n = 12)	66.4 ± 7.6
Faina et al. (1988)	Italia – Amateur (n = 6)	64.1 ± 7.2
Wisløff et al. (1998)	Norway – First League (n = 29)	63.7 ± 3.5
McMillan et al. (2005)	Professional Youth Team/Scotland	63.4 ± 5.6
Apor (1988)	Hungarian Elite Youth	63.2 ± 8.1
Edwards et al. (2003)	Professional English (n = 12)	63.3 ± 5.8
Gil et al. (2007)	Elite Spanish U/17 (n = 32)	62.0 ± 2.0
Puga et al. (1998)	Portuguese 1st Division	59.6 ± 7.7
Urhausen et al. (1996)	German – top-level players	59.5 ± 4.8
Rest of the World		
Chamari et al. (2005)	U/19 elite Senegal/Tunisia	61.1 ± 4.6
Aziz et al. (2000)	Singapore National Team (n = 23)	58.2 ± 3.7
Al-Hazzaa et al. (2001)	Saudi – National Team (n =23)	58.0 ± 4.9
Green (1992)	Australian National League	57.6 ± 3.5
Da Silva et al. (1999)	Brazilian Professional (n =27)	52.52 ± 7.49

are partly due to lower game intensity and number of matches and an inappropriate training stimulus, the higher percentage body fat in amateur participants also contributes to a lower estimated $\dot{V}O_{2max}$ (Gabbett, 2005). Before interpreting information on oxygen uptake and energy expenditure, Winter and Eston (2007) recommended that data should be scaled according to differences in body mass. In field sports such as soccer, $\dot{V}O_{2max}$ values of heavier players tend to be under-estimated whereas values tend to be overestimated in players with a lower body mass (Svensson and Drust, 2005).

Laboratory equipment

The conventional means of measuring maximal oxygen uptake was by using Douglas Bags or meteorological balloons to collect expired air (Cooke, 2003). The participant breathed through a two-way valve and the outlet for expired air was connected to the bag. A single bag was used for each step (see Figure 5.2), typically each collection being over the final 60 s of an individual stage. The oxygen and CO_2 content in a sample of air drawn from the bag was determined using separate gas analysers. The volume of air expired was recorded by passing the air collected through a dry gas meter. Laboratory temperature and ambient pressure were measured and appropriate corrections made to the recordings for the gases. The values for $\dot{V}E$, $\dot{V}CO_2$, $\dot{V}O_2$ were determined using standard calculations and assumptions (see Cooke, 2003).

The original sensors in the analytical equipment were paramagnetic for oxygen and infrared for CO_2. With the development of online gas analysis, fuel cells (using zirconium, for example) came into common use (see Reilly and Brooks, 1982). Pneumotachographs, pressure transducers and demodulators were used for determining volumes of air inspired or expired. Breath-by-breath systems enabled oxygen kinetics to be measured and introduced a new level of sophistication towards studying respiratory responses to exercise (see Figure 5.3).

When face masks were introduced as alternatives to the more cumbersome two-way values, assessment of maximal physiological capacities became more automated. Calibration procedures for gas concentration and volumes are currently controlled by the system's on-board computer. Similarly, face masks are incorporated into the gas analysis systems that are designed for assessments in field conditions.

The advent of short-range telemetry and the design of lightweight portable apparatus have revolutionised applied sports science work. Heart-rate monitoring is now a routine procedure in field settings and as a gauge of maximal effort in performance tests. In contemporary professional soccer, physiological responses such as heart rate and blood lactate are used to monitor and quantify intensity of

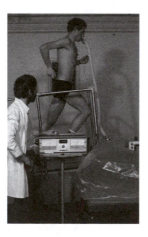

Figure 5.2 Air expired is collected into Douglas Bags for determination of $\dot{V}O_2$

Figure 5.3 Maximal exercise test using online gas analysis for determination of $\dot{V}O_{2max}$ in an international football player

aerobic performace

training drills to provide an appropriate training stimulus for physical development (Carling and Le Gall, 2003; Little and Williams, 2007). Radio telemetry of $\dot{V}O_2$ is also feasible. The analytical equipment containing sensors for measuring gas concentrations and expired air flow can be worn as a backpack. Using these devices in practical set-ups is more convenient than the traditional Douglas Bag method, where the more cumbersome apparatus was likely to hamper the activity being monitored.

Intermittent exercise protocols have been devised to simulate the work rates associated with competitive soccer (Drust et al., 2000b). Motor-driven treadmills may be programmed so that the belt speed is altered automatically, corresponding to the pattern of changes typically observed in a game. The simulation has been used to evaluate nutritional interventions (Clarke et al., 2005), immune responses (Sari-Sarraf et al., (2006) and pre-cooling the body before commencement of exercise (Drust et al., 2000a). Similar programmes may be designed to represent the exercise intensities of other games under laboratory conditions.

SUBMAXIMAL LABORATORY ASSESSMENTS

Running economy

Running economy is indicated by the oxygen cost of locomotion at a fixed exercise intensity. The oxygen uptake is recorded and is expressed relative to body mass in $ml.kg^{-1}$ min^{-1}. It is typically recorded as an accessory measure of submaximal responses to exercise, determined during a steady-rate stage of exercise when the primary purpose may be to assess 'anaerobic threshold'. A reduction in the oxygen consumption at a set exercise intensity in repeated assessments over a season would indicate an improvement in 'economy'.

The mechanical efficiency represents the work done as a percentage of the energy expenditure. The work done can be measured, expressed in watts and converted to joules or work per unit time. Efficiency may be expressed as a gross value, or net when the resting metabolic rate has been taken into account. It may also be expressed as a delta value, by comparing changes in $\dot{V}O_2$ with a known increase in mechanical power output. The calculations are easy to determine in cycle ergometry or other devices where power production can be quantified. These measurements are complex when the mode of exercise is treadmill running and as a result 'running economy' is an accepted alternative to establishing 'efficiency'.

Whilst running economy is in principle applicable to games players, it has not gained wide acceptance among practitioners. This reluctance may reflect a lack of confidence in this variable as a fitness measure, and changes with training are likely to be small. Further research is needed to examine the sports-specific exercise economy of field-games players, for example, when running with the ball (Helgerud et al., 2001) and the effects of specific training interventions on this element of performance. Nevertheless, it can have value in individual cases, for example during rehabilitation when a games player is recovering from an injury.

Anaerobic threshold

The upper level at which exercise can be sustained for a prolonged period is thought to be indicated by the so called 'anaerobic threshold': this variable is usually expressed as the work rate corresponding to a blood lactate concentration of 4 mmol.l^{-1}, the onset of accumulation of lactate in the blood (OBLA) or as a deflection in the relation between ventilation and oxygen consumption with incremental exercise (the ventilatory threshold). The $\dot{V}O_2$ corresponding to a blood lactate concentration of 3 mmol.l^{-1} was found to be about 80% of $\dot{V}O_{2max}$ for both a continuous and an interval test on Danish soccer players running on a treadmill (Bangsbo and Lindquist, 1992). This reference lactate level for the continuous test was significantly correlated with distance covered in a game (see Figure 5.4). Variation in lactate threshold (Tlac) according to positional role has also been reported. Bangsbo (1994) found that elite Danish midfield players and fullbacks had higher lactate thresholds than goalkeepers and central defenders. Whilst the average fractional utilisation of $\dot{V}O_{2max}$ during match play is about 75–80% $\dot{V}O_{2max}$ and is probably close to the 'anaerobic threshold', soccer players at elite level operate at or above this intensity frequently during a game. Lactate threshold has also been shown to fluctuate across the playing season and has been used for monitoring training adaptations via changes in aerobic fitness in elite rugby (Campi et al., 1992) and soccer players (McMillan et al., 2005).

The lactate threshold is determined from responses to a submaximal test. The player runs at four different speeds on a treadmill, each for 4 min. A blood sample is drawn from a fingertip or ear lobe during short pauses between the progressive bouts. The relationship between blood lactate and running velocity is plotted and a reference value of 4 mmol.l^{-1} (or 3 mmol.l^{-1}) may be selected as this concentration is shown to be a good predictor of endurance performance. The running velocity corresponding to this value can be recorded as V-4 mM.

Whilst the lactate response to exercise has been used to indicate the so-called 'anaerobic threshold', there is no universally accepted method for its detection. It may be identified with a mathematical curve-fitting technique to establish the exercise intensity or $\dot{V}O_2$ at which lactate begins to accumulate in the blood. This

aerobic performace

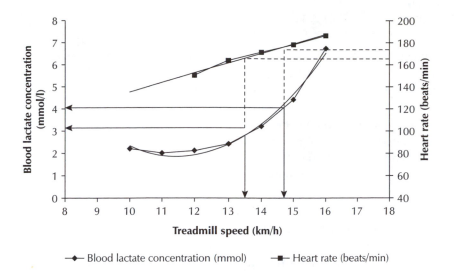

Figure 5.4 The blood lactate response to incremental exercise, with 3-mM and 4-mM 'thresholds' indicated by the arrows. Corresponding heart-rate values are shown in the upper lines (reproduced from Reilly, 2007 with permission)

task is more difficult than calculating the exercise intensity corresponding to a fixed blood lactate concentration, such as 3 mmol.l^{-1} or 4 mmol.l^{-1}. Determination of 'maximal lactate steady state' requires a series of laboratory visits to identify the highest exercise intensity at which blood lactate values stabilise rather than continue to increase. These various methods of determining Tlac have been reviewed by Jones and Doust (2001).

The lactate response is reduced with training as the individual improves in clearing lactate from the system and with endurance exercise producing less lactate within active muscles. A higher lactate threshold theoretically means that a field-games player could maintain a higher average intensity during a match without accumulation of lactate. The result of a training intervention is that the lactate response curve is shifted to the right. In addition to a modification in the running velocity corresponding to Tlac, a marked reduction in heart rate at the same given running velocity is a typical accompanying response to a period of training although the magnitude of error when considering this marker of training status needs to be considered (Lamberts et al., 2004). The lactate curve can also be affected by diet as a similar shift of the curve to the right occurs when carbohydrate stores are lowered, the curve moving to the left following carbohydrate ingestion (Reilly and Bryant, 1986). The latter shift might erroneously be interpreted as a detraining effect and therefore strict control over diet is advised when lactate responses are being monitored.

Australian Rules football (ARF) players are reported to cover large distances in games and carry out frequent sprint and high-intensity actions. Enhancing aerobic endurance capacity is therefore an essential factor for achieving optimal performance. Whilst aerobic fitness is improved during the pre-season period, Bishop and co-workers (2007) investigated whether there were changes in aerobic fitness over the course of seasons in professional ARF players and whether these players were able to maintain or improve their aerobic fitness during the competition season. Eighteen senior members of a professional ARF club were tested in a laboratory at three different time points throughout the season (beginning of pre-season, end of pre-season, end of competitive season). Testing included an incremental treadmill test for the determination of $\dot{V}O_{2max}$, the lactate threshold (increase in lactate >1 mmol.l^{-1}) and running economy at 10 km.h^{-1}. During the pre-season period, there was a significant increase in the lactate threshold, running economy and $\dot{V}O_{2max}$. At the end of the competition season, there was no significant change in these performance factors. The authors concluded that despite less time allocated for fitness training as the season progressed, players were able to maintain their aerobic fitness during the competitive season. Therefore, in-season aerobic training in professional ARF may not be necessary and coaches could allocate training time to other forms of physical or skill-based activities.

Only a small quantity of blood is needed for the current generation of portable lactate analysers. The sports scientist should use gloves for reasons of hygiene and safety when drawing the sample. The fact that the analyses can be done quickly means that assessment of blood lactate is a useful tool in field testing. It also avoids issues associated with the Human Tissues Act (2004) which applies when blood is removed and stored for later analysis. The i-STAT clinical portable analyser (i-STAT Corporation, East Windsor, USA, see http://www.abbottpointofcare.com/) is one example of the current generation of portable lactate analysers. It can accurately and reliably determine in the field-based setting, the concentration of up to 19 haematological analytes of venous or capillary blood within 120 s (Dascombe et al., 2007). The portability and versatility of such systems provide sport scientists with greater diagnostic capabilities of the biochemical responses to exercise in field sports.

A non-invasive method of measuring a phenomenon related to Tlac is to measure ventilatory threshold (Tvent). This point refers to the deflection in the relationship between ventilation and oxygen consumption with incremental exercise. The deflection point is not always clear and other variables, such as $\dot{V}CO_2$, are employed for clarification. The Tvent can be a useful measure to demonstrate submaximal adaptation with training, and has been shown by Casajús (2001) to be more sensitive to seasonal variations in fitness than $\dot{V}O_{2max}$ in a Spanish professional football team. Measurement of Tvent can be incorporated into an exercise protocol for assessment of $\dot{V}O_{2max}$ and hence does not require repeated visits for its identification.

FIELD TESTS

Generic tests – the 20-m shuttle run

Field tests refer to measures that can be implemented in the typical training environment and do not necessarily require a visit to an institutional laboratory for assessment. Such tests enhance the specificity of the evaluation and hence their face validity and are commonly used by coaches and applied sports scientists working with elite players to evaluate game-related performance. An implication is that tests can be performed without recourse to complex monitoring equipment and are therefore accessible to coaches at the lower end of field games. For example, many tests require a simple measuring tape, a Test CD and CD player, running area and cones. Additionally, field tests allow the administrator to assess several players rapidly and simultaneously which is an important factor when taking into account the busy schedules of elite sports performers. However, the problem lies in the standardisation of the test conditions between periods of testing, especially as many tests are undertaken outdoors and are subject to climatic changes or suffer from variations in playing surface type and quality. In addition, heart-rate monitors may also be required to ensure that maximal effort during tests has been achieved (Grantham, 2007).

The Eurofit test battery (Adam et al., 1988) offers a range of fitness items for which norms are available to help in interpreting results. Whilst the tests utilise performance measures such as runs, jumps, throws and so on, they are designed to assess physiological functions such as strength, power, muscle endurance and aerobic power, albeit indirectly.

The validation of the 20-m shuttle run test for estimating maximal oxygen uptake (Léger and Lambert, 1982) marked a step forward for sports science support programmes. Athletes may be tested as a squad in a gymnasium or on open ground such as a car park or synthetic sports surface. The pace of motion between two lines 20 m apart is dictated by signals from an audio tape recorder, giving the name 'the bleep test' to the protocol. The pace is increased progressively, analogous to the determination of $\dot{V}O_{2max}$ on a motor-driven treadmill, until the athlete reaches volitional exhaustion. The final stage reached is recorded and the $\dot{V}O_{2max}$ can be estimated using tables provided by Ramsbottom et al. (1988). For children, the prediction of $\dot{V}O_{2max}$ has been validated by Léger at al. (1988). The test is still widely used at elite levels across a range of field sports. In netball for example, a stage level and shuttle of 12 and 5 respectively (corresponding to a $\dot{V}O_{2max}$ of 55.1 ml.kg^{-1}.min^{-1}) is considered to be the performance standard for English players to attain for playing at national level (Grantham, 2007).

A real advantage of the 20-m shuttle run test is that a sizeable number of individuals can be accommodated together. Therefore, a time period normally used for training can be allocated for administration of the test to an entire squad of team members. A further benefit is that the turns at the end of each 20-m section have relevance for field sports. A limitation is that there is no direct physiological evidence that maximal effort is provided, although monitoring of heart rate can constitute a reasonable basis for evaluating individual input. The test offers only a prediction of $\dot{V}O_{2max}$ rather than a direct measurement as expired air is not usually collected. The development of lightweight portable metabolic measurement systems has facilitated the measurement of oxygen uptake during sports-specific tests (Hoff, 2005) although this may limit the number of individuals that can be assessed at one time. Current lightweight portable systems allow data to be transferred via telemetry to a laptop computer at a distance of up to 1,000 metres (Meyers, 2006). The Cosmed portable gas analyser (K4b^2 Cosmed, Rome, Italy, http://www.cosmed.it/) is commonly used in fitness and performance assessment. In field sports, it has been used to record cardiorespiratory responses to 5-a-side indoor soccer (Castagna et al., 2007b) and during field-hockey play (Bishop et al., 2001). The low weight of this system (under 500 grams) ensures that it does not alter energy demands during exercise. Whilst some problematic assumptions exist with such devices (Atkinson et al., 2005), the reliability and validity of this new generation of systems has been adequately confirmed (Carter and Jeukendrup, 2002; Eisenmann et al., 2003).

Tests of the accuracy of the 20-m shuttle run field test in predicting $\dot{V}O_{2max}$ have indicated contradictory results when compared to observations obtained in graded treadmill tests. The different turning and stopping actions influence the musculature involved in field-test running and therefore energy utilisation will be affected and result in discrepancies in performance when compared to data obtained from steady-state running forward on a treadmill. Metsios and co-workers (2008) proposed a square variation of the 20-m shuttle run test to minimise the effects of turning and stopping on the precision of the protocol and therefore provided a closer resemblance to gold standard treadmill tests used in measuring $\dot{V}O_{2max}$. Prediction of maximal aerobic power from the 20-m multi-stage shuttle run test was shown to underpredict $\dot{V}O_{2max}$ for both male and female athletes (Stickland et al., 2003). Recent work has improved the efficacy of the prediction equations, thus providing increased accuracy in evaluating aspects of fitness (Flouris et al., 2005). As an alternative, the test result can be expressed as the total distance covered (endurance performance) (Stølen et al., 2005). The 20-m shuttle run test may not be sensitive enough to detect changes in $\dot{V}O_{2max}$ and is therefore unsuitable for assessing the effects of a training intervention. This limitation is probably due to the continuous activity pattern which does not reflect the intermittent activity profile of team sports.

Nevertheless, values expressed as $\dot{V}O_{2max}$ obtained from this test protocol tend to distinguish between the various field sports, within teams (often between playing positions) and playing standards. McIntyre (2005) compared aerobic performance of players belonging to a League of Ireland soccer team to that of Gaelic footballers and hurlers at Irish inter-county level. A significantly greater aerobic performance was observed in the soccer players, whereas no difference in performance was observed between hurlers and footballers. In Division I University female lacrosse players, estimated aerobic power was 46.8 ± 4.4 ml.kg^{-1}.min^{-1} with a range of 33.3–57.6 ml.kg^{-1}.min^{-1} for the entire group (Vescovi et al., 2007). Values ranging from 51.8 ml.kg^{-1}.min^{-1} to 59.6 ml.kg^{-1} min^{-1} have been reported across different levels of Rugby Union (Duthie et al., 2003).

Cooper's 12-minute run test

The aim in using this test (Cooper, 1968) is to determine endurance capacity by means of recording distance run in 12 minutes. It is possible also to estimate maximal oxygen uptake from performance in the 12-minute test. A measured outdoor track is required for the conduction of the test. The ideal is a running track with each lap being 400 m. Alternatively, a course marked around playing fields can be used, provided the distance per lap is measured accurately.

The test entails a maximal effort over the 12 minutes and so is dependant on the motivation of the participant. For this reason the pacing of effort is a real challenge. Grouping players according to playing position or to previous determined standards of performance may aid motivation. Participants can set off at fixed intervals between one another and be called to stop in turn as time runs out.

The distance covered in 12 minutes is recorded to the nearest 10 m for each individual. This distance is converted to miles or metres, one mile being equivalent to 1609 metres. For individuals of a high aerobic fitness level, the test tends to overestimate $\dot{V}O_{2max}$ and is more useful as an aerobic performance measure for games competitors. Maximal oxygen uptake ($\dot{V}O_{2max}$) can be predicted from the formula:

$$\dot{V}O_{2max} \, (ml.kg^{-1}.min^{-1}) = \frac{(\text{distance in miles (D)} - 0.3138)}{0.0278}$$

An individual who had covered 2.6 km in the 12 min would have a $\dot{V}O_{2max}$ of:

$$\dot{V}O_{2max} = \frac{(2.6 - 0.3138) \div 0.0278}{1.609} = 46.84 \, ml.kg^{-1}.min^{-1}$$

Cooper's test has been used in field assessments of soccer players and also for purposes of determining the fitness of referees, although more task-specific tests such as the Yo-Yo Intermittent Recovery Test (YYIRT) have recently been devised and validated for use with elite referees (Castagna et al., 2007a). Data have been reported for the Brazilian National soccer team and for professional players in the United States (Raven et al., 1976). The test has not been applied much to games players in recent years, since tests with specificity to the sport have greater utility value.

A related test is the 3-km timed run described for Rugby Union by Scott et al. (2003) and Tong and Wiltshire (2007). This procedure involves the completion of 7.5 laps on a 400-m synthetic running track. Although inexpensive and easy to perform, this test is also limited by being self-paced: it is not possible to know whether the player could have gone faster.

To a certain degree, maximum oxygen uptake expresses the physical capacity of a player, and can be used for comparisons across playing levels and sports. However, the field tests mentioned above may not accurately express the ability to perform prolonged intermittent exercise with alternating intensities as is required in field sports. In addition, maximal oxygen uptake may not be a sensitive enough indicator of fitness for regular use within the competitive season when changes in physiological systems and in performance will be small (Svensson and Drust, 2005). Field tests which have greater validity and are more specific to the physical demands of field games should help to improve sensitivity.

The 15–40 Test

Svensson and Drust (2005) described a shuttle run test with alterations in distance covered before turning and variations in the recovery periods; these changes in activity were designed to suit the intermittent exercise patterns of match-play in soccer. The distances between turning points vary from 15 to 40 m, a variation that gives the name to the test. The test has a submaximal component for assessment of endurance status and a maximal part intended to elicit maximal aerobic power

aerobic performace

with a large anaerobic contribution to the final effort. The heart rate is monitored throughout the entire test. The submaximal stage could be incorporated into the early part of a training session, might be used regularly and has potential for suggesting 'overtraining' by indicating higher than usual heart-rate responses. The complete test to the end of the maximal stage might be used less frequently, for example, at key stages in the competitive season.

The Yo-Yo tests

The Yo-Yo tests were designed to test the capability to sustain high-intensity activity for a long period and are a more football-specific adaptation of the multi-stage fitness test. The test was designed by Bangsbo and Michalsik (2002) for relevance to field games, especially soccer. In the test the participant performs repeated 20-m shuttle runs interspersed with a short recovery period during which the participant jogs. The time allowed for a shuttle is decreased progressively as dictated by audio bleeps from a tape recorder. The test ends when the athlete is unable to continue, the score recorded being the number of shuttles completed.

The Yo-Yo Intermittent Endurance Test evaluates the ability to perform intense exercise repeatedly during prolonged intermittent exercise. A 5-s rest period is allowed between each shuttle and the duration of the test in total is between 10 and 20 min, during which the player must return to the starting point. A warning is given when the player does not complete a successful shuttle out and back in the allocated time. The participant is generally removed from the test the next time he or she does not complete a successful shuttle, although two warnings may also be given.

The ability to recover from intense exercise is evaluated by means of the Yo-Yo Intermittent Recovery Test. The running speeds are higher than in the Yo-Yo Intermittent Endurance Test, but a 10-s period of jogging is permitted between each shuttle. The total duration of the test may range between 2 and 15 min. The sensitivity of the Yo-Yo tests in discriminating players' performances at various competitive levels, between different playing positions and after periods of different types of training has been well demonstrated (Bangsbo et al., 2008). Any field test should be sufficiently sensitive for training-induced improvements to be reflected by improvements in the test (Chamari et al., 2005). Furthermore, while the Yo-Yo Intermittent Recovery Test was initially designed for testing performance in soccer players, its validity for measuring performance in elite professional and semi-professional Rugby League players has been demonstrated (Atkins, 2006). This test also distinguished between selected and non-selected players in elite Australian Rules Football (Young et al., 2005)

Both tests have two levels, one for elite soccer players and another for recreational players with the difference being that the running speeds are higher at level II. For a trained person, the Yo-Yo IR1 test lasts 10–20 min and mainly focuses on an individual's endurance capacity, whereas the Yo-Yo IIR2 test lasts 5–15 min and aims at evaluating a trained person's ability to perform a repeated intense exercise bout that incorporates a high anaerobic energy contribution (Krustrup et al., 2006). The Yo-Yo IR1 test fulfils these purposes for a less trained person. Mohr et al. (2003) described an alternative submaximal version of the Yo-Yo Intermittent Recovery Test lasting 6 min which uses measurements of heart rate to predict performance. The submaximal test used by Impellizzeri et al. (2004) in elite Italian soccer examines the relationship between speed at OBLA and blood lactate concentration at the end of a 6-min run at 13.5 km.h^{-1} to estimate aerobic fitness. These modified non-exhaustive tests are attractive for in-season evaluation as high-energy-demanding maximal efforts are often not welcomed by coaches.

Castagna et al. (2006b) recently investigated the physiological determinants of the Yo-Yo Endurance Test Level 2 (YYETL2) and Yo-Yo Intermittent Recovery Test Level 1 (YYIRTL1) in soccer players. Findings showed that YYETL2 and YYIRTL1, although adopting similar starting and progression speeds and both focusing on endurance capacity, were influenced by different physiological variables and that YYETL2 can be considered more an aerobic fitness-related field test, whereas YYIRTL1 can be regarded as an aerobic–anaerobic soccer-specific field test. This finding is of interest when deciding on a test for determining the effects of a training intervention on a specific energy system. It may also be important when deciding on the most relevant test to assess performance in young players. The Level 1 Yo-Yo Intermittent Endurance Test was shown to be a weak indicator of aerobic power in moderately trained youth soccer players (Castagna et al., 2006a).

It is recommended that the tests are conducted on a football field with the players wearing football boots. The tests can be completed in a relatively short period of time and a whole squad of up to 30 individuals can be tested at the same time. The Yo-Yo Intermittent Recovery Test is used as a compulsory test for football referees in Italy and Denmark, and both tests have been employed in professional teams in a number of European countries.

ALTERNATIVE FIELD OPTIONS

Various options for assessing aerobic performance in field conditions have been described in the literature. They range from attempts to assess aerobic power indirectly to evaluating game-related fitness.

Léger and Boucher (1980) designed a continuous multi-stage track test, known as the Montreal track test. It consisted of lapping an indoor track of 166.7 m. The speed was dictated by audio signals and increased every 2 min. The test constituted a variation of the group's 20-m shuttle run and was constructed to fit local conditions.

Two field tests commonly employed by elite French soccer clubs and other field sports in France include the VAM-EVAL test and the Probst test which are used to determine maximal aerobic velocity ($v\dot{V}O_{2max}$, the lowest velocity that elicits $\dot{V}O_{2max}$ during a graded test). This velocity is a sensitive indicator of aerobic capacity and can then be used to determine individual training intensity as it is arguably the optimal speed to train at to enhance $\dot{V}O_{2max}$ (Jones, 1998). Dupont et al. (2004) demonstrated a significant improvement in the $v\dot{V}O_{2max}$, hence $\dot{V}O_{2max}$, of a professional French soccer team after 10 weeks of in-season high-intensity interval training using runs at 120% of individually determined $v\dot{V}O_{2max}$.

The Probst field test consists of repetitions of 280-m runs including changes in direction separated by a 30-s rest with an initial speed of 8.4 km.h^{-1} and a 0.6.km.h^{-1} increment at each stage (Labsy et al., 2004). Chaouachi et al. (2005) recently described a version of the VAM-EVAL track test. This test requires a 400-m running track with cones placed every 20 m. A pre-recorded soundtrack makes brief sounds the instant when the subject must pass near a cone to maintain the imposed speed. A longer sound marks a change of stage. The first stage is set at 8 km.h^{-1} with subsequent increments of 0.5 km.h^{-1} per 1-min stages. The test is terminated when the subject is unable to maintain the imposed running speed. The speed corresponding to the last completed stage is recorded as $v\dot{V}O_{2max}$ (km.h^{-1}) which is then used to estimate $\dot{V}O_{2max}$. Data on the average $\dot{V}O_{2max}$ of French International soccer teams from U/15 up to U/21 level computed using the VAM-EVAL test are presented in Figure 5.5 (Carling, 2001).

The usefulness of these two tests commonly used in French field games may be limited due to their continuous activity pattern which does not reflect the intermittent activity profile of field sports. Recently, the 30–15 intermittent fitness test based on tests such as the Montreal track test and the VAM-EVAL, but which combines both intermittent and shuttle running has been validated (Buchheit, 2008). In this test, velocity is initially set at 8 km.h^{-1} for the first 30-s run, and speed is increased by 0.5 km.h^{-1} every 30-s stage thereafter. Participants are required to run back and forth between two lines (A and C) set 40 m apart (Figure 5.6) at a pace that is governed by a pre-recorded beep. The pre-recorded beep allows the subjects to adjust their running speed within a 3-m zone placed in the middle and at each extremity of the field. During the 15-s recovery period, participants walk in a forward direction towards the closest line (at either the middle or end of the running area, depending on where their previous run had stopped); they would

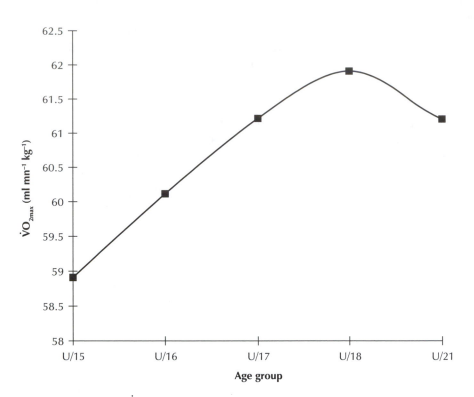

Figure 5.5 Average $\dot{V}O_{2max}$ values of international French soccer players from U/15 to U/21 level (adapted from Carling, 2001)

start the next run stage from this line. Participants are instructed to complete as many stages as possible and the test ends when the subject can no longer maintain the required running speed or when he or she is unable to reach a 3-m zone in time with the audio signal on three consecutive occasions. The maximal intermittent aerobic velocity attained during the last completed stage is recorded. This figure is then used to estimate $\dot{V}O_{2max}$ and can be employed as a basis for programming intermittent training intensities.

Bangsbo and Lindquist (1992) designed a soccer-specific endurance test as a proxy for $\dot{V}O_{2max.}$ The test consisted of intermittent exercise with 15-s bouts of high intensity followed by low-intensity exercise for 10 s. Altogether 40 bouts of the protocol were completed, the overall test taking 16.5 min. The distance covered represented the performance outcome. The Yo-Yo tests can be considered a refinement of this protocol.

Although various tests have been related closely to the physiological load imposed through match-play, they still appear to lack ecological validity with respect to the

aerobic performace

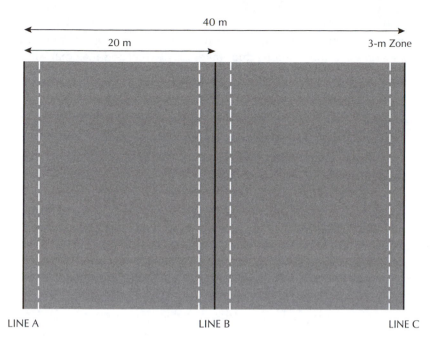

40 m

20 m

3-m Zone

LINE A   LINE B   LINE C

Figure 5.6 Area prepared for the 30–15 Intermittent Fitness Test (30–15IFT) (Buccheit, 2008)

motion types, directions, turns and intensities corresponding to the physical demands of the game, and do not provide sufficiently adapted protocols for the individual playing positions (Bloomfield et al., 2007). These problems may be resolved using motion-analysis methods for determining precise locomotor activities during matches (Carling et al., 2005). The Futsal intermittent endurance test is a free-running test, performed indoors, to simulate the exercise and rest periods observed during Futsal games (Barbero et al., 2005). This test uses a starting speed of 9 km.h^{-1} and shuttle runs over 45 m are carried out at a progressively increased speed controlled by audio beeps from a tape recorder. Between running bouts, the participants have a 10-s active rest (jogging) or 30-s passive rest (standing) period. During the test, eight running bouts with increments of 0.33 km.h^{-1} between each bout are carried out, then the test continues but with 0.2 k.mh^{-1} speed increments after each bout. This test has been shown to tax both the aerobic and anaerobic energy systems of Futsal players.

Kemi et al. (2003) designed a protocol for a soccer-specific field test to assess the highest V̇O$_2$ that could be achieved in the field setting in which the participants dribbled a ball round a multidirectional track. An intensity corresponding to 95% HR$_{max}$ was maintained for 3 min, after which speed was increased then to

aerobic performace

voluntary exhaustion. The test duration was approximately 6–8 min. During the test the heart rate and the oxygen uptake were recorded using separate radio telemetry systems and the highest values taken as field-related maximal values. The authors concluded that these values were typically within 10% of $\dot{V}O_{2max}$ determined under laboratory conditions.

PRACTICAL EXAMPLE 2

Chamari and co-workers (2005) developed a soccer-specific field-based test similar to that used by Kemi et al. (2003) for assessing aerobic performance in soccer. In this test, players must dribble the ball along a 290-m track with various obstacles and changes in direction for 10 min. The purpose of the test is to cover the maximum distance during the 10-min period. Results showed that performance (distance covered) in U/15 youth soccer players was correlated with laboratory measured $\dot{V}O_{2max}$. Training-induced improvements (after scaling) in $\dot{V}O_{2max}$ and running economy of 12% and 10% respectively after an 8-week period of normal soccer training plus specific endurance work were reflected by an improvement in performance of 9.6% in the test. The authors concluded that an achievable goal for U/15 players would be to cover >2100 m at the end of the test as this figure corresponded to a value of $\dot{V}O_{2max}$ >200 ml.kg$^{-0.75}$ min^{-1} which should serve as a minimum for modern soccer. Rupf and co-workers (2007) recently investigated energy expenditure when dribbling the ball in this test. Using a portable Cosmed gas analyser to measure oxygen consumption, they showed that dribbling a ball was associated with an additional increase in oxygen uptake and that the latter was directly related to running speed.

Examples of other soccer-specific field tests are shown in Table 5.2. They range from a series of sprints for incorporating assessment of the ability to recover from intermittent high-intensity exercise, to tests approximating the duration of match-play. The original purpose of each test should be considered before it is adopted for general use by practitioners.

Elferink-Gemser et al. (2004) developed a series of tests for the assessment of performance characteristics of talented young field-hockey players. The battery included a protocol for measuring endurance capacity as expressed in the sport with its intermittent exercise bouts. The test entailed repeated interval shuttle runs, as illustrated in Figure 5.7. The test was capable of discriminating between the elite and sub-elite players among the 126 players studied. The Interval Shuttle Sprint Test (ISST) and the Interval Shuttle Run Test (ISRT)) were used by Lemmink and

aerobic performace

Table 5.2 Examples of some selected soccer-specific field tests of aerobic performance (Svensson and Drust, 2005)

Author	Name of test	Description	Duration of test	Predominantly on components
Ekbolm (1989)	Interval field test	Four laps of a soccer pitch performing forward, backward, sideways and slalom running, including turning and jumping movements	16.5 min	Aerobic
Rico-Sanz, Zehnder, Buchli, Dambach, and Boutellier (1999)	JRS fatigue test	Repeated shuttle running at three different velocities	Until volitional exhaustion	Aerobic
Nicholas, Nuttall and Williams (2000)	Loughborough Intermittent Shuttle Test (LIST)	Running between two lines 20 m apart at various speeds	90 min	Aerobic
Kemi, Hoff, Engen, Helgerud and Wisløff (2003)	Field test (specifically to establish maximal oxygen uptake)	Laps of a course including dribbling, backwards running, turning, jumping	Until volitional exhaustion	Aerobic
Ohashi, Miyagi, Yasumatsu and Ishizaki (2003)	Field test	1- or 4-min set exercise periods with standing, walking, jogging or sprinting in squares (30 × 20 m)	90 min	Aerobic

Visscher (2006) to examine intermittent performance in women field-hockey players. The ISST required the players to perform 10 shuttle sprints starting every 20 s. During the ISRT, players alternately ran 20-m shuttles for 30 s and walked for 15 s with increasing speed. Results showed the different contributions of the aerobic and anaerobic energy systems during each individual test and depending on the aspect of physical performance a coach wants to determine, the ISST or ISRT can be used.

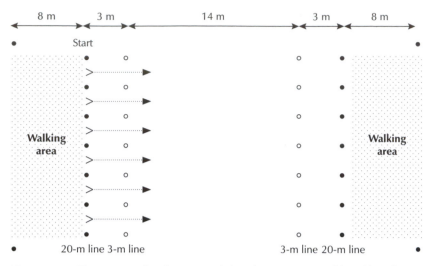

Figure 5.7 The course for the Interval shuttle run test used by Elferink-Gemser et al. (2004) for assessment of young field-hockey players

CONCLUSION

Aerobic fitness is important in field games due to the high tempo of play associated with success. The teams whose players have good endurance capabilities possess an advantage over less fit opponents. Over the years sports scientists have been challenged to design fitness tests that have specificity and practicality for the sport concerned.

A good oxygen-transport system is important for field sports and is represented in the use of maximal oxygen uptake as a fundamental physiological function to assess in laboratory conditions. Blood lactate responses to exercise may be more sensitive to endurance training adaptations than are maximal physiological measures. Variables such as running economy may have value, but most likely only in conjunction with other physiological indices of aerobic fitness.

The emphasis on sports specificity has promoted the design and validation of field-based tests. In some cases physiological responses, submaximal and maximal, complement the performance assessment. Tests such as the 20-m shuttle run can be used to estimate $\dot{V}O_{2max}$ but rely for their validity on the full compliance of subjects to exercise until voluntary exhaustion. The sports scientist operating in the context of competitive teams must choose whether the physiological information derived from classical laboratory tests outweighs the performance data from field assessments. In either case, the deviation from previously established baselines is more important to consider than is a single cross-sectional comparison between individual players.

REFERENCES

Adam, C., Klissouras, V., Ravazzolo, M., Renson, R. and Tuxworth, W. (1988) *EUROFIT: European Test of Physical Fitness*. Rome: Council of Europe, Committee for the Development of Sport.

Al-Hazzaa, H.M., Alumuzaini, K.S., Al-Rafee, A., Sulaiman, M.A., Dafterdar, M.Y., Al-Ghamedi, A. and Khuraji, K.N. (2001) Aerobic and anaerobic power characteristics of Saudi elite soccer players. *Journal of Sports Medicine and Physical Fitness*, 41: 54–61.

Apor, P. (1988) Successful formulae for fitness training. In T. Reilly, A. Lees, K. Davids and W. J. Murphy (eds), *Science and Football* (pp. 95–107). London: E & FN Spon.

Atkins, S.J. (2006) Performance of the Yo-Yo Intermittent Recovery Test by elite professional and semi-professional rugby league players. *Journal of Strength and Conditioning Research*, 20: 222–225.

Atkinson, G., Davison, R.C.R. and Nevill, A.M. (2005) Performance characteristics of gas analysis systems: what we know and what we need to know. *International Journal of Sports Medicine*, 26 (Suppl. 1): S2–S10.

Aziz, A.R., Chia, M. and The, K.C. (2000) The relationship between maximal oxygen uptake and repeated sprint performance indices in field hockey and soccer players. *Journal of Sports Medicine and Physical Fitness*, 40: 195–200.

Bangsbo, J. (1994) The physiology of soccer with special reference to intense intermittent exercise. *Acta Physiologica Scandinavica*, 151 (Suppl. 619): 1–155.

Bangsbo, J. (2000) Physiology of intermittent exercise. In W.E. Garrett and D.T. Kirkendall (eds), *Exercise and Sport Science* (pp. 53–65). Philadelphia, P.A: Lippincott, Williams & Wilkins.

Bangsbo, J. and Lindquist, F. (1992) Comparison of various exercise tests with endurance performance during soccer in professional players. *International Journal of Sports Medicine*, 13: 125–132.

Bangsbo, J. and Michalsik, L. (2002) Assessment of the physiological capacity of elite soccer players. In W. Spinks, T. Reilly and A. Murphy (eds), *Science and Football IV* (pp. 53–62). London: Routledge.

Bangsbo, J., Iaia, F.M. and Krustrup, P. (2008) The Yo-Yo Intermittent Recovery Test: a useful tool for evaluation of physical performance in intermittent sports. *Sports Medicine*, 38: 37–51.

Barbero, J.C., Andrin, G. and Mendez-Villanueva., A. (2005) Futsal-specific endurance assessment of competitive players. *Journal of Sports Sciences*, 23: 1279–1280.

Bishop, D., Spencer, M., Duffield, R., and Lawrence, S. (2001) The validity of a repeated sprint ability test. *Journal of Science and Medicine in Sport*, 4, 19–29.

Bishop, D., Tarbox, B., Schneiker, K., Suriano, R., Wallman, K. and Lim, E. (2007) Changes in aerobic fitness in response to a season of professional Australian Rules Football. In *VIth World Congress on Science and Football, Book of Abstracts* (p. 78). Antalya, Turkey.

Bloomfield, J., Polman R.C.J. and O'Donoghue, P.G. (2007) Physical demands of different positions in FA Premier League soccer. *Journal of Sports Science and Medicine*, 6: 63–70.

Buchheit M. (2008) The 30–15 intermittent fitness test: accuracy for individualizing interval training of young intermittent sport players. *Journal of Strength and Conditioning Research*, 22: 1–10.

Campi, S., Guglielmini C. and Guerzoni P. (1992) Variations in energy-producing muscle metabolism during the competitive season in 60 elite rugby players. *Hungarian Revue of Sports Medicine*, 33: 149–154.

Carling C. (2001) Sports science support at the French Football Federation. *Insight – The Football Association Coaches Journal*, 4(4): 34–35.

Carling, C. and Le Gall, F. (2003). Heart rate monitoring: putting theory into practice. *Insight – The Football Association Coaches Journal*, 7(1): 37–41.

Carling, C., Williams, A.M. and Reilly, T. (2005) *The Handbook of Soccer Match Analysis*. London: Routledge.

Carter, J. and Jeukendrup, A.E. (2002) Validity and reliability of three commercially available breath-by-breath respiratory systems. *European Journal of Applied Physiology*, 86: 435–441.

Casajús, J.A. (2001) Seasonal variation in fitness variables in professional soccer players. *Journal of Sports Medicine and Physical Fitness*, 41: 463–467.

Castagna, C., Impellizzeri, F.M., Belardinelli, R., Abt, G., Coutts, A., Chamari, K. and D'Ottavio, S. (2006a) Cardiorespiratory responses to Yo-yo Intermittent Endurance Test in non-elite youth soccer players. *Journal of Strength and Conditioning Research*, 20: 326–330.

Castagna, C., Impellizzeri, F.M., Chamari, K., Carlomagno, D. and Rampinini, E. (2006b) Aerobic fitness and yo-yo continuous and intermittent tests performances in soccer players: a correlation study. *Journal of Strength and Conditioning Research*, 20: 320–325.

Castagna, C., Abt, G. and D'Ottavio, S. (2007a) Physiological aspects of soccer refereeing performance and training, *Sports Medicine*, 37: 625–46.

Castagna, C., Belardinelli, R., Impellizzeri, F.M., Abt, G.A., Coutts, A.J. and D'Ottavio, S. (2007b) Cardiovascular responses during recreational 5-a-side indoor-soccer. *Journal of Science and Medicine in Sport*, 10: 89–95.

Chamari, K., Hachana, Y., Kaouech, F., Jeddi, R., Moussa-Chamari, I. and Wisløff, U. (2005) Endurance training and testing with the ball in young elite soccer players. *British Journal of Sports Medicine*, 39: 24–28.

Chaouachi, M., Chaouachi, A., Chamari, K., Chtara, M., Feki, Y., Amri, M. and Trudeau, F. (2005) Effects of dominant somatotype on aerobic capacity trainability. *British Journal of Sports Medicine*, 39: 954–959.

Clarke, N.D., Drust, B., MacLaren, D.P.M. and Reilly, T. (2005) Strategies for hydration and energy provision during soccer-specific exercise. *International Journal of Sport Nutrition and Exercise Metabolism*, 15: 625–640.

Cooke, C.B. (2003). Maximal oxygen uptake, economy and efficiency. In R. Eston and T. Reilly (eds), *Kinanthropometry and Applied Exercise Physiology Laboratory Manual: Tests, Procedures and Data*, 2nd edition (pp. 161–191). London: Routledge.

Cooper, K.H. (1968) A means of assessing maximal oxygen intake correlating between field and treadmill running. *Journal of the American Medical Association*, 203: 201–204.

aerobic performace

Dascombe, B.J., Reaburn, P.R.J., Sirotic A.C. and Coutts, A.J. (2007) The reliability of the i-STAT clinical portable analyser. *Journal of Science and Medicine in Sport*, 10: 135–140.

Da Silva, S.G., Kaiss, W., Campos, W. and Ladevig, I. (1999) Decrease in aerobic power and 'anaerobic threshold' variables with age in Brazilian soccer players. *Journal of Sports Sciences*, 17: 823.

Drust, B., Cable, N.T. and Reilly, T. (2000a) Investigation of the effects of pre-cooling on the physiological responses to soccer-specific intermittent exercise. *European Journal of Applied Physiology*, 81: 11–17.

Drust, B., Reilly, T. and Cable, N.T. (2000b) Physiological responses to laboratory-based soccer-specific intermittent and continuous exercise. *Journal of Sports Sciences*, 18: 885–892.

Dupont, G., Akakpo, K. and Berthoin, S. (2004) The effect of in-season, high-intensity interval training in soccer players. *Journal of Strength and Conditioning Research*, 18: 584–589.

Duthie, G., Pyne, D. and Hooper, S. (2003) Applied physiology and game analysis of rugby union. *Sports Medicine*, 33: 973–991.

Edwards, A.M., Clark, N. and Macfadyen, A.M. (2003) Lactate and ventilatory thresholds reflect the training status of professional soccer players where maximum aerobic power is unchanged. *Journal of Sports Science and Medicine*, 2: 23–29.

Eisenmann, J.C, Brisko, N., Shadrick, D. and Welsh, S. (2003) Comparative analysis of the Cosmed Quark b^2 and $K4b^2$ gas analysis systems during submaximal exercise. *Journal of Sports Medicine and Physical Fitness*, 43: 150–155.

Elferink-Gemser, M.T., Visscher, C., Lemmink, K.A.P.M. and Mulder, T.W. (2004) Rotation between multidimensional performance characteristics and level of performance in talented youth field hockey players. *Journal of Sports Sciences*, 22: 1053–1063.

Ekbolm, B. (1989) A field test for soccer players. *Science and Football*, 1: 13–15.

Faina, M., Gallozzi, C., Lupo, S., Colli, R., Sassi, R. and Marini, C. (1988) Definition of the physiological profile of the soccer player. In T. Reilly, A. Lees, K. Davids and W. J. Murphy (eds), *Science and Football* (pp. 158–163). London: E & FN Spon.

Flouris, A.D., Metsios G.S. and Koutedakis, Y. (2005) Enhancing the efficacy of the 20 m multistage shuttle run test. *British Journal of Sports Medicine*, 39: 166–170.

Gabbett, T.J. (2000) Physiological and anthropometric characteristics of amateur rugby league players. *British Journal of Sports Medicine*, 34: 303–307.

Gabbett, T.J. (2005) Science of rugby league football: a review. *Journal of Sports Sciences*, 23: 961–976.

Gil, S., Ruiz, F., Irazusta, A., Gil, J. and Irazusta J. (2007) Selection of young soccer players in terms of anthropometric and physiological factors. *Journal of Sports Medicine and Physical Fitness*, 47: 25–32.

Grantham, N. (2007) Netball. In E.M. Winter, A.M. Jones, R.C.R. Davison, P.D. Bromley and T.H. Mercer (eds), *Sport and Exercise Physiology Testing: Guidelines. Volume I Sport Testing* (pp. 245–255). London: Routledge.

Green, S. (1992) Anthropometric and physiological characteristics of South Australian soccer players. *Australian Journal of Science and Medicine in Sport*, 24: 3–7.

Helgerud, J., Engen, L.C., Wisløff, U. and Hoff, J. (2001) Aerobic training improves soccer performance. *Medicine and Science in Sports and Exercise*, 33: 1925–1931.

Hoff, J. (2005) Training and testing physical capacities for elite soccer players. *Journal of Sports Sciences*, 23: 573–582.

Howley, E.T., Bassett, D.R. Jr and Welch, H.G. (1995) Criteria for maximal oxygen uptake: review and commentary. *Medicine and Science in Sports Exercise*, 27: 1292–1301.

Hughes, M.G., Doherty, M., Tong, R.J., Reilly, T. and Cable, N.T. (2006). Reliability of repeated sprint exercise in non-motorised treadmill ergometry. *International Journal of Sports Medicine*, 27: 900–904.

Impellizzeri, F.M., Marcora, S.M., Castagna, C., Reilly, T., Sassi, A., Iaia, F.M. and Rampinini, E. (2006) Physiological and performance effects of generic versus specific aerobic training in soccer players. *International Journal of Sports Medicine*, 27: 483–492.

Impellizzeri, F.M., Mognoni, P., Sassi, A. and Rampinini, E. (2004) Validity of a submaximal running test to evaluate aerobic fitness changes in soccer players. *Journal of Sports Sciences*, 22: 547.

Jones, A.M. (1998) A five year physiological case study of an Olympic runner. *British Journal of Sports Medicine*, 32(1): 34–43.

Jones, A.M. and Doust, J.H. (2001) Limitations to submaximal exercise performance. In R. Eston and T.Reilly (eds), *Kinanthropometry and Exercise Physiology Laboratory Manual: Test Procedures and Data*. 2nd edition (pp. 235–262). London: Routledge.

Kemi, O.J., Hoff, J., Engen, L. C., Helgerud, J. and Wisløff, U. (2003) Soccer specific testing of maximal oxygen uptake. *Journal of Sports Medicine and Physical Fitness*, 43: 139–144.

Krustrup, P., Mohr, M., Nybo, L., Jensen, J.M., Nielsen, J.J. and Bangsbo, J. (2006) The Yo-Yo IR2 test: physiological response, rehability, and application to elite soccer. *Medicine and Science in Sports and Exercise*, 38: 1666–1673.

Labsy, Z., Collomp, K., Frey, A. and De Ceaurriz, J. (2004) Assessment of maximal aerobic velocity in soccer players by means of an adapted Probst field test. *Journal of Sports Medicine and Physical Fitness*, 44: 375–382.

Lamberts R.P., Lemmink, K.A., Durandt, J.J. and Lambert, M.I. (2004) Variation in heart rate during submaximal exercise: implications for monitoring training. *Journal of Strength and Conditioning Research*, 18: 641–645.

Léger, L. and Boucher, R. (1980) An indirect continuous running multistage field test: the Université de Montreal Track Test. *Canadian Journal of Applied Sports Science*, 5: 77–84.

Léger, L. and Lambert, J. (1982) A maximal 20-m shuttle run test to predict $\dot{V}O_{2max}$. *European Journal of Applied Physiology*, 49: 1–12.

Léger, L.A., Mercier, D., Gadoury, C. and Lambert, J. (1988) The multistage 20-meter shuttle run test for aerobic fitness. *Journal of Sports Sciences*, 6: 93–101.

Lemmink K.A. and Visscher, S.H. (2006) Role of energy systems in two intermittent field tests in women field hockey players. *Journal of Strength and Conditioning Research*, 20: 682–688.

Little T. and Williams A.G. (2007) Measures of exercise intensity during soccer training drills with professional soccer players. *Journal of Strength Conditioning Research*, 21: 367–371.

130

McIntyre, M.C. (2005) A comparison of the physiological profiles of elite Gaelic footballers, hurlers, and soccer players. *British Journal of Sports Medicine*, 39: 437–439.

McMillan, K., Helgerud, J., Grant, S.J., Newell, J., Wilson, J., Macdonald, R. and Hoff, J. (2005) Lactate threshold responses to a season of professional British youth soccer. *British Journal of Sports Medicine*, 39: 432–436.

Mahadevan, V. (2006) The Humaan Tissue Act: implications for anatomical work at the college. *Bulletin of the Royal College of Surgeons of England* 88(8): 264–265.

Metsios, G.S., Flouris, A.D., Koutedakis, Y. and Nevill, M. (2008) Criterion-related validity and test–retest reliability of the 20 m Square Shuttle Test. *Journal of Science and Medicine in Sport*, 11: 214–217.

Meyers, M.C. (2006) Enhancing sport performance: merging sports science with coaching. *International Journal of Sports Science and Coaching*, 1: 89–100.

Mohr, M. Krustrup, P. and Bangsbo, J. (2003) Match performance of high-standard soccer players with special reference to development of fatigue. *Journal of Sports Sciences*, 21: 519–528.

Nicholas, C.W., Nuttall, F.E. and Williams, C. (2000) The Loughborough Intermittent Shuttle Test: a field test that simulates the activity pattern of soccer. *Journal of Sports Sciences*, 18: 97–104.

Ohashi, J., Miyagi, O., Yasumatsu, M. and Ishizaki, S. (2003) Multiple intermittent protocols simulating a soccer match. Communication to the *Fifth World Congress of Science and Football* (p. 174). Madrid: Editorial Gymnos.

Puga, N., Ramos, L., Agostinho, J., Lomba, I., Costa, O. and de Freitas, F. (1993) Physical profile of a First Division Portuguese professional football team. In T. Reilly, J. Clarys and A. Stibble (eds), *Science and Football II* (pp. 40–42). London: E & FN Spon.

Ramsbottom, R., Brewer, J. and Williams, C. (1988) A progressive shuttle run test to estimate maximal oxygen uptake. *British Journal of Sports Medicine*, 22: 141–144.

Raven, P.R., Geltman, L.R., Pollock, M.L. and Cooper, K.H. (1976) A physiological evaluation of professional soccer players. *British Journal of Sports Medicine*, 10: 209–216.

Reilly, T. (2007) *The Science of Training – Soccer: A Scientific Approach to Developing Strength, Speed and Endurance*. London: Routledge.

Reilly, T. and Bangsbo, J. (1998) Anaerobic and aerobic training. In B. Elliot (ed.), *Training in Sport: Applying Sport Science* (pp. 351–409). Chichester: John Wiley & Sons Ltd.

Reilly, T. and Brooks, G.A. (1982) Investigation of circadian rhythms in metabolic responses to exercise. *Ergonomics*, 25: 1093–1107.

Reilly, T. and Bryant, J. (1986) Disassociation of lactate and ventilatory thresholds by glycogen loading. *Journal of Human Movement Studies*, 12: 195–200.

Reilly, T. and Doran, D. (2003) Fitness assessment. In T. Reilly and A.M. Williams (eds), *Science and Soccer*, 2nd edition (pp. 21–46). London: Routledge.

Rico-Sanz, J., Zehnder, M., Buchli, R., Dambach, M. and Boutellier, U. (1999) Muscle glycogen degradation during simulation of a fatiguing soccer match in elite soccer players examined noninvasively by 13C-MRS. *Medicine and Science in Sports and Exercise*, 31: 1587–1593.

Rupf, R., Thomas, S. and Wells, G. (2007) Quantifying energy expenditure of dribbling a soccer ball in a field test, In *VIth World Congress on Science and Football, Book of Abstracts* (p. 132). Antalya, Turkey.

Sari-Sarraf, V., Reilly, T. and Doran, D. (2006) Salivary IgA responses to intermittent and continuous exercise. *International Journal of Sports Medicine*, 27: 849–855.

Scott, A.C., Roeb, N., Coats, A.J.S. and Piepolia, M.F. (2003) Aerobic exercise physiology in a professional rugby union team. *International Journal of Cardiology*, 87: 173–177.

Spencer, M., Bishop, D., Dawson, B. and Goodman, C. (2005) Physiological and metabolic responses of repeated-sprint activities specific to field-based team sports. *Sports Medicine*, 35: 1025–1044.

Stickland, M.K., Petersen, S.R. and Bouffard, M. (2003) Prediction of maximal aerobic power from the 20-m multi-stage shuttle run test. *Canadian Journal of Applied Physiology*, 28: 272–282.

Stølen, T., Chamari, K., Castagna, C. and Wisløff, U. (2005) Physiology of soccer: an update. *Sports Medicine*, 35: 501–536.

Svensson, M. and Drust, B. (2005) Testing soccer players. *Journal of Sports Sciences*, 23: 601–618.

Tong, R.J. and Wiltshire, H.D. (2007) Rugby Union. In E.M. Winter, A.M. Jones, R.C.R. Davison, P.D. Bromley and T.H. Mercer (eds), *Sport and Exercise Physiology Testing: Guidelines. Volume I Sport Testing* (pp. 262–271). London: Routledge.

Urhausen, A., Monz, T. and Kindermann, W. (1996) Sports-specific adaptation of left ventricular muscle mass in athlete's heart. II: an echocardiographic study with 400-m runners and soccer players. *International Journal of Sports Medicine*, 17 (Suppl. 3): 152–156.

Vescovi, J.D., Brown, T.D. and Murray T.M. (2007) Descriptive characteristics of NCAA Division I women lacrosse players. *Journal of Science and Medicine in Sport*, 10: 334–340.

Winter, A. and Eston, R.G. (2007). Surface anthropometry. In E.M. Winter, A.M. Jones, R.C.R. Davison, P.D. Bromley and T.H. Mercer (eds), *Sport and Exercise Physiology Testing: Guidelines. Volume I Sport Testing* (pp. 76–83). London: Routledge.

Wisløff, U., Helgerud, J. and Hoff, J. (1998) Strength and endurance of elite soccer players. *Medicine and Science in Sports and Exercise*, 30: 462–467.

Young, W.B., Newton, R.U., Doyle, T.L.A., Chapman, D., Cormack, S., Stewart, C. and Dawson, B. (2005) Physiological and anthropometric characteristics of starters and non-starters and playing positions in elite Australian Rules Football: a case study. *Journal of Science and Medicine in Sport*, 8: 323–345.

CHAPTER SIX

ANAEROBIC AND MUSCULOSKELETAL PERFORMANCE

INTRODUCTION

Competitive field sports incorporate intermittent high-intensity bouts of activity that may have to be repeated many times during the course of a match with little recovery time between efforts. The demands vary depending on the strength of the opposition, the level of competition, the course of the game and the sport concerned. These patterns apply to the outside sports such as field-hockey, the various football codes, the Gaelic sports of football and hurling and other invasive team games such as lacrosse. They also apply to indoor games such as futsal and to indoor court games such as basketball and netball.

The focus in this chapter is on anaerobic performance where energy must be supplied at a faster rate than can be met by aerobic metabolic pathways. Various tests have been designed for the determination of the power and the capacity of the anaerobic system. In many cases these tests have been modified to be more specific to the sport concerned. Similarly, diagnostic tools originally designed for laboratory assessments have been adapted for use in field settings to determine different aspects of anaerobic performance.

Anaerobic performance can be broken down into its various components that include muscle strength, speed, power, anaerobic capacity and 'repeated sprint ability'. In a games context there is a frequent requirement to change direction of movement rapidly, calling for agility on the part of the participants. Since skills must be executed at speed in a competitive context, technical aspects of the game concerned have been incorporated into many test batteries. The applied sports scientist must strike a balance between an assessment protocol that can be interpreted in physiological terms and one that is purely related to performance in the sport.

In this chapter the physiology of anaerobic metabolism and the processes associated with muscle contraction are first described. Classical tests of anaerobic performance are then considered. The various means of assessing muscle strength are outlined, both laboratory-based and field-based. The biological basis of agility is considered, before tests of this component of performance are related to different sports. The apparatus and equipment necessary to conduct test batteries are incorporated in the test descriptions.

ANAEROBIC PERFORMANCE

Anaerobic metabolism

Metabolism refers to the production of energy within the body. Energy can be produced from aerobic or anaerobic sources, and may be fuelled by different

134

substrates. The immediately available substrates within the muscle cells are the high-energy phosphates, adenosine triphosphate (ATP) and creatine phosphate (CP). ATP is necessary for the muscles to contract. The splitting of this compound yields the energy for muscle contraction, but its stores are limited to supporting only a short sprint. As these stores would be depleted within a few seconds, they must be continually restored for exercise to be maintained.

The next available source of energy is creatine phosphate. Degradation of this substance occurs when sprints must be repeated and there is incomplete recovery in between. The use of creatine monohydrate as an ergogenic aid is designed to boost this system in order to reproduce bouts of high-intensity exercise.

The breakdown of ATP leads to the generation of adenosine disphosphate (ADP). A minor contribution of anaerobic energy is due to a further degradation of ADP to adenosine monophosphate (AMP). This activity is regulated by the enzyme AMP kinase. The AMP can be further broken down to inosine monophosphate (IMP) and ammonia (NH_3). These reactions occur primarily during heavy exercise or towards the end of prolonged exercise.

Another source of energy is glycogen, the form in which carbohydrate is stored within the muscles and in the liver. When the exercise intensity is very high and sustained, as in a long sprint forward from defence to attack (or a track back to head off a counter-attack in field games), muscle glycogen is broken down anaerobically. Lactic acid is produced as a by-product of this reaction and gradually diffuses into the blood. When its production within the active muscles exceeds its clearance rate, lactate accumulates in the blood and is circulated throughout the body in increased concentrations.

It is clear therefore that a number of consequences of anaerobic pathways must be considered when assessment of anaerobic performance is concerned. First, anaerobic power is the highest attainable power output that can be achieved in a maximal effort. In turn this function is influenced by the ability to generate force and the rate of force development. Anaerobic capacity would be reflected in the area under the curve in a sustained maximal effort. Another aspect of anaerobic performance is the ability to recover quickly from an all-out endeavour and repeatedly perform maximally with short recovery periods in between. These functions are assessed in different forms of anaerobic test, the ability to recover in repeated sprints being assessed in a composite measure referred to as the fatigue index.

THE MUSCULOSKELETAL SYSTEM

Skeletal muscle controls the motion of body segments by way of a series of contractions and relaxations. These activities are regulated and coordinated by the nervous system. Voluntary activity is controlled by the motor cortex in the brain, but information about movement is coordinated in the cerebellum whilst afferent nerve fibres from within the muscle spindles provide details about changes in the length of skeletal muscle fibres as they are active.

Each muscle has its own supply of nerves and blood to individual cells that are known as muscle fibres. The muscle is enveloped in an outer layer of connective tissue, the epimysium, but within it there are bundles of fibres organised in fascicles and surrounded by connective tissue referred to as the perimysium. The connective tissue around each muscle fibre is known as the endomysium, beneath which is a thin membrane called the sarcolemma. Each muscle fibre contains several hundred to several thousand myofibrils that consist of long strands of smaller subunits called sarcomeres. The sarcomeres are connected at their ends by Z-discs which appear as dark zones on a light micrograph. Two rod-like protein filaments constitute the contractile machinery of muscle: the thicker filament is made of myosin and is located towards the centre of the sarcomere, whereas the thinner actin filament overlays the end portion of myosin and extends to the Z-disc on each side (see Figure 6.1). The connections between the actin filaments joining at the Z-disc are formed by another protein, α-actinin. Desmin links the Z-discs of adjacent myofibrils and keeps the Z-discs in register. Titin and nebulin are other protein molecules that help to maintain the architecture of the sarcomere.

Cross-bridges are formed between the two protein filaments, actin and myosin and their connection causes muscle tension to be generated. The individual muscle sarcomere is shortened by the attachment of actin to myosin, pulling the former towards the centre of the unit, an event which is repeated along the entire length of the muscle fibre. The 'sliding filament theory' explains how a contraction occurs; it is initiated when an action potential is generated in the muscle fibre. The contractile system is activated by the release of calcium from the sarcoplasmic reticulum across the sarcolemma or thin membrane surrounding the muscle fibre. Its entry frees the myosin heads from inhibition by another protein troponin, lifting the protein tropomyosin off the active sites on the actin filament and allowing actin to become attached to the myosin head. The sliding of actin on the thicker myosin filament is likened to successive strokes of an oar in moving a boat through water. The myosin heads contain ATPase enabling the myosin molecule to bind with ATP for muscle contraction to occur. Relaxation follows with a reversal of these events as calcium is pumped back into the sarcoplasmic reticulum and the deactivation of troponin and tropomyosin once again blocks the connection between myosin heads and actin binding sites. This reversal process also requires use of ATP and is facilitated by the presence of magnesium.

Skeletal muscle can contract in three different ways. First, an isometric contraction occurs when tension is generated but there is no resultant change in the length of

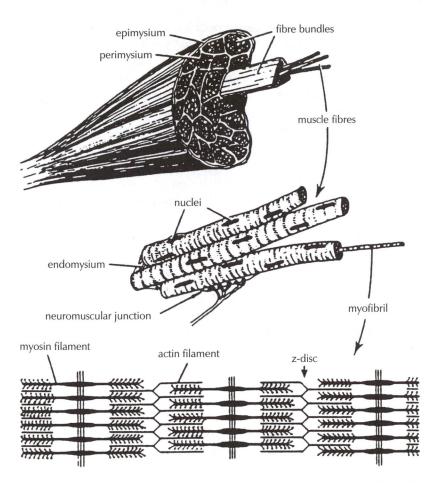

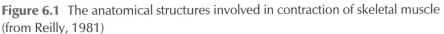

Figure 6.1 The anatomical structures involved in contraction of skeletal muscle (from Reilly, 1981)

the muscle. Second, a concentric contraction occurs when the muscle shortens, as occurs in the quadriceps when kicking a ball or jumping vertically. Third, an eccentric action refers to a stretch of the muscle's length while resisting the force that is being applied: examples are the action of the hamstrings in slowing down limb movement when a ball is being kicked. The fact that a muscle can be increased in length as well as shortened indicates it has elastic as well as contractile elements, which lie in series and in parallel within the muscle and its musculotendinous unit. Each of these types of contraction must be considered relevant to the design of training programmes.

A fundamental relationship is the force–velocity characteristic of muscle. The force generated is a function of the tension developed within the muscle and is related to its cross-sectional area. Force is greater under isometric conditions than when the muscle acts concentrically and decreases as the velocity of contraction increases. Force increases during eccentric contractions beyond maximum isometric tension until there is no overlap between actin and myosin filaments for active tension to be developed. Eccentric contractions require little energy utilisation due to the contribution to tension of the so-called parallel-elastic components that supplement the series-elastic elements of the actin–myosin complex. The force of shortening is increased when a concentric action follows an eccentric contraction in a stretch-shortening cycle such as occurs in a semi-squat motion or counter-movement prior to a jump. Energy generated in lengthening of muscle is stored in the cell's elastic elements and released in the subsequent shortening of the muscle. The outcome is that force is potentiated in the concentric part of the force–velocity curve, reflected in a shift upwards in the right section of the curve shown in Figure 6.2.

The ability of skeletal muscle to store energy and release it in a stretch-shortening cycle is reflected in vertical jump tests. This ability explains why jump performance is better in a counter-movement jump compared to a squat jump. It is important therefore that test conditions are standardised when vertical jumps are used as performance criteria.

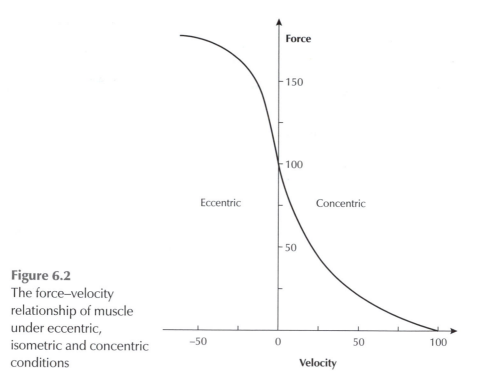

Figure 6.2
The force–velocity relationship of muscle under eccentric, isometric and concentric conditions

anaerobic and musculoskeletal performance

NEUROMUSCULAR FACTORS

Skeletal muscle is supplied with nerves, organised within a highly complex system. The central nervous system accommodates sensory information transmitted via afferent pathways from muscles, tendons and joints as well as efferent pathways to the muscles. A single α-motor neurone supplies a number of muscle fibres distributed throughout the muscle, these fibres forming a motor unit. When a motor neurone is fired, it produces a synchronous electrical discharge through all its axonal branches, causing all the muscle fibres innervated to contract. Muscles that are employed in precise control of fine movements tend to have a small number of nerve fibres per motor unit whereas weight-bearing muscles have a relatively large number of motor units and many fibres per unit.

Neuromuscular mechanisms encompass higher level supraspinal controls known as 'central command' that include afferent feedback. They may also include lower-level controls mediated at a spinal level. With strength training there is an increase in muscle activation, reflected in the percentage of the motor neurone pool that is engaged in the action. More motor units are recruited early with 'explosive' type activity, the rate of force development increases and the time to reach peak torque is decreased.

The intensity of the exercise or the level of force demanded by the active muscle determines the type and number of motor units that are recruited. This concept applies irrespective of the velocity of the action. Only a few motor units are activated when low force is required and these tend to be associated with slow-twitch muscle fibres. At moderate intensities the FTa (Type IIa) fibres are recruited whilst the FTb (Type IIb) fibres are called into play in efforts of maximal strength. Therefore, strenuous efforts for brief repetitions (e.g. 6 × 6-RM) represent a good means of activating the majority of the muscle fibres. Theoretically, if all of the motor units are recruited, the muscle can exert its greatest possible force.

Muscle strength can be increased by a more effective recruitment of muscle fibres contributing to the generation of force and a reduction of neural inhibitory influences. Neural adaptations resulting in increased voluntary activation of muscle account for improvements in strength over the initial weeks of a resistance-training programme (Staron et al., 1994). After about 8 weeks, longer-term effects are generally associated with increases in cross-sectional area of the muscle. These different responses need to be considered whenever muscle strength is being assessed.

There are various sensory organs that detect information about the tension generated during muscle actions. Pacinian corpuscles within the joints sense the forces being transmitted through the joint concerned. Golgi tendon organs are inhibitory, feedback from which causes a reduction in the force generated and thereby protects against injury. Information about the length of muscle and the rate of change in length is sensed by the muscle spindles located within the extrafusal fibres of the tissue. These mechanisms are facilitatory – stimulating the muscle to contract when they are stretched. They are implemented in fast movements when muscles must be activated quickly and are especially important in executing changes in direction and maintaining balance. The vestibular apparatus of the inner ear is also relevant in providing feedback to the cerebellum with respect to postural orientation.

ANAEROBIC PERFORMANCE TESTS

Components of anaerobic performance tests

Anaerobic performance tests embrace simple all-out efforts as in a vertical jump or medicine ball throw, and maintenance of maximal effort until exhaustion. These characteristics reflect anaerobic power and anaerobic capacity, respectively. An extension of these paradigms is the reproduction of short all-out efforts with brief remissions in between, as in the assessment of 'repeated sprint ability'.

In many sports, especially in court games and field sports, movements are not linear in direction but include side-steps, changes in direction and abrupt changes in velocity, both accelerations and decelerations. This characteristic of changing direction quickly is assessed by using agility tests. These can be administered using validated agility tests or incorporated within sport-specific tests. The difficulty in the latter case is that agility and speed are both incorporated in the one test, making interpretation between these faculties indistinct. Maximum running speed and agility in professional soccer players have specific qualities that are unrelated to one another, suggesting that each component should be tested individually (Little and Williams, 2005). Therefore, results from agility tests should be used in conjunction with data from single sprint tests to provide a more objective indication of a player's overall ability to sprint and change direction quickly.

PRACTICAL EXAMPLE 1

In female lacrosse and soccer players, the relationship between sprinting, agility and jump ability was investigated. Altogether, 83 high-school soccer, 51 college soccer and 79 college lacrosse athletes completed tests for linear sprinting, countermovement jump and agility in a single session. Linear sprints (9.1, 18.3, 27.4 and 36.6 m) and agility (Illinois and pro-agility tests) were evaluated using infrared timing gates, while countermovement jump height

140

was assessed using an electronic timing mat. All of the performance scores were statistically correlated with each other; however, the coefficients of determination were low, moderate and high depending on the test pairing. Agility tests, for example, had weak to moderate correlations with static and flying linear sprint times and weak inverse relationships were found between both agility tests and countermovement jump height. The results of this study indicated that linear sprinting, agility and vertical jumping are independent locomotor skills and highlight the complex nature of relationships between tests of physical performance. The authors suggested that a variety of tests ought to be included in an assessment protocol for high-school and college female athletes.

The literature is replete with assessment protocols for anaerobic performance. These tests have been designed for specific purposes and few have gained universal approval (see Table 6.1). Nevertheless those tests that have gained credence in laboratory and field settings can be identified and described. Procedures for measuring muscle strength are covered separately.

The muscular power produced when jumping on a force platform can be used as a measure of maximal anaerobic power. Vertical jumping on a force platform has

Table 6.1 Examples of some soccer-specific field tests of anaerobic performance

Author	Name of test	Description	Duration of test	Predominant demands
Balsom (1990)	Repeated sprint test	20 repeated 10 × 10 × 10-m sprints with 42-s active recovery	Self-paced sprints	Anaerobic
Malomski (1993)	Two-step interval test	15 × 30-m sprints with 5-s recovery performed in two blocks separated by 30 min	Self-paced sprints	Anaerobic
Psotta and Bunc (2003)	Repeated sprint test	10 × 20-m sprints with 20-s recovery	Self-paced sprints	Anaerobic
Wilson (2007)	Liverpool anaerobic speed test	3 × 60-s shuttles over 25-m with 60-s passive recovery	180-s exercise plus 120-s recovery	Anaerobic

also been validated as a means of assessing bilateral strength asymmetry in athletes (Impellizzeri et al., 2007). Such tests require relatively complex equipment, which is not available for routine assessments. Nevertheless jump devices such as the SMARTJUMP system (Fusion Sports, Australia, http://www.fusionsport.com/) can be easily used in the field setting (Figure 6.3). High-speed camera systems using reflective markers placed on participants are also being developed to enable jumping capacity to be assessed.

Peak jumping force, peak jumping velocity, anaerobic power during a jump and the peak height of the jump can easily be obtained using a force platform. The production of power in vertical jumping can be calculated, knowing the player's body mass, the vertical distance through which body mass is moved and the flight time. The vertical distance itself is a good measure of muscular performance, i.e. mechanical work done, and can be measured using the classical Sargent jump technique. This value can also be recorded using a digital system attached to the

Figure 6.3
The SMARTJUMP jumping mat (courtesy of Fusion Sports)

anaerobic and musculoskeletal performance

participant's waist and based on the extension of a cord, which is pulled from its base on the floor as the individual jumps vertically. The vertical jump is preferable to the standing broad jump which is influenced by leg length and which does not permit calculation of power output. An alternative method, the 5-jump test has been used to estimate the muscular anaerobic power of legs in soccer players and is significantly correlated to vertical jump performance (Stølen et al., 2005). This test consists of five consecutive efforts performed from an initial standing position with joined feet.

In elite netball, the ability of players to perform the vertical jump may be assessed to examine differences when reaching with dominant and non-dominant hands (Grantham, 2007). In elite rugby, a sport-specific procedure for assessing leg power in forward players may employ push-tests against a scrummaging machine. The relevance of power assessment is evident as force produced during a vertical jump has been shown to be related to scrummaging force (Robinson and Mills, 2000).

Performance of games players in such tests of jumping ability tends to demonstrate positional influences. Generally, soccer goalkeepers, defenders and forwards perform better than midfield players on a counter-movement jump (vertical jump without use of arms) test (Reilly and Doran, 2003). In contrast, greater vertical jumping ability is observed in elite midfield Gaelic football players compared to backs and forwards (McIntyre and Hall, 2005). Jumping ability is a requirement for gaining possession in the line-out in Rugby Union, but standing height is also an important factor (Rigg and Reilly, 1988).

Another means of measuring mechanical power output in jumping was described by Bosco et al. (1983). The individual jumps repeatedly for a given period, usually 60 s, the flight time and jumping frequency being recorded. The jumps are performed on a touch-sensitive mat, which is connected to a timer. Power output can be estimated knowing the participant's body mass and the time between contacts on the mat. Performance at various parts of the 1-min test can be compared, the tolerance to fatigue as the test progresses being indicative of the anaerobic glycolytic capacity.

Attention must be paid when assessing jump capacity to ensure that performers respect test procedures and do not try to improve their scores by cheating. According to the type of jump employed (for example, counter-movement jump with or without arm swing), the positions of the participant's arms and legs during flight must respect the individual protocol guidelines in order not to increase jump time or height artificially.

The Wingate test

The Wingate Anaerobic test was originally designed at the National Institute in Israel from which it gets its name (Bar-Or, 1996). It is performed on an instrumented cycle ergometer which allows power output to be derived throughout the test (see Figure 6.4). The performance is all-out for 30 s, the peak value for power output reflecting anaerobic power whereas the average value is taken to indicate anaerobic capacity. A comparison of the power output over the final 5 s and that over the initial 5 s generates a fatigue index. For best results the load or resistance is optimised for individual assessments.

The Wingate test has been modified for sports other than cycling. Reilly and Bayley (1988) used the 30-s protocol for assessment of young swimmers using a 'biokinetic swim bench'. The protocol has been applied also for administration to participants using rowing and kayak ergometers (Derham and Reilly, 1993). Nevertheless, peak power and mean power determined on the classical cycle ergometry mode both distinguished between first and second class Rugby Union players (Rigg and Reilly, 1988), power output being important in 'impact' contexts in this sport. The highest values for both measures were found in the back-row players whereas, in soccer,

Figure 6.4 The original Wingate Anaerobic test was performed on a cycle ergometer. The print-out on the left indicates power output in watts for each second throughout the test.

results from the Wingate test have shown that goalkeepers generally demonstrate the highest anaerobic power. A mean power in the Wingate test ranging from 637 to 841 W has been reported across different playing positions and levels of play in soccer (Stølen et al., 2005). Although these results from this test suggest that values vary across playing positions in field sports, no significant differences were observed according to playing position in elite Gaelic footballers (McIntyre and Hall, 2005). The authors suggested that the latter findings were probably the result of a typical common training programme undertaken by all players.

Measurement of power production and anaerobic capacity on a treadmill is generally more appropriate for games players and sprinters than using a cycle ergometer for the traditional Wingate test. Power output may be measured whilst the player runs as fast as possible on a 'non-motorised' treadmill. The speed of the belt is determined by the effort of the participant. The horizontal forces produced can be recorded using a load cell attached to the individual by means of a harness worn around the waist (Lakomy, 1984). Repeated bouts of exercise, such as 6 s in duration may be performed and power profiles determined with different recovery periods.

Without appropriate instrumentation to record time, power output cannot be calculated from the vertical distance jumped. Margaria et al. (1966) designed a stair run for assessment of the power of the muscles' phosphagen system. The participant sprints up a flight of stairs from a 2-m run up, and through two sets of timing lights (Figure 6.5). With knowledge of the time taken, the vertical distance between the

Figure 6.5 A junior athlete sprints up a stairway, contacting two mats linked to a timing device

two sets of photo-cells used as timing devices and the body mass of the participant, the power output could be computed. The test gained credibility as an assessment tool for a time but lack of standardisation of stairways within buildings and issues with health and safety meant it eventually fell out of favour.

Cunningham and Faulkner's test

The test duration of 30 s in a standard Wingate test is likely to be too short to test the anaerobic capacity completely. It may therefore be more appropriate as an anaerobic power test or as an experimental model for laboratory studies.

Cunningham and Faulkner (1969) had originally designed a treadmill test for assessing anaerobic capacity. The protocol involves an all-out run to exhaustion with the belt set at a 20% incline and a speed of 3.58 m.s^{-1}. Typically, athletes last 40–50 s before desisting, a duration that is compatible with anaerobic resources. Although treadmill-based running tests are more appropriate to field sports than those using cycle ergometry, they still lack specificity to the activity profiles of the game. Furthermore, these laboratory tests are generally time-consuming and are therefore unsuitable for testing large groups of players.

A field test commonly employed in elite French soccer to calculate maximal anaerobic power output involves a maximal sprint over 40 m. Using the speed recorded over the last 10 metres of the effort (calculated using photoelectric cells) and the participant's weight and centre of gravity, this means of estimating anaerobic power is probably more appropriate to field sports such as soccer than laboratory-based tests of anaerobic power (Le Gall et al., 2002). Its limitation is that it concentrates on only a part of a maximal anaerobic effort and is not a test of anaerobic capacity.

Speed tests

Speed over short distances is an essential requirement for success in most games. Time–motion analysis of field sports during competition suggests that the mean distance and duration of sprints is between 10–20 m and 2–3 s, respectively (Spencer et al., 2005). In a competitive context, the participant must react quickly to an external stimulus, accelerate up to top speed and maintain it for as long as necessary. Timing and anticipation are important in starting the movement and determining its direction. Maximum speed may not be reached until about 40–60 m before gradually declining. Typically speed tests entail running through a series of timing gates, so that acceleration at 5 m, 10 m and velocity (to 30–40

m) is measured. As sprints are rarely more than 30 m in length, practitioners may consider that maximum speed is not often achieved in competition and may not take this component of performance into consideration when testing players. However, players often initiate sprints when already moving at moderate speeds and maximum speed may be achieved more often than distance and time would otherwise predict (Little and Williams, 2005) and therefore it is useful to measure this component of fitness.

Reaction time may be measured by determining the time taken to register a response to a visual or auditory stimulus. In the classical format the participant had to press a button on seeing a light switched on, or on hearing a sound. Choice reaction time is determined when the correct response is matched to the onset of a stimulus from a whole array. A fast reaction to the starter's gun is important in sprinting but simple reaction tests are not sensitive measures for administration to games players. Whole-body reaction time may be important in some instances, for example when goalkeepers have to shift their position quickly in response to play. The ability to do so is also a characteristic of agility.

Speed and acceleration over short distances are especially important in Rugby Union backs and for all soccer players. Quickness off the mark may decide which player gets to the ball first or whether a pass is intercepted. A comparison of professional soccer players and inter-country Gaelic footballers showed that the two groups were similar in aerobic power, the distinguishing feature being that the soccer professionals were superior in sprints over 10 m and 30 m (Strudwick et al., 2002). If required, devices such as the OptoJump system (Microgate, Bolzano, Italy, http://www.microgate.it/) can provide a detailed breakdown (up to 1/1000 of a second) of the acceleration capacity of players by measuring stride length, stride frequency, contact and flight times over short sprints (Lehance et al., 2005).

It is important to standardise the conditions, equipment and instructions given to participants to ensure quality control of data collection when testing sprint performance. Timing gates should preferably be dual beam and accurate to 0.01 s. Two or three runs with a 1–2 min pause between trials are required to give a reproducible score which reflects a player's sprint ability. The fastest result for the split times is recorded as the score. When examining sprinting ability, the reaction time of the players will affect his or her results. Therefore, a flying start, for example over 15 m may be used to remove this factor and provide a true picture of maximal running speed.

REPEATED SPRINT ABILITY (SPEED-ENDURANCE)

The fitness requirements of games players are quick movements, high speed, fast recovery and an ability to sustain activity. These requirements are also relevant for indoor court games (Figure 6.6). The capacity to recover from and repeat high-intensity actions effectively impacts on individual and team performance. Elite youth soccer players recorded better scores in terms of measures of speed-endurance capacity than did soccer players at sub-elite levels (Reilly et al., 2000). Tests of repeated sprint ability in elite soccer have also been shown to discriminate between different playing positions (Aziz et al., 2008). Speed-endurance training improves the ability to maintain, and repeat, sprint-type activities by increasing the body's ability to produce energy, via the anaerobic energy systems, and improving the ability to recover following high-intensity bouts.

The ability to reproduce high-intensity sprints may be examined by requiring the athlete to reproduce an all-out sprint after a short recovery period. A distance of 30 m is recommended. Timing gates may be set up at the start, after 10 m and at 30 m. There is then a 10-m deceleration zone for the athlete to slow down prior to jogging back to the start line. The recovery period is variable and may have a considerable effect on changes in performance, but 25 s has been recommended

Figure 6.6 A repeated-sprint ability test can be performed indoors when a suitable runway length is available

(Williams et al., 1997). When the interval is reduced to 15 s, test performance is significantly related to the oxygen transport system (Reilly and Doran, 2003). The type of recovery employed between sprints, i.e. active or passive, also affects the decline in performance (Spencer et al., 2005). An active period may hasten the removal of lactate from muscles and its clearance in the blood. Therefore, when designing test protocols, it is important to take into account the recovery period between high-intensity actions as studies of elite match-performance employing motion analysis have shown this to be of an active nature (Carling et al., 2008).

PRACTICAL EXAMPLE 2

Bravo and co-workers (2008) designed a study to compare the effects of a 7-week period of two commonly used types of fitness training in soccer, namely repeated-sprint ability and high-intensity interval training. Their effects on both aerobic and anaerobic physiological variables were investigated in male soccer players. Players were randomly assigned to either the interval training group (ITG) or the repeated-sprint ability training group (RSA). The ITG undertook 4 × 4 min running at 90–95% of maximum heart rate whereas the RST group undertook 3 × 6 maximal shuttle sprints of 40 m. The players' performances were compared across a battery of field tests including the Yo-Yo Intermittent Recovery test, 10-m sprint time, jump height and power, and RSA before and after the training period. Greater improvements were observed in the intermittent test and in the repeated sprint test in the RSA group. Both groups significantly increased their maximal oxygen uptake. These results suggest that the RSA training protocol employed in this study can be used as an effective training method for inducing aerobic and football-specific training adaptations.

The number of sprints will also significantly affect the decrement in performance. Seven sprints are recommended for determining peak acceleration (over 10 m) and speed (time over 30 m). A fatigue index can be calculated for speed over both 10 m and 30 m, based on the drop off in performance over the seven sprints. The fatigue index generally provides an indication of the ability of the player to recover from successive sprints. Hence, this measure indicates how a field player's performance could be affected by preceding bouts of high-intensity exercise during match-play. In match-play, the period between sprints often varies and may be in some instances too short to permit a full recovery before having to sprint again; hence the importance of an increased capacity to recover from high-intensity exercise.

The percentage decrement score is also used to describe a method which compares actual performance to ideal performance, had the best effort been replicated in each sprint. A speed decrement may be expressed as a simple percentage difference. The total sprint time (sum of all sprint times) has also been recommended as being a major measure of performance taken from a repeated-sprint test (Spencer et al., 2006). The mean time for the seven sprints is indicative of the ability to perform several sprints in a short period of time within a game. Generally, the best performances are the first and second sprints, the poorest over the sixth and seventh.

Hughes et al. (2006) demonstrated the high reliability of such tests, although the 'fatigue index' was the least reliable measure. The fatigue index calculated from a repeated sprint test in soccer players has been shown to be influenced by pacing strategies (Psotta and Bunc, 2003). One way around this problem would be to suggest for comparative purposes, that participants complete a single maximal sprint test prior to the repeated-sprint test. In the first sprint of the repeated-sprint test, participants would be expected to achieve a time close to that of their single maximal sprint performance. A time within 0.1 s (or 2%) may represent a suitable criterion score over a distance of 30–40 m (Oliver, 2007).

AGILITY

Agility refers to the ability to change direction quickly or to alter the position of the body in space without loss of balance. It is a composite factor, including elements of strength, balance, coordination and speed of movement. Agility assessment is generally confined to tests of physical components even though this element of performance also includes cognitive components such as visual-scanning techniques, visual-scanning speed and anticipation (Sheppard and Young, 2006). It may be represented in a distinct running pattern, such as in a formal zig-zag test where the player must navigate around cones (Figure 6.7) or in an irregular pattern as might occur in a game.

Agility is typically measured in a shuttle-run, a run around cones with directions of movements altered or in a path dictated by poles set up in a 'T' shape. The most frequently adopted test is the Illinois Agility Run designed by Cureton (1970). This test has been adapted for generic purposes and has been applied to a variety of games players and indoor sports. A modified version of the Illinois test was used to measure agility in high-level university lacrosse players. In this test, the amount of straight-line sprinting was reduced as the authors considered that the original version of the Illinois test may be heavily influenced by the ability to sprint quickly over short distances instead of measuring the ability to change directions (Vescovi et al., 2007). Nevertheless, the Illinois test has been used as part of a battery of tests

150

Figure 6.7 A games player performs a zig-zag agility test

for talent identification in female field-hockey (Keogh et al., 2003) and distinguishes between rugby performers of varying standards (Gabbett, 2002).

A 'T' test as described by Seminick (1990) is applicable to a number of sports. It has the advantage of being easy to set up and administer, indoors or outdoors on a consistent surface. The participant sprints from a standing start to a cone placed 9 m away, then side-shuffles leftwards without crossing the feet. The participant touches the cone, then side-shuffles 9 m along the top of the 'T' course to touch this third cone, side-shuffles to the middle cone before sprinting back to the start. Usually two attempts are allowed, the fastest one being recorded as the score. Tests that are more specific to the individual demands of various field sports have also been developed and are covered later in this chapter.

FLEXIBILITY

Speed of movement may be impaired when flexibility is poor. Flexibility refers to range of movement around a joint. It can be regarded as a component of agility, since poor flexibility would render the individual to perform badly also in agility tasks. Flexibility is also a predisposing factor in injury, since inflexibility in hamstrings and adductor muscle groups have been found to be risk factors for injury in soccer players (see Reilly, 2007). Tests of flexibility in elite soccer and Gaelic football players and hurlers indicated a greater level of flexibility in soccer players (McIntyre, 2005). This result may be due to specific training and conditioning programmes or physical adaptations to match-play. However, poor flexibility in elite soccer players has been observed (Witvrouw et al., 2003) and notably during pre-season testing (Bradley and Portas, 2007).

Range of motion at each joint can be measured using a variety of techniques. The posture is controlled from start to completion of the motion and the measurement protocol follows standard procedures. In performance-orientated assessments of flexibility, complex three-dimensional motion patterns may be analysed in a broad field of view (Borms and Van Roy, 2001). Such measurements are useful in technical sports events and are more relevant to clinical applications in games players. Gross motions of body segments and coupled motions might be analysed for diagnostic purposes.

Equipment used in assessing flexibility may be simple or highly sophisticated. The simplest forms of devices are portable goniometers, hygrometers or conventional flexometers. These devices are used to measure the angle through which the joint has moved. Three-dimensional electrogoniometers are both complex to interpret and expensive to use and are restricted mainly to dynamic movements and research purposes. The uses and limitations of a range of instruments for assessing flexibility were reviewed elsewhere by Borms and Van Roy (2001).

Bradley and Portas (2007) used the following protocol to determine the effect of pre-season range of motion on muscle strain injury during the competitive season in English Premier League soccer players. A stationary video camera (Panasonic SHM20; Matsushita Electric Corp. of America, Secaucus, N.J.) operating at a frame rate of 25 Hz was placed perpendicular to the plane of motion at a distance of 10 m. On each player, reflective skin markers were placed in the sagittal plane at the trunk (base of the 10th rib); hip (greater trochanter); knee (femur/tibia joint line); ankle (lateral malleolus); heel (calcaneous) and the foot (head of the 5th metatarsal). These markings then were digitised manually using customised software (Digi-TEESer; University of Teesside, UK) to identify pelvic, thigh, shank and foot positions and corresponding joint angles.

Probably the best-known field test is the sit-and-reach method of measuring flexibility. It incorporates a number of muscle groups, but can identify hamstring tightness as well as stiffness in the lower back. Nevertheless, it is a crude indication of flexibility and results require more specific follow up. A variation of this test is

152

the stand-and-reach in which the athlete stands on a raised platform and slowly stretches down to move a marker with his/her fingertips. The marker is moved over a scale graded in centimetres, and the score is based on where the marker finally rests.

The stage of the season and the overall fitness of the player should be taken into consideration when the individual's flexibility data are evaluated. The time of day at which measurements are made is also relevant, since there is a clear diurnal variation in flexibility (Reilly et al., 1997).

SOCCER-SPECIFIC APPLICATIONS

Some of the more skilful movements in field games may be incorporated into field tests. Soccer-dribbling tests can include a sprint as fast as possible over a zig-zag course whilst dribbling a ball. This procedure incorporates an agility component, calling for an ability to change direction quickly. Such tests formed part of a battery designed for monitoring young players by Reilly and Holmes (1983) and have been employed in contemporary talent identification programmes (Reilly et al., 2000).

The slalom dribble designed by Reilly and Holmes (1983) calls for total body movement in which the participant has to dribble a ball around a set obstacle course as quickly as possible. Obstacles comprise plastic conical skittles 91 cm high with a base diameter of 23 cm. Two parallel lines, 1.57 m apart, are drawn as reference guides. Intervals of 1.83 m are marked along each line, and diagonal connections of alternate marks 4.89 m long are made. Five cones are placed on the course itself, and a sixth is positioned 7.3 m from the final cone, exactly opposite to and 9.14 m from the starting line. On the command, go, each participant dribbles the ball from behind the starting line to the right of the first cone and continues to dribble alternately around the remainder in a zig-zag fashion to the sixth, where the ball is left and the participant sprints back to the starting line. The time elapsed between leaving and returning past the start line is recorded to the nearest 0.1 s and indicates the individual's score. Participants are forced to renegotiate any cones displaced in the course of the test. A demonstration by the experimenter and a practice run by the participant are undertaken before four trials are performed, with a rest of 20 min between trials, the aggregate time representing the participant's score.

An alternative test is the 'straight dribble', which has been used to discriminate between elite young soccer players and their sub-elite counterparts (Reilly et al., 2000). In the test, five cones are placed in a straight line perpendicular to the start line: the first is 2.74 m away, the middle two separated by 91 cm and the remainder 1.83 m apart. Players dribble around alternate obstacles until the fifth is circled and then must return through the course in similar fashion. The ball has to be dribbled from the final obstacle to the start line, which now constitutes the finish. The aggregate score from four test trials constitutes the overall test result.

Another field test that combines running movement and skill evaluation is the Loughborough Soccer Shooting test (Ali et al., 2007). Performance criteria are based on points scored per shot, time taken to complete each shot sequence and ball speed per shot. The reliability and validity of this test have been achieved for assessing performance in elite soccer players.

The capability to change the direction of the body abruptly, then quickly dodge and sidestep opponents in field games calls for good motor coordination and is reflected in an agility run test. Professional soccer players in the North American Soccer League were found to have performances on the Illinois Agility Run that were on average above the 99.95 percentile for the test norms (Raven et al., 1976). The test distinguished the soccer players as a group from the normal population better than any field test used for strength, power and flexibility. From the same test, the same conclusion can be extended to elite young soccer players who recorded better results compared to sub-elite players (Reilly et al., 2000). Measures of varying agility according to player age, quality and position have also been reported in soccer (Gil et al., 2007a, 2007b).

Other simple tests of agility for soccer include the modified Balsom run and the 'M' run test (see Barnes, 2007). A 40-m sprint fatigue test with an agility component has been incorporated into a battery of fitness assessment tasks for soccer, although the speed and agility components were not differentiated (Williams et al., 1997). A 20-m soccer-specific agility test which requires participants to sprint a zig-zag course around four cones that deviates to the left by 4 m then to the right by 4 m and is completed four times is depicted in Figure 6.7. Agility is assessed in this test but without the inclusion of a skills component.

Wilson (2007) designed an anaerobic endurance test specifically for soccer that consisted of 25-m shuttle runs for 60 s. The test incorporated a push-pass before turning at the end of each 25-m sprint. A 60-s rest period was permitted between efforts before completing three 60-s shuttles in total, the score being indicated by the total distance covered. The test was found to be sensitive to the detraining effect that can occur in players in Islamic countries during the holy month of Ramadan.

FIELD TESTS IN FIELD-HOCKEY

Field-hockey is a sport where players must be capable of controlling the ball and dribbling with it when given the opportunity. They may have to turn quickly past

anaerobic and musculoskeletal performance

opponents or change direction to shield the ball from them. Posture is unorthodox when dribbling with the ball, the player in possession stooping to keep it under control. Field tests relevant to the game have incorporated use of the ball to assess the composite abilities required of players.

The tests designed for US college women by Wessel and Keonig (1971), described in a review on field-hockey by Reilly and Borrie (1992), included a dribble, a dodge, a circular tackle and a drive. Other non-standardised tests were built around two or more of the fundamental game skills but failed to provide the physiological stress of match-play under which the skills must be executed (Reilly and Borrie, 1992).

Reilly and Bretherton (1986) used two field tests in their evaluation of English elite female players. The first was a 'T' run over a 60-yard (54.5 m) course, dribbling a leather hockey ball around skittles (Figure 6.8). The test involved as many circuits of the T-shaped course as possible in 2 min. According to Åstrand and Rodahl (1986) sports which engage large muscle groups for 1 min or more may tax $\dot{V}O_{2\,max}$ and so this test implies a high aerobic loading. The use of reversed sticks is excluded and the best of three trials is recorded. Performance on the test was found to correlate significantly both with aerobic and anaerobic power and to differentiate between elite- and county-level players.

The second field test was a distance and accuracy test (Reilly and Bretherton, 1986). This entailed a combination of dribbling a ball and hitting it at a target, a set sequence being repeated as often as possible within 2 min. Distance travelled was measured to the nearest 2.5 yards (2.27 m) and relative accuracy was calculated

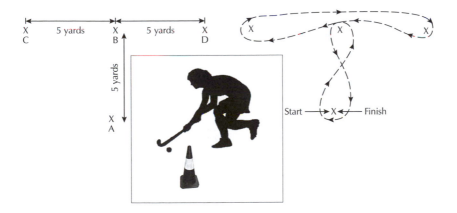

Figure 6.8 Field tests for assessment of fitness of female hockey players incorporating dribbling (from Reilly and Bretherton, 1986)

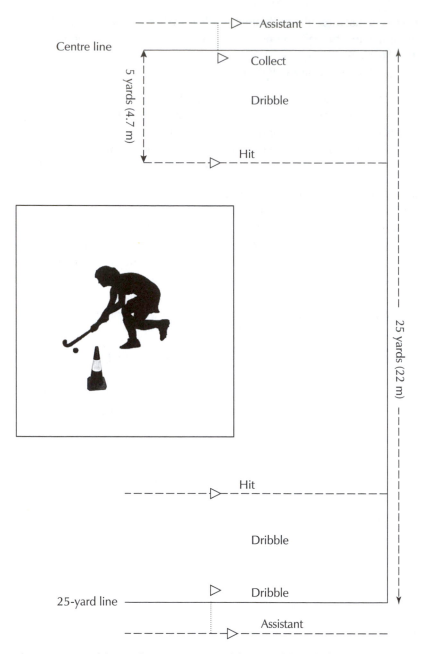

Figure 6.9 Field tests for assessment of fitness of female hockey players incorporating speed and accuracy (from Reilly and Bretherton, 1986)

anaerobic and musculoskeletal performance

by the number of accurate shots as a percentage of the number of hits (Figure 6.9). Accuracy on this test was significantly related to the somatotype of participants, ectomorphy and accuracy being highly correlated.

Many hockey practitioners may find it convenient to eliminate hockey skills from field tests in evaluating fitness of players. In such instances sprint times over 30–50 m (Reilly and Bretherton, 1986) and the 20-m shuttle run test to predict $\dot{V}O_{2\,max}$ are examples of feasible tests. These tests imply anaerobic and aerobic performance capability, respectively. It should be recognised that these are dependant on motivational compliance of participants and are not true indicants of physiological limits of players.

Lemmink et al. (2004) evaluated the reliability of two field-hockey-specific field tests for dribbling and sprinting. The shuttle SDT (speed and dribble test) required players to perform three 30-m shuttle sprints while carrying a hockey stick alternated with short rest periods: after a 5-min rest, the protocol was repeated whilst dribbling a hockey ball. A variation of this test was the slalom SDT in which the players ran a slalom course and, after a 5-min rest, dribbled the same slalom route with a hockey ball. Both tests were found to be reliable measures of sprint and dribble performance for young field-hockey players, with skill and fitness integrated within the tests.

RUGBY UNION AND LEAGUE

Distances of 15 and 30 m have been employed as field tests for Rugby Union, on the basis that these distances represent typical all-out efforts during a game. Repeated-sprint ability tests (6 s with 25–30 s recovery) are also relevant for both codes of rugby. Face validity is improved when field tests incorporate games skills. Examples of mean fitness scores for various anaerobic components of performance in elite Rugby League players are presented in Table 6.2.

Table 6.2 Examples of mean fitness test results for various components of anaerobic performance in elite Rugby League players (data cited in Breivik, 2007)

Test	Forward	Back
Vertical jump (cm)	49	51
Bench press (kg)	119	113
Speed 10 m (s)	2.0	1.9
Speed 20 m (s)	3.1	2.9
Speed 40 m (s)	5.6	5.3
Agility	6.0	5.8

McLean (1992) developed a shuttle run test with players required to maintain shuttle running at 85% $\dot{V}O_{2\ max}$. The recovery period of 30 s was designed to represent the average exercise to rest ratio observed in competitive play. Backs from the Scotland national team could maintain the test velocity for nine shuttles on average, the forwards performing as few as five shuttles at various times during the season.

Later McLean (1993) designed a functional field test for the national team in Scotland. It included slalom runs across a football field over a well-marked course. Fifteen points were marked by flags, round or past which the players ran. Games skills were incorporated, including passing the ball, driving a tackle dummy over 2 m backwards, driving to win the ball on the ground and so on. The forwards took about 30 s to complete the test, the backs being an average of 2 s faster.

A 300-m shuttle run test has been validated as a field test for measuring anaerobic capacity in Rugby Union players (Moore and Murphy, 2003). A significant correlation was found between laboratory-determined maximally accumulated oxygen deficit (a means of estimating anaerobic capacity) and 300-m shuttle run test times.

A sport-specific test of anaerobic endurance for application in Rugby League that simulates the high-intensity physical performance and movement demands placed on players during a match has recently been described (Holloway et al., 2008). This field test, known as the Triple 120-metre Shuttle (T120S) test incorporates the movements of the game associated with defensive play. Performance is judged on the total time taken to complete a full set (three runs with a 60-s rest interval between efforts) of the test.

The agility characteristics of elite Rugby League male, female and junior players have been measured using agility tests such as the L Run and the 505 Run test which incorporate movement patterns of Rugby League (see Gabbett, 2005, 2007; Gabbett et al., 2007). An alternative agility test (glycolytic agility test) has recently been employed in elite female Rugby League to determine and compare the glycolytic capacity of players across playing positions and between selected and non-selected players (Gabbett, 2007).

Modifications of these tests could be made with face validity for the other football codes. Nevertheless, the scores have to be interpreted with caution. Results are difficult to express in physiological terms once skills are added to the demands of locomotion. Importantly also, there is no clear indication that players are performing to their limits and their compliance with the all-out nature of the test is crucial.

158

NETBALL

Netball is a court game for females, requiring many of the characteristics of basketball. Grantham (2007) described a battery of tests for the sport that can be performed on court. The tests include generic items such as the vertical jump, 10-m sprint, '777' agility test, multi-stage 20-m shuttle run, upper-body performance test and a speed-endurance test. The upper-body performance test is performed with a medicine ball from a position seated on a chair. The '777' agility test involves three 7-m sprints with two 90° turns. Whilst these tests may be considered generic in nature, standards have been laid down for national squads. The agility and speed endurance tests are considered to incorporate the repeated accelerations, decelerations and changes of direction that occur in the game.

The speed-endurance test is designed to tax anaerobic mechanisms. The start line is 1 m behind two timing gates set 2 m apart. The player sprints alternately to one of two markers on a line 10 m from the timing gates, returning to a third maker placed between the two timing gates. The first sprint is from the right side, the second from a start position on the left. This sequence is continued with a sprint every 10 s until ten repetitions have been completed. Fastest and slowest times, average and total times are calculated to form the assessment.

Agility, whilst generally considered as the capability to change direction quickly, relies on factors such as timing, perception, reaction time and anticipation. Therefore, Farrow and co-workers (2005) developed a new method for the measurement of agility in netball that was considered more ecologically valid than previous agility tests. The reactive agility performance of players of different standards when responding to a life-size interactive video display of a netball player initiating a pass was compared to a traditional pre-planned agility movement where no external stimulus was present. Results showed that the reactive test condition was more likely to differentiate between the differing skill levels. A similar investigation on Australian Football players employed a reactive agility test which included anticipation and decision-making components in response to the movements of a tester. As in the study on netball, the test distinguished between players of differing performance levels in Australian football (Sheppard et al., 2006).

MUSCLE STRENGTH

Relevance of muscle strength

Muscle strength is a critical component of anaerobic power production, power being defined as force per unit of time. Assessments of muscle strength and power have ranged from use of performance tests such as squats and bench press and measurement of isometric strength to contemporary dynamic measures using computer-linked isokinetic equipment. Strength in the lower limbs is clearly important in field games: the quadriceps, hamstrings and triceps surae groups must generate high forces for jumping, kicking, tackling, turning and changing pace. Sustained forceful contractions are also relevant for retaining balance, for example, when being challenged for possession of the ball. Isometric strength is also an important factor in maintaining a player's balance on a slippery pitch and in controlling the ball. Almost all the body's muscle groups are used by goalkeepers in executing the skills of this positional role in soccer, field-hockey and Gaelic games. For outfield players the lower part of the trunk, the hip flexors and the plantarflexors and dorsiflexors of the ankle are used most. Upper-body strength is employed in throw-ins in soccer, in scrummaging in Rugby Union and in wielding the stick in hockey. The strength of the neck flexors is important in heading the ball forcefully in soccer and in contact situations in Rugby Union and Rugby League. Rugby players are required to have high muscular strength to perform effectively the tackling, lifting, pushing and pulling tasks that occur during match-play (Meir et al., 2001). Strength in the upper body should help prevent the player from being knocked off the ball. High levels of muscular strength are also useful in reducing the risk of injury.

Isokinetic assessments

It is common to monitor the muscle strength of games players using isokinetic apparatus and such assessment on a regular basis is important (see Figure 6.10). These machines offer facilities for determining torque-velocity curves in isokinetic movements and joint-angle curves in a series of isometric contractions. The more complex systems allow for measurement of muscle actions in eccentric as well as concentric and isometric modes. However, these are often expensive and require trained personnel. It is also possible to measure the relationship between joint angular velocity and physical functions using a gyro-sensor (Arai et al., 2008). Isokinetic apparatus may be complemented by electromyographic evaluations to investigate muscle kinematics during game actions such as kicking.

In eccentric actions the limb musculature resists a force exerted by the machine: the muscle is lengthened in the process and hence produces an eccentric contraction. Traditionally, isokinetic assessment was concentrated almost exclusively on muscle groups of the lower limb and on concentric contractions. Isokinetic dynamometry is widely used in assessments of muscle strength in different sports. In rugby, peak force at high contraction speeds in international French Rugby

160

Union backs have been reported to be similar to those reported in international sprinters (Miller et al., 1996). Members of the National youth soccer team of Greece presented higher maximal isometric force than sub-elite and recreational young soccer players of the same age (Gissis et al., 2006). Findings from isokinetic testing of soccer players generally indicate that high absolute muscle strength in the lower limbs is an important component of fitness and a desirable characteristic for successful soccer play (Svensson and Drust, 2005). Nevertheless, some authors view it as not reflecting the specificity of limb movement noted during performance of games skills, advocating instead the use of functional tests in performance assessment (Wisløff et al., 1998). Such tests might include maximal lifts as in a squat, a power clean or a bench press. The various methodological limitations associated with isokinetic assessment have previously been covered in Svensson and Drust (2005) and detailed guidelines for protocols are provided in Blazevich and Cannavan (2007).

Isokinetic dynamometry is accepted as clinically relevant for assessing deficits and imbalances in muscle strength (Cometti et al., 2001). As approximately 75% of injuries in soccer are to the lower extremities (Morgan and Oberlander, 2001), high levels of muscular strength in the hamstrings relative to quadriceps would

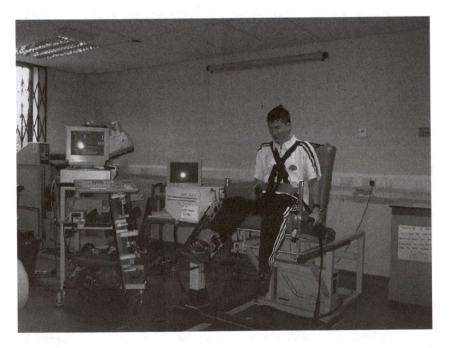

Figure 6.10 Isokinetic dynamometry is used for assessment of strength of the knee extensors in this set-up

seem important in stabilising the knee and reducing the risk of injury (Fried and Lloyd, 1992). The possession of strong hamstrings, particularly in eccentric modes, is an important requirement for playing field games. Improper balance between hamstrings and quadriceps strength may predispose players towards injury. At slow angular velocities and under isometric conditions, a knee flexor-extensor ratio of 60–65% has been recommended (Oberg et al., 1986). This ratio is increased at the higher speeds of commercially available apparatus. Graham-Smith and Lees (2002) have applied a model of risk assessment for hamstring injury termed the dynamic control ratio. Expressed as the eccentric hamstring to concentric quadriceps ratio, it provides a functional assessment of potential injury risk.

Assessment of isokinetic strength also allows asymmetries in lower-limb muscular strength to be identified; generally where imbalances are present, the weaker limb is the one most liable to injury (Fowler and Reilly, 1993). In games, where rapid accelerations, decelerations, angled runs and side-stepping manoeuvres can apply substantial mechanical loading to the knee joint, any inter- or intra-limb asymmetries in knee extensor strength can predispose towards injury, particularly where the knee is inadequately stabilised (Besier et al., 2001). However, there is contrasting evidence of muscle imbalances at elite levels of play in soccer. No evidence was reported of muscle imbalances in extensor and flexor muscle groups and hamstring to quadriceps ratios between the right and left legs in professional Greek soccer players with dominance on one or both legs (Zakas, 2006), whereas several members of a group of English professional soccer players demonstrated a strength imbalance in one or more leg muscle groups (Rahnama et al., 2005). These differences may reflect training histories of players, test protocols and familiarisation of participants with test procedures. Isokinetic test profiles are also important in monitoring muscle strength gains during rehabilitation using the uninjured side as reference. These comparisons to identify asymmetry, weakness or progress within an individual player may be more important than comparisons between teams or between team members.

STRENGTH PERFORMANCE TESTS

Absolute strength is important in many contexts of field games, but especially in contact situations. One of the most important physical qualities for success in elite Australian Rules Football was shown to be the greater upper-body strength of players (Keogh, 1999). In American Football, Rugby Union and Rugby League, performance is reflected in the ability to hit opponents hard in these circumstances and also to take 'hits' when tackled by opponents. For these players, the assessment of functional strength by means of performance tests may be more acceptable than use of clinical tests such as are available on isokinetic dynamometers.

Assessment of strength can be determined using the repetition-maximum (RM) principle. For example, the 1-RM indicates the maximum load that can be lifted once only, 6-RM refers to the maximum load that can be lifted six times, and so on. The loads corresponding to 6-, 10- and 12-RM represent about 78, 61 and 53% of the 1-RM value, respectively (Klausen, 1990). Lees (1997) presented the following protocol for determining 1-RM. This test is performed after a warm-up and some repetitions of the exercise to be assessed using a lower weight. After a rest period of 3–5 min, an attempt should be made at a 1-RM using a weight that is judged to be close but just below the player's maximal level. If this load is successfully lifted, the exercise should be repeated after a further 3–5 minute rest with a higher weight. The 1-RM value is the highest weight that can be lifted successfully.

The monitoring of muscle strength is therefore relevant in the field games that employ weight training in their conditioning programmes. The choice of test may be determined by the strength training regimens employed, for example Olympic lifts are more likely to be used by Rugby Union and Rugby League players than by hurlers or lacrosse or hockey players. Tests for the upper, lower and whole body should be considered.

The bench press and back squat were recommended as suitable exercises for testing 1-RM strength of Rugby League players. The basis for the choice was that these muscles activate the upper- and lower-body 'pushing muscles' (Breivik, 2007). According to Meir (1993), these exercises replicate sport-specific actions adequately for this game. For Rugby Union players, Tong and Wiltshire (2007) advocated bench-press, bench pull, half squat and chin-ups. Typically, the higher values are expected for front-row players, followed in rank order by those in the back row, lock forwards, inside backs and outside backs. It seems that there is variation in the test specification used in the sport, ranging from 1-RM to 5-RM. Irrespective of the number of repetitions used, the lifting technique should be executed correctly. Particular care and attention must be made when assessing muscular strength especially when using maximal loading. Players should be warmed up thoroughly and familiar with the procedures. Assessments must be carried out in a technically sound manner in the presence of a suitably qualified assessor. If practitioners prefer to avoid the use of maximal loading in strength testing, there are possibilities to estimate performance using a sub-maximal lift combined with an accelerometer device. Detailed advice and guidelines on the different procedures and techniques for assessing strength performance across a wide range of field sports can be found in Winter et al. (2007).

CONCLUSION

Sports science laboratories provide a controlled environment in which physiological assessments of physical fitness can be carried out with great precision. This requirement explains why many methodological studies have been conducted in search of a 'gold standard' test for determining anaerobic performance. These tests are proposed, then validated and the exercise protocols are standardised. The application of scientific principles to field testing has progressed to a point where existing tests are continually refined and new tests designed. In such instances, one difficulty is that baseline and reference data become obsolete with the use of new versions of a particular test. Applied sports scientists ultimately have to choose between protocols that allow direct physiological interpretation of results or have proven utility for determining game-related performance. It is inevitable that practitioners will seek to have available tests that have validity for assessing performance capabilities in their sport. Competitive performance is not a static concept, and performance profiles in field games are altered in a progressive upward spiral as intensity of competition increases. Whilst field tests have been used widely due to administrative ease, attention to detail is essential for quality control. Laboratory tests are needed where a physiological interpretation of fitness changes is called for, particularly when related to anaerobic characteristics.

REFERENCES

Ali, A., Williams, C., Hulse, M., Strudwick, A., Reddin, J., Howarth, L., Eldred, J., Hirst, M. and McGregor, S. (2007) Reliability and validity of two tests of soccer skill. *Journal of Sports Sciences*, 25: 1461–1470.

Arai, T., Obuchi, S., Shiba, Y., Omuro, K., Nakano, C. and Higashi, T. (2008) The feasibility of measuring joint angular velocity with a gyro-sensor. *Archives of Physical and Medical Rehabilitation*, 89: 95–99.

Åstrand, P.O. and Rodahl, K. (1986) *Text Book of Work Physiology: Physiological Basis of Exercise*. New York: McGraw Hill.

Aziz, A.R., Mukherjee, S., Chia, M.Y. and Teh, K.C (2008) Validity of the Running Repeated Sprint Ability Test among playing positions and level of competitiveness in Trained Soccer Players. *International Journal of Sports Medicine*, in press.

Balsom, P.D. (1990) A field test to evaluate physical performance capacity of association football players. *Science and Football*, 3: 9–11.

Barnes, C. (2007) Soccer. In E.M. Winter, A.M. Jones, R.C.R. Davison, P.D. Bromley and T.H. Mercer (eds), *Sport and Exercise Physiology Testing: Guidelines. Volume I Sport Testing* (pp. 241–248). The British Association of Sport and Exercise Sciences Guide. London: Routledge.

Bar-Or, O. (1996) Anaerobic performance. In D. Doherty (ed.), *Measurements in Paediatric Exercise Science* (pp. 161–182). Champaign, IL: Human Kinetics.

Besier, T.F., Lloyd, D.G., Cochrane, J.L. and Ackland, T.R. (2001) External loading of the knee joint during running and cutting manoeuvres. *Medicine and Science in Sports and Exercise*, 33: 130–137.

Blazevich, A.J. and Cannavan, D. (2007) Strength testing. In E.M. Winter, A.M. Jones, R.C.R. Davison, P.D. Bromley and T.H. Mercer (eds), *Sport and Exercise Physiology Testing: Guidelines. Volume I Sport Testing* (pp. 130–137). The British Association of Sport and Exercise Sciences Guide. London: Routledge.

Borms, J. and Van Roy, P. (2001) Flexibility. In R.G. Eston and T. Reilly (eds), *Kinanthropometry and Exercise Physiology Laboratory Manual* (pp. 117–147). London: E & FN Spon.

Bosco, C.P., Luhtanen, P. and Komi, P. (1983) A simple method for measurement of mechanical power in jumping. *European Journal of Applied Physiology*, 50: 273–282.

Bradley P.S. and Portas, M.D. (2007) The relationship between preseason range of motion and muscle strain injury in elite soccer players. *Journal of Strength and Conditioning Research*, 21: 1155–1159.

Bravo, D.F., Impellizzeri, F.M., Rampinini, E., Castagna, C., Bishop, D. and Wisløff, U. (2008) Sprint vs. interval training in football. *International Journal of Sports Medicine*, 29: 668–674.

Breivik, S.L. (2007) Rugby League. In E.M. Winter, A.M. Jones, R.C.R. Davison, P.D. Bromley and T.H. Mercer (eds), *Sport and Exercise Physiology Testing: Guidelines. Volume I Sport Testing* (pp. 256–261). The British Association of Sport and Exercise Sciences Guide. London: Routledge.

Carling, C., Bloomfield, J., Nelsen. L. and Reilly, T. (2008) The role of motion analysis in elite soccer: contemporary performance measurement techniques and work-rate data. *Sports Medicine*, 38: 839–862.

Cometti, G., Maffiuletti, N.A., Pousson, M., Chatard, J.C. and Maffulli, N. (2001) Isokinetic strength and anaerobic power of elite, sub-elite and amateur French soccer players. *International Journal of Sports Medicine*, 22: 45–51.

Cunningham, D.A. and Faulkner, J.A. (1969) The effect of training on aerobic and anaerobic metabolism during a short exhaustive run. *Medicine and Science in Sports*, 1: 65–69.

Cureton, T.K. (1970) Illinois agility run. In T.K. Cureton (ed.), *Physical Fitness and Workbook for Adults* (pp. 105–118). Champaign, IL: Stipes Publishing Co.

Derham, S. and Reilly, T. (1993) Ergometric assessments of kayak paddlers. In W. Duquet and J.A.P. Day (eds), *Kinanthropometry IV* (pp. 150–156). London: E & FN Spon.

Farrow, D., Young, W. and Bruce, L. (2005) The development of a test of reactive agility for netball: a new methodology. *Journal of Science and Medicine in Sport*, 8: 52–60.

Fowler, N. and Reilly, T. (1993) Assessment of muscle strength asymmetry in soccer players. In E.J. Lovesey (ed.), *Contemporary Ergonomics* (pp. 327–332). London: Taylor & Francis.

Fried, T. and Lloyd, G.J. (1992) An overview of common soccer injuries. Management and prevention. *Sports Medicine*, 14: 269–275.

Gabbett, T.J. (2002) Physiological characteristics of junior and senior rugby league players. *British Journal of Sports Medicine*, 36: 334–339.

Gabbett, T.J. (2005) Science of rugby league football: a review. *Journal of Sports Sciences*, 23: 961–976.

165

Gabbett, T.J. (2007) Physiological and anthropometric characteristics of elite women rugby league players. *Journal of Strength and Conditioning Research*, 21: 875–881.

Gabbett, T., Kelly, J., Ralph, S. and Driscoll, D. (2007) Physiological and anthropometric characteristics of junior elite and sub-elite rugby league players, with special reference to starters and non-starters. *Journal of Science and Medicine in Sport*. Dec 3 (Epub ahead of print).

Gil, S.M., Gil, J., Ruiz, F., Irazusta, A. and Irazusta J. (2007a) Physiological and anthropometric characteristics of young soccer players according to their playing position: relevance for the selection process. *Journal of Strength and Conditioning Research*, 21: 438–445.

Gil, S.M., Ruiz, F., Irazusta, A., Gil, J. and Irazusta, J. (2007b) Selection of young soccer players in terms of anthropometric and physiological factors. *Journal of Sports Medicine and Physical Fitness*, 47: 25–32.

Gissis, I., Papadopoulos, C., Kalapotharakos, V.I., Sotiropoulos, A., Komsis, G. and Manolopoulos, E. (2006) Strength and speed characteristics of elite, subelite, and recreational young soccer players. *Research in Sports Medicine*, 14: 205–214.

Graham-Smith, P. and Lees, A. (2002) Risk assessment of hamstring injury in rugby union place kicking. In W. Spinks, T. Reilly and A. Murphy (eds), *Science and Football IV* (pp. 183–189). London: Routledge.

Grantham, N. (2007) Netball. In E.M. Winter, A.M. Jones, R.C.R. Davison, P.D. Bromley and T.H. Mercer (eds), *Sport and Exercise Physiology Testing: Guidelines. Volume I Sport Testing* (pp. 245–255). The British Association of Sport and Exercise Sciences Guide. London: Routledge.

Holloway, K.M., Meir, R.A., Brooks, L.O. and Phillips, C.J. (2008) The triple-120 meter shuttle test: a sport-specific test for assessing anaerobic endurance fitness in rugby league players. *Journal of Strength and Conditioning Research*, 22: 633–639.

Hughes, M.G., Doherty, M., Tong, R.T., Reilly, T. and Cable, N.T. (2006) Reliability of repeated sprint exercise in non-motorised treadmill ergometry. *International Journal of Sports Medicine*, 27: 900–904.

Impellizzeri, F.M., Rampinini, E., Maffiuletti, N. and Marcora, S.M. (2007) A vertical jump force test for assessing bilateral strength asymmetry in athletes. *Medicine and Science in Sports and Exercise*, 39: 2044–2050.

Keogh, J. (1999) The use of physical fitness scores and anthropometric data to predict selection in an elite under-18 Australian Rules football team. *Journal of Science and Medicine in Sport*, 2: 125–133.

Keogh, J.W., Weber, C.L. and Dalton, C.T. (2003) Evaluation of anthropometric, physiological, and skill-related tests for talent identification in female field hockey. *Canadian Journal of Applied Physiology*, 28: 397–409.

Klausen, K. (1990) Strength and weight training. In T. Reilly, N. Secher, P. Snell and C. Williams (eds), *Physiology of Sports* (pp. 41–67). London: E & FN Spon.

Lakomy, H. (1984) An ergometer for measuring the power generated during sprinting. *Journal of Physiology*, 354: 33.

Lees, A. (1997) Strength training for football. *Insight – The Football Association Coaches Journal*, 1(2): 32.

Le Gall, F., Beillot, J. and Rochcongar, P. (2002) The improvement in maximal anaerobic power of soccer players during growth. *Science & Sports*, 17: 177–188.

anaerobic and musculoskeletal performance

Lehance, C., Croisier, J.L. and Bury, T. (2005) Optojump system efficiency in the assessment of lower limbs' explosive strength. *Science & Sports*, 20: 131–135.

Lemmink, K.A., Elferink-Gemser, M.T. and Visscher, C. (2004) Evaluation of the reliability of two field hockey specific sprint and dribble tests in young field hockey players. *British Journal of Sports Medicine*, 38: 138–142.

Little, T. and Williams, A.G. (2005) Specificity of acceleration, maximum speed, and agility in professional soccer players. *Journal of Strength and Conditioning Research*, 19: 76–78.

Malomski, E.J. (1993) Physiological characterisation of physical fitness of football players in field conditions. In T. Reilly, J. Clarys and A. Stibbe (eds), *Science and Football II* (pp. 81–85). London: E & FN Spon.

Margaria, R., Aghemo, P. and Rovelli, E. (1966) Measurement of muscular power (anaerobic) in man. *Journal of Applied Psychology*, 21: 1662–1664.

McIntyre, M.C. (2005) A comparison of the physiological profiles of elite Gaelic footballers, hurlers, and soccer players. *British Journal of Sports Medicine*, 39: 437–439.

McIntyre, M.C. and Hall, M. (2005) Physiological profile in relation to playing position of elite college Gaelic footballers. *British Journal of Sports Medicine*, 39: 264–266.

McLean, D.A. (1992) Analysis of the physical demands of international Rugby Union. *Journal of Sports Sciences*, 13: 13–14.

McLean, D.A. (1993) Field testing in Rugby Union football, In D.A. Macleod, R.J. Maughan, C. Williams, C.R. Madeley, J.C.M. Sharp and R.W. Nutton (eds), *Intermittent High Intensity Exercise: Preparation, Stresses and Damage Limitation* (pp. 79–84). London: E. & FN Spon.

Meir, R. (1993) Evaluating players' fitness in Rugby League: reducing subjectivity. *Strength and Conditioning Coach*, 1: 11–17.

Meir, R., Newton, R., Curtis, E., Fardell, M. and Butler, B. (2001) Physical fitness qualities of professional rugby league football players: determination of positional differences. *Journal of Strength and Conditioning Research*, 15: 450–458.

Miller, C., Quievre, J. and Gajer, B. (1996) Characteristics of force/velocity relationships and mechanical power output in the French national rugby team and elite sprinters using 1/2 squats. In P. Marconnet (ed.), *First Annual Congress, Frontiers in Sport Science, the European Perspective*; May 28–31, Nice. European College of Sport Science, 494–5.

Moore, A. and Murphy, A. (2003) Development of an anaerobic capacity test for field sport athletes. *Journal of Science and Medicine in Sport*, 6: 275–284.

Morgan, B.E. and Oberlander, M.A. (2001) An examination of injuries in major league soccer. *American Journal of Sports Medicine*, 29: 426–430.

Oberg, B., Moller, M., Gillquist, J. and Ekstrand, J. (1986) Isokinetic torque levels in soccer players. *International Journal of Sports Medicine*, 7: 50–53.

Oliver, J.L. (2007) Is a fatigue index a worthwhile measure of repeated sprint ability? *Journal of Science and Medicine in Sport*, in press.

Psotta, R. and Bunc, V. (2003) Intermittent anaerobic running test (IANRT) reliability and factor validity in soccer players. *Communication to the Fifth World Congress of Science and Football* (p. 94). Madrid: Editorial Gymnos.

167

Rahnama, N., Lees, A. and Bambaeichi, E. (2005) Comparison of muscle strength and flexibility between the preferred and non-preferred leg in English soccer players. *Ergonomics*, 48: 1568–1575.

Raven, P.R., Gettman, L.R., Pollock, M.L. and Cooper, K.H. (1976) A physiological evaluation of professional soccer players. *British Journal of Sports Medicine*, 10: 209–216.

Reilly, T. (1981) *Sports Fitness and Sports Injuries*. London: Faber and Faber.

Reilly, T. (2007) *Science of Training: Soccer*. London: Routledge.

Reilly, T. and Bayley, K. (1988) The relation between short-term power output and sprint performance of young female swimmers. *Journal of Human Movement Studies*, 14: 19–29.

Reilly, T. and Borrie, A., (1992) Physiology applied to field hockey. *Sports Medicine*, 14: 10–26.

Reilly, T. and Bretherton, S.L. (1986) Multivariate analysis of fitness of female field hockey players. In J.A.P. Day (ed.), *Perspectives in Kinanthropometry* (pp. 135–142). Champaign, IL: Human Kinetics.

Reilly, T. and Doran, D. (2003) Fitness assessment. In T.Reilly and A.M. Williams (eds), *Science and Soccer* (pp. 21–46). London: Routledge.

Reilly, T. and Holmes, M. (1983) A preliminary analysis of selected soccer skills. *Physical Education Review*, 6: 64–71.

Reilly, T., Atkinson, G. and Waterhouse, J. (1997) *Biological Rhythms and Exercise*. Oxford: Oxford University Press.

Reilly, T., Williams, A.M., Nevill, A. and Franks, A. (2000) A multidisciplinary approach to talent identification in soccer. *Journal of Sports Sciences*, 18: 695–701.

Rigg, P. and Reilly, T. (1988) A fitness profile and anthropometric analysis of first and second class Rugby Union players. In T. Reilly, A. Lees, K. Davids and W.J. Murphy (eds), *Science and Football* (pp. 194–200). London: E & FN Spon.

Robinson, P.D.R. and Mills, S.H. (2000) Relationship between scrummaging strength and standard field tests for power in rugby. In Y. Hong and D.P. Johns (eds), *Proceedings of the XVIII International Symposium on Biomechanics in Sports* (p. 980). Hong Kong: Chinese University of Hong Kong.

Seminick, D. (1990) The T-Test. *National Strength and Conditioning Association Journal*, 12: 36–37.

Sheppard, J.M. and Young, W.B. (2006) Agility literature review: classifications, training and testing. *Journal of Sports Sciences*, 24: 919–932.

Sheppard, J.M., Young, W.B., Doyle, T.L, Sheppard, T.A. and Newton R.U. (2006) An evaluation of a new test of reactive agility and its relationship to sprint speed and change of direction speed. *Journal of Science and Medicine in Sport*, 9: 342–349.

Spencer, M., Bishop, D., Dawson, B. and Goodman, C. (2005) Physiological and metabolic responses of repeated-sprint activities specific to field-based team sports. *Sports Medicine*, 35: 1025–1044.

Spencer, M., Fitzsimons, M., Dawson, B., Bishop, D. and Goodman, C. (2006) Reliability of a repeated-sprint test for field hockey. *Journal of Science and Medicine in Sport*, 9: 181–184.

Staron, R.S., Karapondo, D.L., Kraemer, W.J., Fry, A.C., Gordon, S.E., Falkel, J.E., Hagerman, F.C. and Hikida, R.S. (1994) Skeletal muscle adaptions during early phase of heavy-resistance training in men and women. *Journal of Applied Physiology*, 76(3): 1247–1255.

Stølen, T., Chamari, K., Castagna, C. and Wisløff, U. (2005) Physiology of soccer: an update. *Sports Medicine*, 35: 501–36.

Strudwick, A., Reilly, T. and Doran, D. (2002) Anthropometric and fitness profiles of elite players in two football codes. *Journal of Sport Medicine and Physical Fitness*, 42: 239–242.

Svensson, M. and Drust, B. (2005) Testing soccer players. *Journal of Sports Sciences*, 23: 601–618.

Tong, R.J. and Wiltshire, H.D. (2007) Rugby Union. In E.M. Winter, A.M. Jones, R.C.R. Davison, P.D. Bromley and T.H. Mercer (eds), *Sport and Exercise Physiology Testing: Guidelines. Volume I Sport Testing* (pp. 262–271). The British Association of Sport and Exercise Sciences Guide. London: Routledge.

Vescovi, J.D., Brown, T.D. and Murray, T.M. (2007) Descriptive characteristics of NCAA Division I women lacrosse players. *Journal of Science and Medicine in Sport*, 10: 334–340.

Vescovi, J.D. and McGuigan, M.R. (2007) Relationships between sprinting, agility, and jump ability in female athletes. *Journal of Sports Sciences*, 26: 97–107.

Williams, A.M., Borrie, A., Cable, T., Gilbourne, D., Lees, A., MacLaren, D. and Reilly, T. (1997) *Umbro: Conditioning for Football*. London: TSL Publishing.

Wilson, D. (2007) Training and fitness measures in Islamic soccer players during Ramadan. Unpublished Ph.D. thesis, Liverpool John Moores University.

Winter, E.M., Jones, A.M., Davison, R.C.R., Bromley, P.D. and Mercer, T. (eds) (2007) Sport & Exercise Physiology Testing Guidelines: Sport Testing. *The British Association of Sport & Exercise Sciences Guide*. London: Routledge.

Wisløff, U., Helgerud, J. and Hoff, J. (1998) Strength and endurance of elite soccer players. *Medicine and Science in Sports and Exercise,* 30: 462–467.

Witvrouw, E., Danneels, L., Asselman, P., D'Have, T. and Cambier, D. (2003) Muscle flexibility as a risk factor for developing muscle injuries in male professional soccer players. A prospective study. *American Journal of Sports Medicine*. 31: 41–46.

Zakas, A. (2006) Bilateral isokinetic peak torque of quadriceps and hamstring muscles in professional soccer players with dominance on one or both two sides. *Journal of Sports Medicine and Physical Fitness*, 46: 28–35.

CHAPTER SEVEN

THE MEANING AND MEASUREMENT OF BODY COMPOSITION

INTRODUCTION

The physical composition of the body is relevant in the preparation of games players for competitive performance. Lean tissue such as skeletal muscle contributes to the production of power output during exercise of high intensity. Extra fat mass constitutes an added load to be lifted against gravity when running and jumping. For participants at a recreational level excessive fat deposits lead to becoming overweight and a continuation of this trend leads towards obesity. Appropriate training programmes, together with a controlled diet and favourable genetics, can contribute to the optimal body composition of participants in competitive games. Therefore, measurement of lean and fat tissues, representing a breakdown of the body into two compartments, is of interest to games players, their coaches and scientific support staff. This interest remains even if body composition is not strictly

170

a fitness measure, although its components are influenced by physical training and the balance between energy intake and expenditure.

Measurements of body composition may therefore be pertinent for evaluating nutritional status. Changes in body mass have been used as a practical means of monitoring dehydration in the field in elite soccer players (Harvey et al., 2007). The body composition of games players may also change in a seasonal pattern, fat depots increasing in the off-season and major losses occurring during the pre-season period as training is stepped up. Measures of body composition may be employed as criteria for studying the effects of nutritional strategies and dietary interventions. There are likely to be changes in body composition also during injury and rehabilitation, when the normal high levels of energy expenditure due to training are reduced. The muscle mass also changes according to the amount and nature of strength training, and during lay offs.

In field sports, observations of performance and physiological characteristics of players are influenced by differences in body size and consequently results need to be adjusted for this factor. Allometric scaling is the technique that is used to make these adjustments and is especially important in activities where body mass is unsupported and must be carried (Winter and Eston, 2006). Shields et al. (1984) stated that among position groups from professional American football players a low percentage of body fat was correlated with a high level of cardiovascular fitness. In elite soccer (Stølen et al., 2005; Chamari et al., 2005) and rugby players (Duthie et al., 2003), the importance of adjusting maximal oxygen uptake and muscular strength according to body mass (or preferably lean body mass) has previously been discussed when evaluating players' capacities and designing appropriate training interventions.

The individual's 'frame size' affects skeletal mass, which is also influenced by impact loading associated with training and competing in the sport in question. These respective components of body composition – fat, muscle, bone – are also susceptible to change with experience in the sport and eventually with ageing. The assessment of body composition can also be useful for monitoring and evaluating changes in composition and skeletal mass according to growth and maturation of youth players.

Information on body composition is subject to the individual's personal sensitivities which must be respected. Cultural differences may preclude the acquisition of some or all measurements in participants (Stewart and Eston, 2007). The manner in which the information is acquired, presented and received will be of concern to the professionals involved in care of the athlete – whether physiologist, dietician or counsellor and psychologist in certain cases. The matter is of special relevance in young players, and in individuals prone to eating disorders. In their consensus statement on body fat, the Steering Group of the British Olympic Association attempted to harmonise ways of treating the data in dialogue with athletes and mentors so the feelings of the individual concerned are not hurt (Reilly et al., 1996).

In this chapter, various methods of body composition are described and their applications to games players illustrated. Analysis at whole-body level is first presented, prior to an exposition of the levels of organisation that allow body compartments to be structured conceptually. Methods of body composition assessment are then described according to an anatomical or chemical approach. Contemporary technologies are contrasted with anthropometry in their current applications to sports participants.

ANTHROPOMETRIC MEASURES

The conceptual separation of the body into two or more compartments overcomes some of the limitations of using combinations of whole-body measurements for estimating body composition. The simplest of these indices is the body mass index (BMI) in which stature (m) is divided by body mass squared (kg^2). The index combines a linear measure with another which reflects a cubic rather than squared dimension, so it is hardly surprising that the relationship breaks down when BMI values are very large or very low. Nevertheless, the BMI has been adopted by the World Health Organisation in its population studies (see Table 7.1).

Whilst the BMI measure has proved useful in quantifying the obesity epidemic in developed populations, its application to elite athletes participating in field games is questionable. The calculation fails to distinguish between muscle and fat as constituents of body mass. A Rugby Union forward, for example, who increases muscle mass as a result of weight training, can be wrongly interpreted as overweight. Similarly, a hockey player who ceases training completely during the off-season may lose muscle mass whilst gaining fat mass: in this instance there may be an increase

Table 7.1 The relationship between body mass index (BMI) and health-related weight categorisation according to the World Health Organisation

BMI	Weight categorisation
<18.5	Underweight, Thin
18.5 – 24.9	Healthy weight, Healthy
25.0 – 29.9	Grade 1 Obesity, Overweight
30.0 – 39.9	Grade 2 Obesity, Obese
>40.0	Grade 3 Obesity, Morbidly obese

(or no overall change) in BMI. Awareness of the limitations of BMI is important when the consequences of training throughout the season, especially the types of training interventions adopted by games players, are being evaluated.

Muscle development is unlikely to be pronounced in adolescents so that a high BMI should indicate a greater than normal level of body fat. However, in maturing children, for whom the ratio of muscle and bone to height is constantly changing, BMI values can be misleading and results must therefore be interpreted with caution. In the adolescent population BMI may nevertheless be useful in identifying both health-related consequences and impairments in performance capability. Sjolie (2004) reported that lower-back pain was associated with higher than average BMI values in adolescents in eastern Norway. The relationship was particularly evident in young girls.

An alternative health-related measure to BMI is the waist-to-hip ratio (WHR). Accepted values differ between men and women, since men tend to put on extra weight in the abdominal region whilst women accumulate extra fat mainly on the hips. The cause of this sexual dimorphism is the differential pattern of oestrogen receptors located in these two regions in females, allowing the latter to store fat preferentially in the hips. A WHR value of 1.0 is deemed acceptable for men; the corresponding average figure for adult females being 0.85. However, there are no standardised values across the field sports.

A comprehensive anthropometric profile of athletes embraces measurements of limb lengths, bone breadths and limb girths. Combining two or more measures allows a picture of body proportions to be built up. It is good practice to record the basic measures to provide at least a restricted profile for young players as part of a talent-development programme. Training in anthropometric assessment is required for such endeavours, in accordance with procedures outlined in Eston and Reilly (2009) and in ISAK (2001). Such assessments are relevant for many competitive sports, since level of ultimate performance and positional role may be determined by anthropometric characteristics.

A study on prospective elite junior Australian footballers reported significant differences between a group of selected and non-selected players when height and mass were compared (Veale et al., 2008). Similar findings have been obtained when junior elite and sub-elite Rugby League players were compared for height and mass (Gabbett, 2005). Results in young soccer players indicate that around the time of puberty, parameters associated with physical maturity such as height and body size are instrumental in determining whether they are successful or not in future selection processes (Gil et al., 2007). The findings from these studies suggested that selection for participation at elite levels in field sports appears to be related to a generally higher profile across a range of measures including anthropometric characteristics. In Rugby Union, a larger body size correlates significantly with scrummaging force and competitive success (Duthie et al., 2003).

Regional differences in the physical make-up of soccer teams across Four European professional soccer leagues are shown to exist with players from the German Bundesliga, reporting higher values for body mass and BMI than players from the English Premier League, Spanish La Liga Division and Italian Serie A (Bloomfield et al., 2005). In addition, there may be anthropometric predispositions for the different positional roles within team sports. Significant differences in a variety of anthropometric characteristics, most notably stature and body mass, have previously been reported for soccer players (Reilly et al., 2000), suggesting that these variables denote a morphological optimisation within soccer and that anthropometric measurement of players should therefore be an integral part of a performance-profiling programme (Hencken and White, 2006). For example, taller soccer players may be considered more suitable for central defensive positions and goalkeepers tend to be tall. In junior Rugby League players, props were shown to be significantly taller and heavier and to have greater skinfold thicknesses compared to all the other positions (Gabbet, 2005). Defensive line players in the Turkish American Football League were significantly heavier than running, corner and quarter-backs (Koz and Balci, 2007). Whilst greater amounts of body fat may provide a level of protection against injury in collision sports such as rugby (Brewer and Davis, 1995), carrying excess body fat will adversely affect player mobility and speed so a suitable balance should be met (Breivik, 2007).

PRACTICAL EXAMPLE

Gabbett (2007) investigated the physiological and anthropometric characteristics of elite women Rugby League players and developed physical performance standards for these athletes. Significant differences were detected between forwards and backs for body mass and skinfold thickness. The hit-up forwards positional group were heavier, and had greater skinfold thickness than the adjustables and outside backs positional groups. No significant differences were detected between selected and non-selected players for any of the anthropometric characteristics. The results of this study also showed that elite women Rugby League players had greater body mass and skinfold thickness and had lower physical capacities than previously reported for other elite women team-sport athletes. The author suggested that improvements in such performance-related factors are required to allow elite women Rugby League players to tolerate the physiological demands of competition more effectively, reduce fatigue-related errors in skill execution and decrease the risk of injury.

174

The physique is another factor that is evident at whole-body level. The accepted method of recording physique or body shape is the somatotype approach outlined by Duquet and Carter (2001). The somatotype can be described by means of three components – endomorphy, representing fatness; mesomorphy, representing muscularity; and ectomorphy, representing leanness or linearity. These measures can be derived from data on stature, body mass, bone breadth, limb girths (corrected by skinfold thicknesses) and skinfold thicknesses.

The somatotype is essentially the description of a phenotype. Specialists at elite level in individual sports tend to cluster at a particular part of the somatochart, a two-dimensional picture of the individual's body shape. There is more variability in games players, due to positional roles. Tracking of International Rugby Union players over three decades (Olds, 2001) has yielded valuable insights into how the game has changed, in accordance with the physiques of its elite performers (see Figure 7.1). Whilst both backs and forwards have increased muscular make-up and reduced fatness, the backs of the professional era are more muscular than the amateur forwards of two decades earlier.

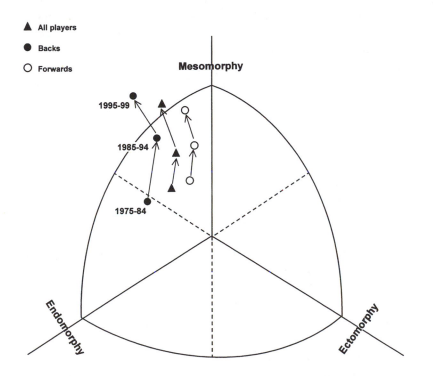

Figure 7.1 The expanding universe of physiques in international Rugby Union (from Olds, 2001)

The values for mesomorphy are highest among the field games that entail physical contact with opponents (see Table 7.2). These games include both Rugby football codes, and American football. The 'expanded universe' of physiques is also extended to Gaelic football players and to contemporary professional soccer players whereby the somatotypes displayed tend to be dissociated from the general population (Reilly, 2005). A mainly muscular make-up is not necessarily advantageous in all the playing positions in games contexts: Rienzi et al. (1999) reported that international Rugby-Sevens players with high values for mesomorphy displayed lower work-rate values in matches compared with their remaining team-mates. The prevailing physique may therefore influence the types of performance tasks to which the individual player is best suited. It reflects also that forward players benefit from added muscle mass in the scrums and mauls but are disadvantaged in more open play in the 7-a-side version of the game.

These whole-body measurements provide useful comparisons between sports and between individuals in certain sports. Their sensitivity in detecting changes in body composition is insufficient for regular use in practical settings. For this purpose, specific tools are needed that are reliable, objective and valid. There is also a need to understand the limitations of the techniques, the assumptions their calculations require and the biological foundations for their use. This is especially important as values of body composition are highly dependent on the method employed and caution should be shown when interpreting results from different techniques, especially on an individual basis when estimation procedures are employed. For these reasons, the different levels of organisation of the body are described as background for the various methods that have been designed for the analysis of body composition.

LEVELS OF ORGANISATION

The integration of the various physiological systems is reflected in the effective functioning of the organism at the whole-body level. The physiological systems may be assessed by functional tests, such as maximal aerobic power ($\dot{V}O_{2\,max}$) for the oxygen transport system and isokinetic peak torque for specific skeletal muscle groups. Physiological systems are comprised of functional aggregates of tissues. The main categories of tissue are connective, epithelial, muscular and nervous. Adipose and bone tissue are forms of connective tissue that, with muscle (skeletal, cardiac and smooth), form about 75% of total body mass. Adipose tissue contains adipocytes, mostly lipid or fat, and external depots are located in subcutaneous layers. There are also quantities of lipid stored in internal depots, as supportive packing around central organs, in the interstices within muscles and in the yellow marrow of bone.

176

the meaning and measurement of body composition

Table 7.2 Somatotype and estimated body fat percentage in different groups of male games players

	Author	Nationality	Level	n	Age (years)	Somatotype	Body fat (%)
Soccer	White et al. (1988)	English	Professional: Top Division	17	23.3 ± 0.9	2.6–4.2–2.7	19.3 ± 0.6
	Rienzi et al. (2000)	South American	Professional International	11	26.1 ± 4.0	2.1–5.4–2.2	10.6 ± 2.6
	Casajús (2001)	Spanish	Professional: Top League	15	26.3 ± 3.1	2.6–4.9–2.3	8.2 ± 0.91
	Gil et al. (2007)	Spanish	High-level youth	32	17.8 ± 0.9	2.4 ± 0.1	11.6 ± 0.2
Gaelic football	Reilly and Doran (2003)	Irish	Inter-county	33	23.0 ± 5.0	2.7–5.7–1.9	12.3 ± 2.9
Rugby Sevens	Rienzi et al. (1999)	International	Professional	27	–	2.3–5.9–1.5	11.7 ± 2.3

Skeletal muscle refers to the tissue level, but the individual muscle fibre represents the cellular level. At this level the body can be divided into total cell mass, extracellular fluid (ECF) and extracellular solids (ECS). The different types of cells comprising total cell mass include adipocytes, myocytes and osteocytes. The ECF compartment includes intravascular plasma and interstitial fluid. The ECS includes organic substances such as collagen and elastin fibres in connective tissue, and inorganic elements like calcium and phosphorus found largely in bone. The ECS compartment may be estimated using the technique of neutron activation analysis. Analysis at cellular and tissue levels represents an anatomical approach to body composition analysis.

The anatomical approach is in contrast with a chemical approach towards the analysis of human body composition. There are over 100,000 chemical components at molecular level. These may be presented as five main groupings – lipids, water, protein, carbohydrates and minerals. Lipids are molecules that are insoluble in water, but are extractable with ether. Besides triglycerides, which constitute the main energy reserve of the body and have a higher energy density than carbohydrates, other forms of lipid are found in cell membranes and nervous tissue and are known as essential lipids. In a two-compartmental model, the lean body mass includes these essential lipids whereas the fat-free mass (FFM) does not. The FFM assumes all fat is removed and is composed of fat-free muscle, fat-free bone, fat-free adipose tissue and other fat-free remaining tissues.

The deepest view of body composition is at the atomic level, indicative of the 50 or so elements of the body. The combination of oxygen, carbon, hydrogen, nitrogen, calcium and phosphorus comprises 98% of total body mass. The main elements can be estimated using tissue ionising radiation, but the instrumentation is expensive and scarce and inaccessible except for specialised research. Whole-body potassium-40 (^{40}K) counting utilises scintigraphy for determining total body potassium, and neutron activation has been used to estimate the body's nitrogen stores with total body protein then estimated from nitrogen content.

The only direct method of analysing body composition is by means of cadaver dissection. The methods that are in clinical or practical use have typically been validated against cadaver material. This process has generated reference methods, based on a chemical approach, such as measurement of body water or potassium counting, that incorporates quantitative assumptions. Other methods have evolved that have based their calibrations on correlations with these reference methods, and hence are referred to as doubly indirect (see Table 7.3). An awareness of these methods is important in understanding their limitations when applied to active athletes.

178

Table 7.3 Different methods of body composition assessment

Underwater weighing	The person is weighed underwater in a tank and his/her body density is determined. Body density is proportional to % body fat. The higher the body density the less the body fat.
Potassium counting	The amount of naturally occurring potassium 40 (K^{40}) in muscles is measured in a special whole-body counter. The amount of K^{40} is proportional to the lean body mass (LBM). Body fat is determined by subtraction (body weight – LBM = fat).
Isotopic dilution	Total body water (TBW) is measured by dilution procedures. Blood or urine samples are collected for analysis after introduction of the dilutant in the body. Lean body mass contains 73.2% water, and body fat is determined by subtractions.
Dual-energy X-ray absorptiometry	A dual-energy low-radiation beam is passed through a supine body from a source underneath the bed. Detectors above the subject measure the beam's attenuation and either the whole body or selected regions are scanned. The dual energy of the beam allows quantification of the body components in each pixel.
Medical imaging	Ultrasound, X-ray, NMR – a picture of either fat, muscle and/or bone is obtained. These regional pictures (or estimates) of fat and muscle thickness are converted to estimates of total body fat using statistical and mathematical relationships.
Anthropometry	Regional measurements (girths, skinfolds, body widths) are taken at specific body sites. Site location and measurement technique are very important. Conversion of regional measurements to estimates of total body fat and LBM are done using statistical and mathematical relationships.

Densitometry (underwater weighing)

The hydrostatic or underwater weighing method is taken as the reference standard for body composition assessment. It operates from Archimedes' principle that a 'solid heavier than a fluid will, if placed in it, descend to the bottom of the fluid, and the solid will, when weighed in the fluid, be lighter than its true weight by the weight of the fluid displaced'. It is not usual to measure the water spilled over: instead the body is weighed in air and again under water in a tank. The participant is suspended in a sling attached to a scale and is retained long enough under the water for measurement to be recorded. The participant exhales before being immersed and holds his or her breath whilst under water after emptying the lungs as far as possible (see Figure 7.2). A number of immersions, maybe up to ten, are required for accurate recording of data. The amount of air remaining in the lungs is known as residual volume (RV) and this can be measured using standard physiological procedures. Air in the gastrointestinal tract is assumed to be 100 ml, irrespective of body size.

179

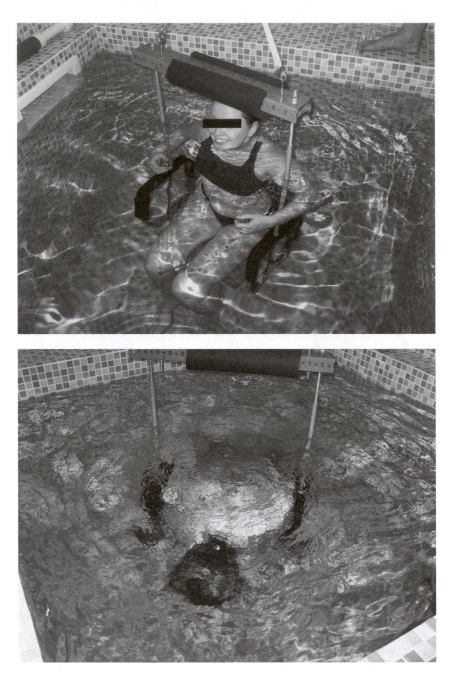

Figure 7.2 Subject is in water tank prior to (top) and during (bottom) immersion for weighing underwater

the meaning and measurement of body composition

It is assumed that body fat has constant density of 0.9 and that the density of the FFM is 1.1. The formula used to compute body density from the body weight in air (BWa) and the weight in water (BWw) is:

$$\text{body density} = \frac{\text{BWa}}{\dfrac{(\text{BWa} - \text{BWw}) - \text{RV} + 100\ \text{ml}}{\text{Dw}}}$$

Once the body density has been calculated, this figure can be translated into a body fat value using a regression equation. There are many such equations in the literature, the most commonly used being those derived by Siri (1956) and Brozek et al. (1963). Siri's equation for calculating percentage body fat from the whole body density is:

$$\%\ \text{body fat} = \frac{495}{\text{density}} - 450$$

Air displacement (plethysmography)

Body volume is measurable by utilising Archimedes' principle to record the amount of air or water that the body displaces. Equipment for measurement of gas displacement consists of a test chamber large enough to hold an adult, separated by a diaphragm from a reference chamber. Pressure changes induced by vibration of the diaphragm allow the test chamber volume to be determined first with and then without the participant. The recordings allow the body volume to be calculated, from which density is computed and then body fat estimated using equations such as that of Siri (1956) or Brozek et al. (1963).

Plethysmography using air displacement is the principle employed by commercial systems such as the BOD POD device (Life Measurement Instruments Inc., Concord, CA, http://www.bodpod.com/) purchased by some professional sports clubs. The accuracy of currently available systems is against its wider acceptance. It is subject to the quantitative assumptions about the constancy of FFM and other compartments that are inherent in densitometry. The large errors that result make its use questionable in games players for the detection of small changes in body composition.

Chemical methods

Body composition may be determined from measurements of total body water. As fat cells contain little water, an individual with a relatively large amount of water will have more lean tissue and less fat than the norm. The isotope dilution method of body composition assessment refers to the procedure whereby the participant drinks a known amount of an isotope, usually tritiated water or deuterated water (with deuterium oxide). After 3–4 hours to allow for the distribution of the isotope throughout body water pools, a sample of body fluid is obtained for measurement of the isotope's concentration. How much water is needed within the body to achieve that concentration is then calculated.

Another chemical procedure for the body composition assessment is potassium counting. Potassium (K) is located primarily within the body's cells. The gamma rays of one of its naturally occurring radioactive isotopes, usually ^{40}K, can be measured in a whole-body scintillation counter. Since emissions are proportional to the amount of lean tissue, this constancy is utilised in computing lean body mass (LBM). The amount of fat is obtained by subtraction.

Both methods of chemical analyses are impractical for use within a battery of measures in profiling athletes. The equipment is expensive, especially for ^{40}K counting, and the procedures too technical for routine use. They are mainly used as research and clinical tools, or in validation studies of other methods.

Another chemical method that has gained acceptance in clinical contexts is dual-energy X-ray absorptiometry or DXA. Originally designed for assessing risk of osteoporosis, the technique incorporates a three-component model of the body – bone, fat and bone-free fat-free mass. This scanner is able to divide the body's non-mineral content into fat and lean compartments based on the X-ray attenuation properties of the different molecular masses. Dual-energy X-ray absorptiometry has fast become the reference method for assessing percent body fat, particularly as it does not rely on the quantitative assumptions associated with underwater weighing. This technique is non-invasive, with a good precision, low radiation exposure and a quick scanning and analysis time. It also removes the errors associated with the selection of skinfold prediction equations and reduces the bias and error of the assessor. Wallace et al. (2006) compared values of percentage fat in 30 females between DXA scans and hydrodensitometry, reporting a close agreement and strong correlation ($r = 0.974$) between the methods. Similarly, skinfold values in a squad of players belonging to a Premier League soccer club obtained through DXA scans were highly comparable to those obtained on the same players but using the traditional calliper method (Wallace et al., 2007). Whilst the DXA machine is expensive, the method has been applied in monitoring the body composition of professional games players throughout a season of competition (Wallace et al., 2008). Its uses in assessing bone health are covered later in the chapter.

Body imaging techniques

There is a family of techniques by which images or pictures of the body and its specific tissues can be constructed. These range in terms of sophistication and cost. They include clinical methods such as X-ray and ultrasound, and computer-aided imaging, for example tomography and nuclear magnetic resonance.

An X-ray or roentgen may provide a picture of the width of fat, tissue and bone. Historically, it has been used to trace the growth of these tissues over time. Body fat can be estimated from X-ray measurements at a number of sites using a multiple regression equation. This is a somewhat impractical approach to body composition assessment, especially nowadays when ethical issues associated with giving repeated doses of low radiation are considered.

Ultrasound devices are used to distinguish between tissue layers. The machines act both as a signal emitter and receiver. Echoes of sound waves passing through tissue are analysed. The current systems have been used for measuring volumes of various organs and cross-sectional areas of muscle rather than for assessing body fat.

Computerised axial tomography (computer tomography or CT) and nuclear magnetic resonance imaging techniques are both expensive to purchase and to use. Computed tomography entails exposure of the participant to ionising radiation and so is not ethical for use in repeated monitoring of athletes. Nuclear magnetic resonance or magnetic resonance imaging (MRI) refers to the transmission of electromagnetic waves through the tissue whilst the body is placed within a large magnetic field. Nuclei absorb and release energy at a particular frequency, this resonant frequency being dependent on the type of tissue. Computer analysis of the signal enables detailed images of specific tissues to be produced and their volumes calculated. These methods are used mainly for research purposes and are not really appropriate for routine body composition analysis. The MRI technique has been used to detect absolute and relative changes in skeletal muscle size in response to a period of heavy resistance training (Abe et al., 2003). Results showed that resistance training induced larger increases in skeletal muscle mass than in fat-free mass, indicating that MRI can be useful in determining the effects of a particular type of training on body composition. Nevertheless, magnetic resonance imaging is more often employed in assessment of the extent of injury to internal structures on players across professional field sports.

TOBEC and BIA

Total body electrical activity (TOBEC) employs the principle that lean tissue and body water conduct electricity better than fat does. An electrical current is injected into a large cyclindrical coil within which the participant is placed. The body composition of the participant affects the electromagnetic field developed in the space enclosed by the cylindrical coil.

Bioelectric impedance analysis (BIA) utilises the same principle as TOBEC, but the instrumentation is small enough to be portable. Two electrodes are placed on the right foot and two on the right hand. The current at 50 Hz is passed through the body and the resistance to it is recorded. This value is then used along with measures of frame size and other anthropometric details to estimate percentage body fat. The portable systems are linked to a computer whose software is determined by the supplier. It is thought that the resistivity should be related to the square of body stature to take account of the length of the body through which the signal travels.

Bioelectric impedance analysis may hold promise for routine assessment of body fat, provided the conditions in which measurements are made are controlled. The requirements include a normal state of hydration and so results are affected by exercise prior to observation. Emptying the bladder in between measurements can cause a change in estimated body fat of up to 2.5% of body weight. Measurements are recommended for early in the day, with the bladder emptied. Therefore, factors such as eating, hydration status, fluid distribution, temperature, time of day and exercising must be controlled when using this method as they can introduce con-siderable error in the resistance measurements. The method correlates reasonably well with others. For example, in a group of 84 participants, the correlation between BIA results and those derived for skinfolds was 0.683 (Reilly and Sutton, 2008). This level of agreement is too low to detect small changes in body composition with sufficient confidence for assessment of elite athletes. There is still work to be done on the most appropriate anthropometric corrections to the conductivity (or resistance) values before BIA can be recommended unequivocally.

Multi-frequency BIA has been developed in an attempt to discriminate between body water pools, in addition to estimating percentage body fat (see Figure 7.3). This application to assess hydration status is likely to be more useful in a football context than estimation of body fat. The difficulties of establishing satisfactory control over the participants prior to its use would raise questions about the quality of any data generated for body composition. Segmental multi-frequency bioelectrical impe-dance has recently been employed to evaluate the composition of the body and its different segments in professional soccer players, and describe differences across teams and playing positions (Melchiorri et al., 2007). This technique uses an 8-point

184

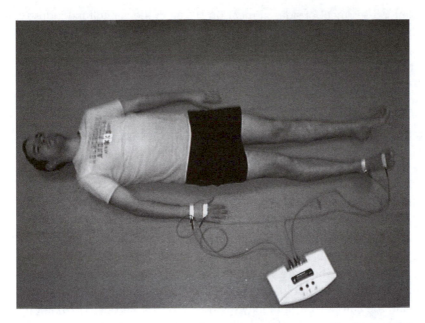

Figure 7.3 Multi-frequency bioelectric impedance is applied to an athlete lying supine for determination of body water, from which percentage body fat is estimated

tactile electrode method with two electrodes placed on each hand and foot, and by regulating impedance via on-off switches the composition of individual body segments can be detected. Whilst the system was deemed to be accurate in determining body fat, low impedance was observed in the trunk in very lean or obese subjects, leading to a higher error of measurement (Salmi, 2003).

Infrared interactance

Near infrared machines have been developed commercially with the express purpose of assessing body fat. The principle of this approach is the differential absorption and reflection of light by the various layers of body tissue. A portable low-cost instrument, the Futrex 5000 (FTX) gathers light-interactance data by means of a fibre-optic probe based over the belly of a muscle (http://www.futrex.com/). The system most used selects the biceps muscle site for placement of the probe.

The first validation of the infrared interactance technique was completed at the National Institute of Health at Bethesda, Maryland. The single site proved acceptable for assessment of sides of meat on behalf of the agricultural industry. Predictions of total body fat from a single peripheral site is not likely to be very accurate in humans (Clarys et al., 1987). In order to overcome this problem, the interactance data are entered along with anthropometric values (height, weight, frame size) and activity levels into a regression equation to estimate percentage body fat. Skinfold measures give more information and predict body fat more accurately than do infrared devices such as the Futrex 5000 system, especially at the extremes of the body fat continuum. For this reason some attention is now given to measurement of skinfolds.

THE SKINFOLD: MYTH AND REALITY

Since almost half of the body's fat is stored subcutaneously, it was thought that total body fat might be predictable if enough representative sites of the body are sampled for skinfold thicknesses. There are over 100 equations in the scientific literature for predicting body fat from skinfold measures. The one mostly used in the United Kingdom and the European Community (Durnin and Wormersley, 1974) adopts four sites for measurement of skinfold thicknesses. These are known as the triceps, biceps, supra-iliac and subscapular sites. From these four measurements the percentage body fat is predicted, making allowance for the participant's age and sex.

The most comprehensive examination of the validity of skinfolds for assessment of body composition has been the Brussels Cadaver Study (Clarys et al., 1987). The Brussels group of researchers had access to a large number of cadavers and the possibility of quantifying the magnitude of various tissues. They were able to look at the relation between external and internal fat deposits, and the distribution of fat throughout the body which is otherwise known as fat patterning. Subcutaneous and internal fat stores are significantly related, but the correlation is not perfect. The distribution of fat is noticeably different between males and females, and is especially pronounced in middle-age when males store excess fat, predominantly in the stomach, females in the thighs. This trend of abdominal deposition of fat is not so pronounced in female participants. It should be noted, however, that the best single predictor of total body fat is the skinfold thickness at the anterior thigh (Eston et al., 2005). This site is not included in most of the prediction equations.

Clarys and co-workers also examined the effect that compression of the adipose tissue layer has on the measurement made. The skinfold thickness pinched within the fingers of the operator and compressed by the callipers must include two layers of skin and two layers of adipose tissue. These layers are compressed

186

whilst the measurements are being made, the compressibility depending on the site involved.

The use of skinfold callipers (see Figure 7.4 for example) requires training of the operator. Otherwise the data are unreliable. It is important also to use a calliper accepted by the International Biological Programme and the International Society for the Advancement of Kinanthropometry (ISAK, 2001). Acceptable models include those of Harpenden, John Bull and Lafayette. The cheap plastic devices have a sensitivity of 1 mm (compared to 0.1 mm on the spring-loaded system) and most of them are not easy to use. Guidelines for the use of callipers and instructions for measurement at different anatomical sites are available from Eston and Reilly (2009) and Stewart and Eston (2007). Advice for application at different sites is summarised in Table 7.4.

The interpretation of skinfold thickness data should be done with caution. Whilst the sum of skinfold may be used to estimate percentage body fat, its limitations as a doubly indirect method of doing so should be acknowledged. The measurement and prediction errors should be recognised when any prescriptions for body-weight control are being considered. It is preferable to use the sum of skinfolds as a measure and monitor changes in this composite variable in repeated test profiles alongside other fitness data.

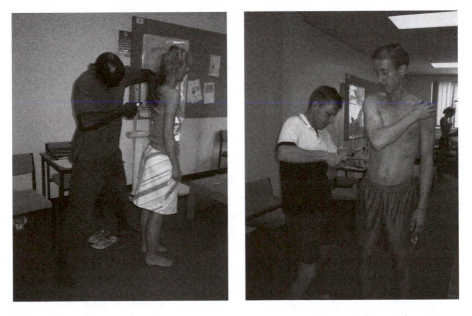

Figure 7.4 Skinfold thicknesses at subscapular (left) and supra-iliac (right) sites are recorded

Table 7.4 Guidelines for assessing skinfold thicknesses at different sites

Technique

- Measurement should be taken on dry skin. Moist skin can impair the measurement.
- The subject should keep the muscles relaxed during the measurement.
- Measurement should be taken on the right side of the body.
- The skinfold should be firmly grasped by the thumb and index finger, using the pads at the tip of the thumb and finger.
- The callipers should be placed perpendicular to the fold, on the site marked, dial up, at approximately 1 cm below the finger and thumb. While maintaining the grasp of the skinfold, the callipers should be released so that full tension is placed on the skinfold. The dial should be read to the nearest 0.1 mm, 1-2 s after the grip has been fully released.
- The callipers should not be placed too close to the subject's body or too far away on the tip of the skinfold. It is helpful to visualise the location of a true double fold of skin thickness, and to place the callipers there.
- A minimum of two measurements should be taken at each site. If repeated tests vary by more than 1 mm, conduct the measurements again. If consecutive measurements become increasingly smaller, this suggests the fat is being compressed.
- The final value recorded should be the average of the two that best seem to represent the skinfold site.
- Record each skinfold as it is measured.
- Tables for transforming skinfold thicknesses to percent body fat values are contained in the publication of Durnin and Wormersley. They are also incorporated in the manuals provided with the callipers by its suppliers.

Skinfold sites

- Biceps: A vertical fold on the anterior surface of the biceps midway between the anterior axillary fold and the antecubital fossa.
- Triceps: A vertical fold on the posterior midline of the upper arm, over the triceps muscle, halfway between the acromion process (bony process on top of the shoulder) and olecranon process (bony process on the elbow).
- Subscapular: The fold is taken on the diagonal line coming from the vertebral border to between 1 cm and 2 cm from the inferior angle of the scapula. (A diagonal fold about 1-2 cm below the point of the shoulder blade and 1-2 cm towards the arm).
- Supra-iliac: A diagonal fold above the crest of the ilium at the spot where an imaginary line would come down from the anterior axillary line (just above the hip bone and 2-3 cm forward).
- Anterior thigh: A vertical fold on the anterior aspect of the thigh, midway between the hip and knee joints (on the front of the thigh half-way between the hip joint where the leg bends when the knee is lifted, and the middle of the knee cap). The leg should be straight and relaxed. This measurement is best made with the subject seated if difficulty is experienced in isolating a double layer of skinfold with the subject standing.

The most accessible method for acquiring data on body composition of games players is by means of measuring skinfold thicknesses using callipers. The scientific steering groups of the British Olympic Association recommended five anatomical sites: these were biceps, triceps, subscapula, supra-iliac and anterior thigh (Reilly et al., 1996). This approach was subsequently confirmed by Eston et al. (2005) who found that skinfolds from the lower body are highly related to percentage body fat. The values can be summed to provide an index of subcutaneous adipose tissue. Using the first four of these sites and referring to the age of the individual, the percentage of the body weight in the form of fat can be estimated. This value is most useful in setting targets for the amount of weight comprising fat to be lost. It will be especially useful in any input of nutritional advice to the players. Whilst there is a large range in the number and location of skinfold sites employed in estimating percentage body fat, what is more important is the accuracy of the measurements.

Figures for percentage body fat in female field-hockey players range from 16 to 26% (Reilly and Borrie, 1992) with the lowest figures reported at the elite end of the game (Wassmer and Mookerjee, 2002). This decrease in body fat as playing level increases is generally evident across all field sports. As mentioned earlier, differences in percentage body fat exist across the various playing positions. In Rugby Union, lower body fat figures were reported in rugby backs compared to forwards (Rigg and Reilly, 1988), values which may also reflect the higher speed requirements of these players (Duthie et al., 2003). The average value for a male in his mid-twenties is 16% body fat. Professional games players may have values in excess of this average on return from their off-season break. Indeed, 20 years ago the average value reported for the entire squad of one of the top London soccer teams was 19% (White et al., 1988). Nowadays, it would be expected that early in the season, figures of below 12% are evident (see Table 7.2).

MASS

Muscle mass

Measurement of muscle mass may have relevance in a range of sports. The body imaging methods have been utilised in studies of cross-sectional areas of skeletal muscle. These have largely been concerned with investigating effects of strength training, relations with muscle fibre types or muscle characteristics and other research questions.

A traditional method of assessing muscle development was the measurement of limb girth or circumference. The assessment may be made using an anthropometric tape. Upper arm and lower leg circumferences are used in the measurement of somatotype, the girths being corrected for skinfold thicknesses and related to body size. For monitoring muscular development due to strength training, the tape measure would be too crude an instrument to be helpful.

Martin and co-workers (1990) provided an equation for estimating muscle mass in men. This is the only cadaver-validated equation that is currently available and it yields values that are consistent with all known dissection data. The anthropometric measures needed for predicting muscle mass include stature, thigh circumference (corrected for front thigh skinfold thickness), forearm circumference and calf circumference (corrected for medial calf skinfold thickness). The method has been applied to distinguish between specialist sports groups (Spenst et al., 1993) and is related to performance in strenuous muscular efforts.

The formula of Martin et al. (1990) may overestimate true muscle mass, largely because the prediction was based on cadaver data from a non-athletic population. In an attempt to validate the equation, Cattrysse et al. (2002) found that the sum of the separate compartments (fat, muscle, bone) amounted to an overestimate of total body mass. Nevertheless, the equation has proved to be useful in distinguishing between different games sports (Spenst et al., 1993). Players can be monitored during the course of a weight-training programme to quantify the increase in muscle mass to the exclusion of changes in other body compartments. Those engaged in physical contact – in Rugby football, soccer and Gaelic football – demonstrate much higher values than non-athletic controls of the same age (see Table 7.5). Muscle mass is beneficial in generating power and in vigorous contact and is not necessarily a disadvantage when a high work rate is required. In their study of elite South American soccer players with an average estimated muscle mass of 63% body weight, Rienzi et al. (2000) found a significant correlation ($r = 0.53$) between muscle mass and distance covered in a game.

Skeletal mass and bone mineral density

Anthropometry can be used to estimate skeletal mass from breadth measurements taken over the body's surface. A sturdy skeleton is important in games, rendering it more difficult to knock the player off the ball. The measurement of a player's bone mass and mineral density may also have implications for health as it can be useful in determining the susceptibility of the individual to the risk of bone fractures and injuries. Bones respond to the stresses imposed on them by increasing their mineral content. Female athletes in particular lose bone minerals when their diets are inadequate or when experiencing prolonged hypoestrogenia. Whilst secondary amenorrhea is no more common in female games players than in the general population its consequences for bone health should be recognised when normal

190

Table 7.5 Estimated muscle mass in various groups of male games players and reference groups

Sport		n	Mass (kg)	% muscle mass	Source
Basketball	University	10	89.8 ± 12.5	60.9 ± 2.5	Spenst et al. (1993)
Belgian males	Nurses	159	73.2 ± 11.2	48.6 ± 8.6	Cattrysse et al. (2002)
Gaelic football	Inter-county	33	79.2 ± 8.2	60.7 ± 2.4	Strudwick et al. (2002)
Non-athletes	–	13	71.4 ± 10.2	56.5 ± 3.4	Spenst et al. (1993)
Rugby Sevens	International	20	84.7 ± 10.4	62.4 ± 4.1	Rienzi et al. (1999)
	Forwards	17	93.5 ± 7.8	61.8 ± 3.7	Rienzi et al. (1999)
	Backs	13	78.6 ± 7.1	62.9 ± 4.5	Rienzi et al. (1999)
Soccer	High-level Youth	32	74.0 ± 1.5	47.7 ± 0.2	Gil et al. (2007)
Soccer	International	17	74.5 ± 4.4	63.0 ± 4.0	Rienzi et al. (2000)
Soccer	Premier League	19	77.9 ± 8.9	62.4 ± 3.3	Strudwick et al. (2002)
Various sports	University	48	74.1 ± 3.9	58.4 ± 5.2	Coldwells et al. (1993)

menstrual cycles are disturbed. A recent study on menstrual function and bone mineral density in female high-school athletes confirmed that the rate of bone mineralisation is highly dependent upon normal menstrual function, and brief periods of amenorrhea during this critical time may compromise bone health and increase the risk of stress fractures (Nichols et al., 2007). The authors suggested that young female athletes should be evaluated periodically and be advised of the possible adverse effects of menstrual irregularity on bone health.

Bone mineral density is measured by means of dual-energy X-ray absorptiometry (DXA). This technique entails placing the participant supine on a bed while a dual-energy X-ray beam passes through the body from a source beneath to a detector on top (Figure 7.5). The body is scanned along its longitudinal axis and the density of bone is computed. The system uses a three-compartment chemical model of the body, separating it into fat, bone and lean (fat-free, bone mineral-free) mass. Regional data in the arms, ribs, thoracic spine, lumbar spine, legs and pelvis can be provided for bone mineral content and bone mineral density. The machines are expensive but are available for monitoring professional teams on a regular basis in

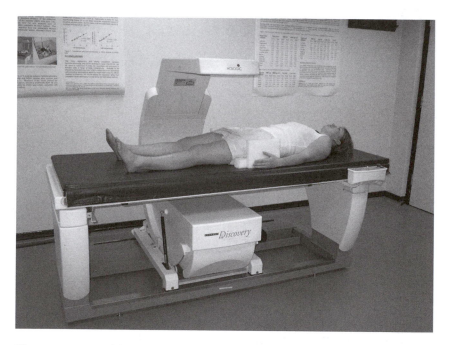

Figure 7.5 An athlete is supine on the bed for assessment using dual-energy X-ray absorptiometry. Body fat, bone mass, bone mineral content and bone mineral density can be determined from a whole-body scan

emerging technologies

specialised sports-science laboratories. A squad of 30 players can easily be accommodated within a 3-hour period. Since the DXA technique provides two clinical measurements (bone mineral density and fat distribution) in one examination and is associated with less physical and psychological stress, it has been suggested to be a superior technique compared to all the other methods (Norcross and Van Loan, 2004). An example of output from the assessment is shown in Figure 7.6.

In a comprehensive study of Premier League soccer players, Egan et al. (2006b) showed how body composition changes reflected seasonal shifts in emphasis of training. Positive changes in body composition that were observed in the pre-season period were partly lost before the end of the competitive season but were

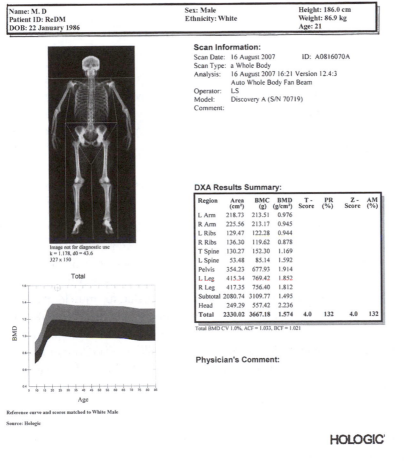

Name: M. D	Sex: Male	Height: 186.0 cm
Patient ID: ReDM	Ethnicity: White	Weight: 86.9 kg
DOB: 22 January 1986		Age: 21

Scan Information:
Scan Date: 16 August 2007   ID: A0816070A
Scan Type: a Whole Body
Analysis: 16 August 2007 16:21 Version 12.4:3
        Auto Whole Body Fan Beam
Operator: LS
Model: Discovery A (S/N 70719)
Comment:

Image not for diagnostic use
k = 1.178, d0 = 43.6
327 x 150

Total

DXA Results Summary:

Region	Area (cm²)	BMC (g)	BMD (g/cm²)	T- Score	PR (%)	Z- Score	AM (%)
L Arm	218.73	213.51	0.976				
R Arm	225.56	213.17	0.945				
L Ribs	129.47	122.28	0.944				
R Ribs	136.30	119.62	0.878				
T Spine	130.27	152.30	1.169				
L Spine	53.48	85.14	1.592				
Pelvis	354.23	677.93	1.914				
L Leg	415.34	769.42	1.852				
R Leg	417.35	756.40	1.812				
Subtotal	2080.74	3109.77	1.495				
Head	249.29	557.42	2.236				
Total	2330.02	3667.18	1.574	4.0	132	4.0	132

Total BMD CV 1.0%, ACF = 1.033, BCF = 1.021

Physician's Comment:

BMD

Age

Reference curve and scores matched to White Male

Source: Hologic

HOLOGIC

Figure 7.6 Output of assessment using DXA

restored by the start of the subsequent competitive season. Bone mineral density was higher than reference values, confirming that professional soccer players have a markedly greater skeletal mineral content than age-matched controls (Wittich et al., 1998).

The accrual of bone minerals due to training is dependent on the loading characteristics of the sport. In a study of female sports participants, runners, netball players and Rugby Union players were found to have higher bone density than control subjects (Egan et al., 2006a). The Rugby players had elevated values in all upper-body regions and in whole-body values whereas the superior values of the netball players and runners were evident only in the legs, femoral neck and inter-trochanter regions. Values for bone mineral density over a range of sports are shown for young adult eumenorrheic females in Table 7.6.

CONCLUSION

There is a body of evidence that sports participants must be suited anthropo-metrically to their chosen sport. Athletes may gravitate towards the sport or playing position to which their body build deems them best suited. Sports such as soccer accommodate a heterogeneity of body types, but positional roles generally contain less variability. In contrast, body size is a requirement in certain roles in some sports, an obvious example is Rugby Union forward play, where height may be more important than jumping ability, although the two in combination complete the requirements (Rigg and Reilly, 1988).

Anthropometric features such as height are largely determined by genetics whilst body composition is subject to environmental influences such as diet, training and lifestyle. Weight-control is important for games players at recreational level and for elite performance there is likely to be an optimal body composition at which they feel best prepared for competitive performance. This value for muscle mass and body fat is likely to vary between sports and even between individuals. The technologies available for assessment of body composition vary from laboratory-based methods to portable devices such as skinfold callipers. The former provide greater precision for detecting small changes in groups subjected to year-long training programmes, but their use is generally restricted to practitioners at the elite end of the game. The field methods are of practical use, provided that quality control is applied in data collection and the recorders are formally trained (and not just experienced) in the use of the techniques. Furthermore, these latter methods to assess body composition are often accessible to recreational, lower-tier and semi-professional teams.

194

Table 7.6 Summary of whole-body, femoral neck and lumbar spine BMD values for cross-sectional studies in young adult eumenorrheic females (from Egan et al., 2006a)

Sport	Author	Age	n	Whole-body (% above controls)	Femoral neck (% above controls)	Lumbar spine (% above controls)
Volleyball	Lee et al. (1995)	19.4 ± 1.3	11	6.9	11.4	17.9
	Fehling et al. (1995)	19.5 ± 1.3	8	16.2	17.4	19.6
	Risser et al. (1990)	19.6 ± 1.5	12	–	–	14.7
Basketball	Lee et al. (1995)	19.9 ± 1.6	7	7.8	20.0	13.7
	Risser et al. (1990)	19.6 ± 1.1	9	–	–	12.2
Rugby Union	Egan et al. (2006a)	21.4 ± 1.9	30	13.5	21.7	16.5
Weightlifting	Heinonen et al. (1993)	24.6 ± 4.6	18	–	10.1	14.8
Body builders	Heinrich et al. (1990)	25.7 ± 5.2	11	–	14.7	12.0
Squash	Heinonen et al. (1995)	25.0 ± 3.9	18	–	18.9	14.8
Gymnastics	Fehling et al. (1995)	19.6 ± 1.0	13	9.9	17.4	14.7
Netball	Egan et al. (2006a)	20.7 ± 1.3	20	6.3	14.5	12.4
Speed skaters	Heinonen et al. (1995)	21.4 ± 8.6	14	–	6.2	7.4
Runners	Duncan et al. (2002)	17.6 ± 1.4	15	8.6	9.7	12.2
	Egan et al. (2006a)	21.5 ± 2.6	11	6.3	13.3	3.0

REFERENCES

Abe, T., Kojima, K., Kearns, C.F., Yohena, H. and Fukuda, J. (2003) Whole body muscle hypertrophy from resistance training: distribution and total mass. *British Journal of Sports Medicine*, 37: 543–545.

Bloomfield, J., Polman, R., Butterly, R. and O'Donoghue P. (2005) Analysis of age, stature, body mass, BMI and quality of elite soccer players from 4 European Leagues. *Journal of Sports Medicine and Physical Fitness*, 45: 58–67.

Breivik (2007) Rugby. In E.M. Winter, A.M. Jones, R.C.R. Davison, P.D. Bromley and T.H. Mercer (eds), *Sport and Exercise Physiology Testing: Guidelines. Volume I, Sport Testing* (pp. 76–83). The British Association of Sport and Exercise Sciences Guide. London: Routledge.

Brewer, J. and Davis J. (1995) Applied physiology of rugby league. *Sports Medicine*, 20: 129–135.

Brozek, J., Grande, F., Anderson, J.T. and Keys, A. (1963) Densitometric analysis of body composition: revision of some quantitative assumptions. *Annals of the New York Academy of Sciences*, 110: 113–140.

Casajús, J.A. (2001) Seasonal variation in fitness variables in professional soccer players. *Journal of Sports Medicine and Physical Fitness*, 41: 463–467.

Cattrysse, E., Zinzen, E., Caboor, D., Duquet, W., Van Roy, P. and Clarys, J.P. (2002) Anthropometric fractionation of body mass: Matiegka revisited. *Journal of Sports Sciences*, 20: 717–723.

Chamari, K., Moussa-Chamari, I., Boussaïdi L., Hachana, Y., Kaouech, F. and Wisløff, U. (2005) Appropriate interpretation of aerobic capacity: allometric scaling in adult and young soccer players. *British Journal of Sports Medicine*, 39: 97–101.

Clarys, J.P., Martin, A.D., Drinkwater, D.T. and Marfell-Jones, M.J. (1987) The skinfold: myth and reality. *Journal of Sports Sciences*, 5: 3–33.

Coldwells, A., Atkinson, G. and Reilly, T. (1993) The influence of skeletal muscle mass on dynamic muscle performance. In A.L. Claessens, J. Lefevre and B. Vanden Eynde (eds), *World-wide Variation in Physical Fitness* (pp. 50–53). Leuven, Belgium: Institute of Physical Education.

Duncan, C.S., Blimkie, C.J.R., Cowell, C.T., Burke, S.T., Briody, J.N. and Howman-Giles, R. (2002) Bone mineral density in adolescent female athletes: relationship to exercise type and muscle strength. *Medicine and Science in Sports and Exercise*, 34: 286–294.

Duquet, W. and Carter, J.E.L. (2001) Somatotyping. In R. Eston and T. Reilly (eds), *Kinanthropometry and Exercise Physiology Laboratory Manual: Tests, Procedures and Data. Volume 1 Anthropometry* (pp. 47–64). London: Routledge.

Durnin, J.V.G.R. and Wormersley, J. (1974) Body fat assessed from total body density and its estimation from skinfold thickness: measurements on 481 men and women aged from 16 to 72 years. *British Journal of Nutrition*, 32: 77–97.

Duthie, G., Pyne, D. and Hooper, S. (2003) Applied physiology and game analysis of rugby union. *Sports Medicine*, 33: 973–991.

Egan, E., Reilly, T., Giacomoni, M., Redmond, L. and Turner, C. (2006a) Bone mineral density among female sports participants. *Bone*, 38: 227–233.

Egan, E., Wallace, J., Reilly, T., Chantler, P. and Lawlor, J. (2006b) Body composition and bone mineral density changes during a Premier League season as measured by dual-energy x-ray absorptiometry. *International Journal of Body Composition Research*, 4(2): 61–66.

Eston, R.G. and Reilly, T. (2009) *Kinanthropometry and Exercise Physiology Laboratory Manual. Volume 1 Anthropometry*, 3rd edition. London: Routledge.

Eston, R.G., Rowlands, A.V., Charlesworth, S., Davies, A. and Hoppitt, T. (2005) Prediction of DXA-determined whole body fat from skinfolds: importance of including skinfolds from the thigh and calf in young, healthy men and women. *European Journal of Clinical Nutrition*, 59: 695–702.

Fehling, P.C., Alekel, L., Clasey, J., Rector, A. and Stillman, R.J. (1995) A comparison of bone mineral densities among female athletes in impact loading and active loading sports. *Bone*, 17: 205–210.

Gabbett, T.J. (2005) Science of rugby league football: a review. *Journal of Sports Science*, 23: 961–976.

Gabbett T.J. (2007) Physiological and anthropometric characteristics of elite women rugby league players. *Journal of Strength and Conditioning Research*, 21: 875–81.

Gil, S.M., Gil, J., Ruiz, F., Irazusta, A. and Irazusta, J. (2007) Physiological and anthropometric characteristics of young soccer players according to their playing position: relevance for the selection process. *Journal of Strength and Conditioning Research*, 21: 438–45.

Harvey, G., Meira, R., Brooks, L. and Holloway, K. (2007) The use of body mass changes as a practical measure of dehydration in team sports. *Journal of Science and Medicine in Sport*, in press.

Heinonen, A., Oja, P., Kannus, P., Sievanen, H., Haapasalo, H., Manttari, A. and Vuori, I. (1995) Bone mineral density in female athletes representing sports with different loading characteristics of the skeleton. *Bone*, 17: 197–203.

Heinonen, A., Oja, P., Kannus, P., Sievanen, H., Manttari, A. and Vuori, I. (1993) Bone mineral density of female athletes in different sports. *Bone and Mineral*, 23: 1–14.

Heinrich, C.H., Going, S.B., Ramenter, R.W., Perry, C.D., Boyden, T.W. and Lohman, T.G. (1990) Bone mineral content of cyclically menstruating female resistance and endurance trained athletes. *Medicine and Science in Sports and Exercise*, 22: 558–563.

Hencken, C. and White, C. (2006) Anthropometric assessment of Premiership soccer players in relation to playing position. *European Journal of Sport Science*, 6: 205–211.

International Society for the Advancement of Kinanthropometry (2001) *International Standards for Anthropometric Assessment*. North West University (Potchefstroom Campus), Potchefstroom 2520, South Africa ISAK (revised 2006).

Koz, M. and Balci, V. (2007) Body size and composition of Turkish National American Football League players. *Journal of Sports Science and Medicine*, 6 (Suppl. 10): 56.

Lee, E.J., Long, K.A., Risser, W.L., Poindexter, H.B.W., Gibbons, W.E. and Goldzieher, J. (1995) Variations in bone status of contralateral and regional sites in young athletic women. *Medicine and Science in Sports and Exercise*, 27: 1354–1361.

Lohman, T.G., Roche, A.F. and Martorell, R. (eds) (1992) *Anthropometric Standardization Reference Manual*. Champaign, IL: Human Kinetics.

Marfell-Jones, M., Olds, T., Stewart, A. and Carter, J.E.L. (2006) *International Standards for Anthropometric Assessment*. ISAK: Potchefstroom, South Africa.

Martin, D.D., Spenst, L.F., Drinkwater, D.T. and Clarys, J.P. (1990) Anthropometric estimation of muscle mass in men. *Medicine and Science in Sports and Exercise*, 22: 729–733.

Melchiorri, G., Monteleone, G., Andreoli, A., Callà, C., Sgroi, M. and De Lorenzo, A. (2007) Body cell mass measured by bioelectrical impedance spectroscopy in professional football (soccer) players. *Journal of Sports Medicine and Physical Fitness*, 47: 408–412.

Nichols, J.F., Rauh, M.J., Barrack, M.T. and Barkai, H. (2007) Bone mineral density in female high school athletes: interactions of menstrual function and type of mechanical loading. *Bone*, 41(3): 371–377.

Norcross, J. and Van Loan, M.D. (2004) Validation of fan beam dual energy x-ray absorptiometry for body composition assessment in adults aged 18–45 years. *British Journal of Sports Medicine*, 38: 472–476.

Olds, T. (2001) The evaluation of physique in male Rugby Union players in the twentieth century. *Journal of Sports Sciences*, 19: 253–262.

Reilly, T. (2005) Science and football: a history and an update. In T. Reilly, J. Cabri and D. Araujo (eds), *Science and Football V* (p. 3–12). London: Routledge.

Reilly, T. and Borrie, A. (1992) Physiology applied to field hockey. *Sports Medicine*, 14: 10–26.

Reilly, T. and Doran, D. (2003) Fitness assessment. In T. Reilly and A.M. Williams (eds), *Science and Soccer*, 2nd edition (pp. 21–46). London: Routledge.

Reilly, T. and Sutton, L. (2008) Methods and applications of body composition analysis. In P.D. Bust (ed.), *Contemporary Ergonomics* (pp. 491–495). London: Taylor & Francis.

Reilly, T., Bangsbo, J. and Franks, A. (2000) Anthropometric and physiological predispositions for elite soccer. *Journal of Sports Sciences*, 18: 669–683.

Reilly, T., Maughan, R.J. and Hardy, L. (1996) Body Fat Consensus Statement of the Steering Groups of the British Olympic Association. *Sports Exercise and Injury*, 2: 46–49.

Rienzi, E., Drust, B., Reilly, T., Carter, J.E.L. and Martin, A. (2000) Investigation of anthropometric and work-rate profiles of elite South American soccer players. *Journal of Sports Medicine and Physical Fitness*, 40: 162–169.

Rienzi, E., Reilly, T. and Malkin, C. (1999) Investigation of anthropometric and work-rate profiles of Rugby Sevens players. *Journal of Sports Medicine and Physical Fitness*, 39: 160–164.

Rigg, P. and Reilly, T. (1988) A fitness profile and anthropometric analysis of first and second class Rugby Union players. In T. Reilly, A. Lees, K. Davids and W.J. Murphy (eds), *Science and Football* (pp. 194–200). London: E & FN Spon.

Risser, W.L., Lee, E.J., Leblanc, A., Poindexter, H.B.W., Risser, J.M.H. and Schneider, V. (1990) Bone density in eumenorrheic female college athletes. *Medicine and Science in Sports and Exercise*, 22: 570–574.

Salmi, J.A. (2003) Body composition assessment with segmental multi-frequency bioimpedance method. *Journal of Sports Science and Medicine* 2 (Suppl. 3): 1–29.

Shields, C.L. Jr, Whitney, F.E. and Zomar, V.D. (1984) Exercise performance of professional football players. *American Journal of Sports Medicine*, 12: 455–459.

198

Siri, W.E. (1956) Body composition from fluid spaces and density: analysis of methods. *University of California Radiation Laboratory Report*, UCRL No. 3349.

Sjolie, A.N. (2004) Low-back pain in adolescents is associated with poor hip mobility and high body mass index. *Scandinavian Journal of Medicine and Science in Sports*, 14: 168–175.

Spenst, L.F., Martin, A.D. and Drinkwater, D.T. (1993) Muscle mass of competitive athletes. *Journal of Sports Sciences*, 11: 3–8.

Stewart, A. and Eston, R.G. (2007) Surface anthropometry. In E.M. Winter, A.M. Jones, R.C.R. Davison, P.D. Bromley and T.H. Mercer (eds), *Sport and Exercise Physiology Testing: Guidelines. Volume I, Sport Testing* (pp. 76–83). The British Association of Sport and Exercise Sciences Guide, London: Routledge.

Stølen, T., Chamari, K., Castagna, C. and Wisløff, U. (2005) Physiology of soccer: an update. *Sports Medicine*, 35: 501–536.

Strudwick, A., Reilly, T. and Doran, D. (2002) Anthropometric and fitness profiles of elite players in two football codes. *Journal of Sports Medicine and Physical Fitness*, 42: 239–242.

Veale, J.P., Pearce, A.J., Koehn, S. and Carlson, J.S. (2008) Performance and anthropometric characteristics of prospective elite junior Australian footballers: a case study in one junior team. *Journal of Science and Medicine in Sport*, 11: 227–230.

Wallace, J., Egan, E., Lawlor, J., George, K. and Reilly, T. (2008) Body composition changes in professional soccer players in the off-season. In M. Marfell-Jones and T. Olds (eds), *Kinanthropometry X* (pp. 127–134). London: Routledge.

Wallace, J.A., George, K. and Reilly, T. (2006) Validity of dual-energy x-ray absorptiometry for body composition analysis. In P.D. Bust (ed.), *Contemporary Ergonomics* (pp. 513–515). London: Taylor & Francis.

Wallace, J., Marfell-Jones, M., George, K. and Reilly, T. (2007) A comparison of skinfold thickness measurements and dual-energy x-ray absorptiometry analysis of percent body fat in football players. In *VIth World Congress on Science and Football, Book of Abstracts* (p. 66). Antalya, Turkey.

Wassmer, D.J. and Mookerjee, S. (2002) A descriptive profile of elite U.S. women's collegiate field hockey players. *Journal of Sports Medicine and Physical Fitness*, 42: 165–71.

White, J.E., Emery, T.M., Kane, J.E., Groves, R. and Risman, A.B. (1988) Pre-season fitness profiles of professional soccer players. In T. Reilly, A. Lees, K. Davids and W.J. Murphy (eds), *Science and Football* (pp. 164–171). London: E & FN Spon.

Winter, A. and Eston, R.G. (2006) Surface anthropometry. In E.M. Winter, A.M. Jones, R.C.R. Davidson, P.D. Bramley and T.H. Mercer. (eds), *Sport and Exercise Physiology Testing Guidelines* (pp. 76–83). London: Routledge.

Wittich, A., Mautalen, C.A., Oliveri, M.B., Bagur, A., Somoza, F. and Rotemberg, E. (1998) Professional football (soccer) players have a markedly greater skeletal mineral content, density and size than age- and BMI-matched controls. *Calcified Tissue International*, 63: 112–117.

CHAPTER EIGHT

EMERGING TECHNOLOGIES

INTRODUCTION

Technological advances and the development and refinement of procedures have been and continue to be a hallmark of sport and exercise science (Winter et al., 2007). In the fast-changing world of technologies, it is therefore important for sports scientists and coaches to be able to look ahead and position themselves at the forefront of new developments so that these may become part of everyday assessment of training and competition. The technology used to measure performance will no doubt continue to move forward in the way it already has done over recent years. New and improved methods based on 'state-of-the-art' computer technology and robotic automation for measuring and analysing performance are being continually developed and commercialised to help in the relentless

pursuit of success in elite sport. The broad range of research programmes in sport and exercise would benefit enormously from an ability to collect data unobtrusively and without hindering movement or performance (Armstrong, 2007). Technology has already gone some way in improving this first step in the assessment process by opening doors for major advances that have ultimately led to miniaturisation, increased reliability, user-friendliness and cost reduction of measurement equipment. The processing of data and reporting of results and their practical application have also vastly improved thanks to greater calculation power, speed and interactivity of computer equipment.

In this chapter we briefly look to the future at emerging areas for sports scientists and coaches such as the use of the Internet, Virtual Reality and the evolution of techniques in field-based monitoring of performance. We also touch on DNA testing and various artificial intelligence disciplines involved in aiding the decision-making process such as expert systems, fuzzy logic and artificial neural networks. Practical examples of sports performance assessment systems and scientific research are provided throughout the chapter.

PHYSIOLOGICAL MEASUREMENTS

Portable laboratories

The equipment used to measure physiological responses to exercise has evolved over recent years leading to more portable, fast, reliable and accurate onsite testing facilities. For example, the intensity of play during training and competition is now easily and effectively monitored through short-range radio telemetry, microchips and GPS systems worn by players as described in Chapter 4. The measurement of heart rate in the field setting is now commonplace thanks to these lightweight systems. Work is also underway in various research laboratories around the world to develop mobile 'lab in a box' systems containing urinalysis instruments for analysis of urine content, blood gases and immunochemical markers with the aim of providing more information to further our understanding of sports performance and its consequences.

PRACTICAL EXAMPLE 1

The OmegaWave Sport Technology System has been designed to improve onsite physiological testing of the elite athlete (see http://www.omega wave.com/). It is a mobile assessment technology that provides information on

201

an athlete's current functional state. This system is now employed by a number of professional soccer teams across Europe. The OmegaWave system reports on the cardiac regulatory system, energy metabolism system, central nervous system and regulatory mechanisms of the gas exchange and cardiopulmonary systems. Simple electrodes, placed on the athlete's body, are connected to a hardware device (which in turn is connected to a laptop computer). Electrical activity in the heart and slow 'omega' brain waves are analysed at rest to provide an 'inside look' at how an athlete's body is functioning, quickly and non-invasively (see Figure 8.1). Propriety software is then used to analyse the data which can then be compared to norms established from the results of monitoring thousands of elite athletes throughout the world. Based on an analysis of the athlete's functional state, the system suggests training loads and intensities as well as target heart-rate zones for development, maintenance, recovery and rehabilitation in training. An initial investigation on the reliability and validity of this system has provided support for the use of OmegaWave in measuring heart-rate variability in elite American track-and-field athletes (Berkoff et al., 2007).

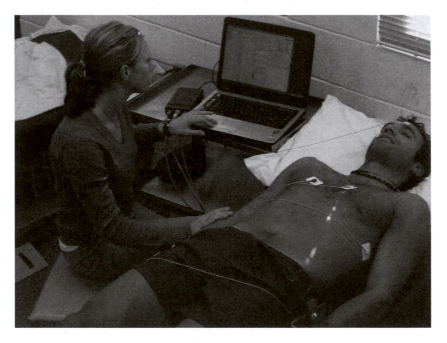

Figure 8.1 The OmegaWave Sport and STAR+ system (courtesy of OmegaWave Technologies, LLC)

emerging technologies

Wireless technology

Technological advances have already gone some way towards solving the issues of compactness and size; sensors, microprocessors and memory devices for processing and collecting the physiological data are now miniaturised (Armstrong, 2007). However, portability and cabling (for data collection and electrical power) between assessment devices still remain a major issue as movement during exercise may be impeded. The linking of nanotechnology (engineering on a scale of individual atoms to make new materials or to improve properties such as size and weight of existing materials) measuring/sensing devices with high-speed microelectronic reporting networks now allows a more efficient remote monitoring of performance. Recent work has been aimed at developing suitable transmission technologies centred on wireless devices. Based on its beneficial properties with regard to power consumption, range, data security and network capability, the worldwide standard radio technology Bluetooth is used to transmit measurements of data collected synchronously from multiple points across the body (Moor et al., 2005).

Rasid and Woodward (2005) recently developed a Bluetooth system to monitor ECG signals (measurement of rate, rhythm and heart muscle blood flow), blood pressure, body temperature and saturation of peripheral oxygen (SpO_2). These signals are digitised in a Bluetooth-enabled processing unit worn on the participant's body and then transmitted remotely to a Bluetooth-capable mobile phone. The data can then be sent via a General Packet Radio Service (GPRS) mobile network to any computer for data analysis.

In many sporting settings, measuring other physiological responses to exercise using traditionally invasive methods is not practical and often obtrusive. For example, measuring lactate accumulation in blood or body temperature responses to exercise during competition is not feasible. Performers must leave the field of play and therefore stop participation which will affect the reliability of results. Receiver units are now being linked through a new wireless connectivity standard known as Zigbee, optimised for connection to sensor probes worn by players. The latest sensor probes work using electrochemical detection methods and have fast responses and high sensitivity. For example, it will soon be possible for physiologists and medical staff to make observations on lactic acid levels using sweat samples during field-based exercise. These measurements could also be combined with information on heart- and work rate data to provide a comprehensive picture of players' efforts. Zigbee technology is reportedly already replacing the Bluetooth component in wireless timing-light systems for measuring running speed, accelerations/decelerations and agility (see www.fusionsport.com). Information on the Fusionsport website claims that the benefits of Zigbee are numerous, including superior performance and reliability, battery life and ease of use. A further advance in wireless technology is the Wibree protocol which has recently been under development by the Nokia Corporation. This protocol is designed for applications such as in healthcare and sports performance monitoring where ultra-low power consumption, small size and low cost are the critical requirements (see: http://www.wibree.com/use_cases/).

An alternative device known as the Biotrainer has recently been produced by Citech Holdings Pty Ltd (http://www.citechholdings.com/) and is attempting to take the analysis and comprehension of athletic performance one step further. This device is described by the company as a disposable patch, similar to a Band-aid, worn by the athlete. It provides movement tracking data on areas such as distance run and speed, both indoor and outdoor, as well as supplying real-time biofeedback on nine physiological outputs such as body temperature, heart and respiration rate and level of hydration. This system is currently undergoing trials in both American Football and Basketball contests.

Ingestible sensors

Another developing technique is the use of ingestible temperature-sensor capsules and DNA chips with the ultimate aim of developing a complete laboratory within a microchip. For example, investigation of the candidate genes involved in endurance exercise is now becoming possible using ingestible DNA chips. Ingestible capsules sensitive to temperature have already been applied successfully in numerous sport and occupational applications such as the continuous measure-ment of core temperature in deep-sea saturation divers, distance runners and soldiers undertaking sustained military training exercises (Byrne and Lim, 2007). Gant and co-workers (2006) discussed how ingestible temperature-sensor capsules are a promising alternative to traditional rectal temperature measurements during intermittent-type efforts, which are a common feature of exercise in team sports. When using this technology, care should be taken to ensure adequate control over sensor calibration and data correction, timing of ingestion and electromagnetic interference (Byrne and Lim, 2007).

DNA analysis

Technology is now allowing scientists to look at the functions at cellular level and to understand gene expression under a variety of stimuli. Microarray analysis offers a set of analytical platforms that provide rapid, affordable and substantial infor-mation at the DNA, RNA or protein level (Fehrenbach et al., 2003). Arrays for analyses of RNA expression allow gene expression profiling for use in exercise physiology and provide new insights into the complex molecular mechanisms of

the exercise-induced stress response, adaptation to training and modulation of immune function. Gene-expression profiling and genetic screening may help sport and exercise scientists to assess, characterise and predict the responses of individuals to training. For example, enhanced skeletal muscle mitochondrial function following aerobic exercise training is related to an increase in mito-chondrial transcription factors, DNA abundance and mitochondria-related gene transcript levels (Chow et al., 2007). Gene expression fingerprints can also serve as a powerful research tool to design novel strategies for diagnosis and treatment of exercise-related injury and stress (Zieker et al., 2005).

Many of the variables that determine athletic performance are partially inherited (Spurway, 2007) and, therefore, the use of genetic tests to predict performance potential may be viable. However, the pace and progress of genetic research in the realm of sport and exercise science is slow, primarily because the number of laboratories and scientists focused on the role of genes and sequence variations in exercise-related traits continues to be quite limited (Rankinen et al., 2006). Furthermore, genetic investigations of this nature often bring with them uncomfortable ethical questions and fears of misuse. Nevertheless, experimental work has already demonstrated highly significant associations between the ACTN3 genotype (colloquially known as the gene for speed) and athletic performance (MacArthur and North 2007). Frequency distribution of ACTN3 (R577X) genotypes associated with sprint and power capacity has recently been investigated in professional Spanish soccer players and compared to sedentary controls and elite endurance athletes (Santiago et al., 2008). The proportion of this 'fast' genotype was significantly higher in the majority of professional soccer players than in the other groups, which at face value may suggest that individuals are inherently predisposed towards performance in specific sports. An investigation of the ACE I allele candidate gene found in the renin-angiotensin pathway (which plays a key role in the regulation of both cardiac and vascular physiology) has provided evidence that this genetic marker is associated with athletic excellence (Gayagay et al., 1998). Whilst gene testing may help researchers to identify markers that can predict components of performance, it may not be able to predict actual performance in field sports, particularly given that the latter is dependant on a rich tapestry of multifaceted components.

Another recent advance at gene level is the Gensona™ General Nutrition Genetic test which analyses variations in various genes that influence how the body uses vitamins and micronutrients (see http://www.ilgenetics.com/content/products-services/gensona.jsp). For example, genes involved in vitamin B utilisation and which are significant in managing oxidative stress especially in endurance sports, where the efficiency of oxygen transport is vital, are currently under investigation. Knowing genetic variations associated with nutrient and vitamin metabolism can help the development of a personalised health and diet plans for elite athletes and sports participants.

VIRTUAL REALITY

As technology evolves and people explore novel ideas, new and more creative applications are being developed (Katz, 2001). Virtual Reality (VR) offers the potential to enhance sports performance and fitness by creating realistic simulations of real or imagined environments that can be experienced visually in three dimensions with sound, tactile and other forms of feedback. Virtual Reality involves immersing an individual in a simulated environment through the use of equipment such as cyber eyeglasses (see Figure 8.2), data-generating gloves and simulators (for various examples of sports-related VR equipment, see http://www.virtalis.com/).

PRACTICAL EXAMPLE 2

The simulation of football plays in a Virtual Football Trainer has been shown to be a useful and promising application in the training of the decision-making skills of American football players for specific aspects of the game (see http://www-VRL.umich.edu/project/football/). This concept of a Virtual Football Trainer based on a Cave Automatic Virtual Environment (CAVE) developed by the University of Michigan, immerses the participant in situations where he or she experiences and participates in the game from a first person perspective (i.e. the participant is surrounded by virtual players on the field and these are presented in full scale and in stereo; see Figure 8.3). The CAVE provides an ultimate immersion experience and an extremely wide field of view through its surrounding walls. Peripheral vision is well supported and instrumental for orientation, navigation and, most of all, for the perception of movements that occur in the periphery. These aspects of the CAVE are instrumental for the Virtual Football Trainer. The objective is to train a player for the correct visual perception of play situations and improve the estimation of distances and awareness of the locations of other players. It also aims to improve recognition of other players and to speed up reactions to their movements.

Currently, the Virtual Football Trainer system (http://www-VRL.umich.edu/project/football/) relies on the manual creation in two dimensions of animated plays and training drills by coaches which are then transformed into three-dimensional situations for playback in the virtual simulator. A future version could be adapted

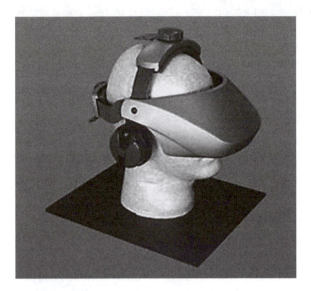

Figure 8.2 A head-mounted display for immersion in a virtual environment (courtesy of www.5dt.com)

Figure 8.3 Immersion in the Virtual Football Trainer Cave (courtesy of University of Michigan Virtual Reality Lab)

to make use of motion analysis and action data obtained in real competition conditions from the tracking systems previously mentioned in Chapter 4. These data would allow the creation of more objective and true-to-life match situations in which participants can be actively immersed to assess tactical decision-making and technique.

Carling et al. (2005) suggested that VR simulators could be used to evaluate and correct technique. For example, a player who is struggling to strike the ball properly could be aided as the VR system assesses technical movements by detecting errors (such as the position of feet and head and where the ball should be struck) through comparing them to an expert model. The system can then work on correcting these errors by guiding the player through the exact movements required using computer-linked VR suits or playing equipment. Coaches can also use simulation models to test their latest theories and then athletes can first experiment with the new manoeuvres in a virtual environment that will allow for error without risk of injury (Katz, 2001). Virtual reality has already been used to design and reproduce standardised situations in a controlled environment to analyse links between kinematics of the handball throws and the goalkeeper's reactions (Bideau et al., 2004). This particular system allowed the measurement and recording of the effects of small changes in the throwing movements through the isolation of visual elements in the thrower's gestures and could be adapted for various field sports. Williams (2000) described how Virtual Reality set-ups were useful in identifying anticipation as a key factor in talented young players and in some characteristics of 'game intelligence'. On the downside, one side effect players may experience when immersed in a virtual environment is the feeling of cybersickness, which is a form of motion sickness where disorientation, disequilibria and nausea can occur. In addition, the development of these systems is still relatively expensive and coaches may be reluctant to adopt such technologies. For further information on the applications and complexities of Virtual Reality in sport, see review by Katz et al. (2006) and book chapter by Ward et al. (2006).

THE INTERNET

The Internet is playing an increasingly important role in the performance assessment process. Katz (2002) suggested that the Internet can play a part in not only improving sports performance, but in reducing the risk of injury and improving health. The rapid development over the last decade or so of this worldwide computer network allows much more flexibility in the way data on performance are collected, transferred and made available for viewing. For example, analysis of performance is now possible from anywhere in the world due to faster connection speeds (broadband) allowing real-time data collection from video or captors sent

emerging technologies

over the Internet. It is now possible for athletes and coaches to access and retrieve physiological data remotely and many aspects of performance can be monitored at distance. This development is radically reducing the need, and therefore cost of transporting staff and equipment. Some of the latest software packages for performance assessment provide options to publish data automatically into Web format that can then be uploaded and displayed on a website address for visualisation by coaches and players, anytime and anywhere in the world. For a review on Web-based applications for the sports sciences, see Katz (2002).

Online databases

Various companies are providing access to online databases containing information on many aspects of game performance. Coaches, from wherever they are, can query the database to provide current and previous performances by looking at and comparing trends in the data. One such example is the use by coaches and athletes of online assessment tools to provide information on diet quality and physical activity status. The Departments of Agriculture and Health and Human Services in the United States have jointly developed the MyPyramid Tracker system (http://www.mypyramidtracker.gov/). The online dietary assessment evaluates and provides information on diet quality and provides relevant nutritional messages and information. The physical activity assessment evaluates physical activity status and provides relevant information on energy expenditure and educational messages. Another online-based assessment of sports performers is the Ottawa Mental Skills Assessment Tool (see http://www.mindeval.com/). This tool is used to assess the mental strengths and weaknesses of athletes and design relevant training programmes for performance improvement. The test protocol was created to help researchers investigate the effectiveness of intervention programmes to develop the mental skills of athletes. However, the accuracy and objectivity of online (as with traditional) questionnaires are questionable and caution should be observed when interpreting results.

Remote coaching

The 'remote coaching' model is an exciting development that is greatly enhancing our abilities to communicate expertise across vast distances without the expense and time of travel. For example, the performance of a player may be digitally recorded and transmitted over the web so that it can be viewed by other experts for analysis and feedback using dedicated software for technique analysis. These experts can then make notations or drawings on the video and send it back with explanations as to how to correct the error, all within a matter of minutes. This technological approach is already being used by professional cricket coaches and will no doubt be adopted for use in other professional field sports. Another novel approach is the real-time remote assessment of training. Liebermann and Franks (2004) discussed how coaches can supervise athletes undertaking computerised exercise programmes on fitness machines by controlling speed, resistance and other parameters from a remote location. In the future, this kind of application will no doubt be extended to the remote assessment and supervision of performance in the field. 'Virtual trainers' presented as a digital humanoid format linked to sensors placed on players have been developed to assess and provide real-time verbal feedback on performance. A virtual trainer may use an interactive expert knowledge base to correct movement automatically, adjust the physical efforts of the player and suggest ways of optimising performance.

Simulated Internet-enhanced instruction

Another area currently being investigated in various research projects around the world is the effectiveness of simulated Internet-enhanced instruction compared to traditional instruction on the pitch. Players may log on to the Internet and see graphical and video examples of their own tactical and technical performance compared to expert models. The players can view on their computer screens, the actions from any angle or a number of different angles and at different speeds and even immerse themselves to become part of the action. This approach may be useful in helping them to see and assess the skills they were supposed to be trying to perform and can give them something to focus on during training. Virtual Learning Environments based on online E-learning modules created by coaches could also be employed to question players' knowledge of different aspects of their performance and what they learnt from the video. The Sportspath application (http://www.sportspath.com/) designed for the development of participants in soccer is one such example of an E-learning environment for sport and exercise. Another is the recent development of online learning modules for obtaining qualifications in Sports Psychology by the Football Association (www.thefa.com).

EXPERT SYSTEMS, ARTIFICIAL NEURAL NETWORKS, GENETIC ALGORITHMS AND HYBRID SYSTEMS

Expert systems

Applications that use a knowledge base of human expertise to aid in solving problems by making decisions using artificial intelligence (the science and engineering of making machines to automate tasks requiring intelligent behaviour) are being employed for decision-making, modelling performance and predicting behaviour. Expert Systems are considered as a means to analyse and elucidate sports performance and develop the most efficient and optimal training methods. In theory, an 'expert system' could provide advice on how performance can be improved by delivering information on areas such as fitness and designing tailor-made training schedules. This procedure will be possible as these systems can combine and explain qualitative information derived from the knowledge and expertise of coaches and other support staff (e.g. fitness trainer, defensive coach) and by mining quantitative data obtained from assessing performance in training and competition.

An Expert System could evaluate progress made in competitive conditions, answer various questions from coaches and players, supply explanations on performance-related issues and apply or perhaps suggest ways of improving the training model. Such systems may be useful for cases in which a situation has to be analysed and the situation has too many variables to account for everything with complete precision. Expert Systems may also play a future part in helping coaches to analyse performance in real-time. For example, a system can be programmed to provide intelligent information on performance (using both past and current data) and make real-time suggestions which are then practically translated into coaching terms allowing coaches to make informed decisions. Although it is next to impossible to model all the variables in a sporting event completely, current statistical approaches used in Expert Systems can be utilised to analyse past results in order to make educated predictions about future events. However, in a recent review, Bartlett (2006) reported that the usage of Expert Systems remains relatively rare in the field of sports science.

Fuzzy logic

Expert Systems often use an approach based on fuzzy logic to aid in the complex decision-making processes involved in field sports. Fuzzy logic entails a simple rule-based approach (IF X AND Y, THEN Z) for data processing and systems control to arrive at a definite conclusion. This approach has been employed for determining the appropriate features which would qualify a soccer player for a specific tactical position (Wiemeyer, 2003). A coach would determine that a player, who scores many goals, has good heading ability and is a risk-taker, should play as a striker. This application of such rules reflects the logic structure of the decision rules proposed by fuzzy logic. However, the complexity of applying fuzzy logic requires a great deal of time and computer expertise as well as agreement on the relative weightings of formulation and management of rules between sports experts (James, 2006).

Artificial Neural Networks

The fuzzy logic-based Expert System approach generally uses sets of pre-defined rules and data to produce a decision or recommendation. Artificial Neural Networks (ANNs), on the other hand, attempt to simulate intelligence by mimicking the natural neural networks of the human brain by collecting and processing data for the purpose of remembering, learning or making decisions. The primary difference between fuzzy logic and an ANN is that the latter can adapt its criteria to provide a better match to the data it analyses; it 'learns' to recognise patterns instead of being given a set of rules, while Expert Systems tend to produce results without adjusting for changes in the data analysed. ANNs can model complex relationships between input variables and output categories and aid in finding patterns in data such as pictures, processes and situations and in the selection of actions. In sports assessment, ANNs can be described as being non-linear programs that represent non-linear systems, such as the human movement system, and, from a notational analysis perspective, games (Bartlett, 2006).

A special type of ANN known as a Kohonen Feature Map (KFM) has generally been employed for the modelling of relationships. The KFM neural network learns by forming clusters of neurones in response to a set of training patterns which allows it to identify other arbitrary patterns by associating these patterns with one of the already learned clusters within the network (McGarry and Perl, 2004). However, the problem of the KFM is that it requires a large amount of training data and lacks the necessary dynamics for continuous learning as its learning behaviour is fixed by the starting rules and the parameters that are used. Once trained, it can only be used for testing, not further learning, as would be necessary if the input patterns themselves changed over time. This weakness has led to the development of dynamically controlled neural networks (DyCoNs). Such systems only require several hundred data to coin a pattern, where a conventional KFM normally needs about 10 to 20 thousand data points (Perl, 2002). This type of ANN learns continuously and so can recognise and analyse time-dependent pattern changes, for example, the tactical changes of a team over a season. For further information on the functioning of ANNs, see articles by Perl (2002, 2004).

Neural networks have been used to analyse instep kicks by two soccer players for distance and accuracy (Lees et al., 2003) and to reduce the complexity of joint kinematic and kinetic data, which form part of a typical instrumented gait assessment (Barton et al., 2006). They have also been employed to reconstruct the three-dimensional performance space in a typical one-versus-one subphase of rugby and shown to be instrumental in identifying and assessing pattern formation in team sports generally (Passos et al., 2006). In predicting the outcome of soccer matches, ANNs have produced accurate predictions that recognised the combined

212

and individual effects of a multitude of variables ranging from home advantage to current form and playing strength (Reed and O'Donoghue, 2005). They have also been used to study game intelligence (Memmer and Perl, 2005) and to model creativity (Perl et al., 2006) in young players. At the turn of the century, ANNs were described as one of the most important paradigms for the modelling of learning in the field of computer science (Perl, 2001). However, according to Bartlett (2006), the full value of ANNs remains unclear and progress in applying these techniques to sport has been slow. The slow uptake is perhaps partly due to the conceptual complexity associated with the method and also the difficulty in obtaining sufficient data to establish a reasonable classification of movement (Lees, 2002). Therefore, ANNs still have little place to date in the assessment of elite sports performance as coaches seemingly find it difficult to appreciate the practicality and application of such assessment methods within daily training and competition.

PRACTICAL EXAMPLE 3

One of the most practical examples reported concerning an intelligent system using artificial neural networks is the MilanLab Scientific Centre employed at AC Milan Football Club and co-developed with Computer Associates. Its central purpose is to achieve and maintain top-level athletic performance by helping medical staff predict injury and giving the coach support when picking the team. The system is capable of evaluating the players' condition and fitness needs, based on objective data, numbers and metrics, while at the same time providing a foundation on which to construct a knowledge base. The machine collects physiological data from radio transmitters during training sessions and integrates the observations with other records such as players' biomedical and psychological data, nutritional habits and signs of illness. The data are fed into a neural network which is capable of 'learning' from stored data to predict likely outcomes such as potential injuries, much more quickly and effectively than a doctor or coach may be able to. Reports available on the Internet (see www.ca.com) have indicated a 90% reduction in injury frequency in the 2003 season when compared to the five previous years of data, although this finding has not been formally validated.

Genetic algorithms and evolutionary strategies

These systems constitute an interdisciplinary field of artificial intelligence research where geneticists and computer scientists try to integrate their knowledge in order to simulate evolution and establish new methods of finding solutions to complex problems. Based on mutations, crossovers and selective fitness functions these algorithms can be applied to improve the performance of a complex system (Wiemeyer, 2003). A genetic algorithm generally operates by creating a population of randomly chosen individuals who are then evaluated on a defined function. The individuals are given a score based on how well they perform the given task. Two individuals may then be selected based on their fitness – the higher the fitness, the higher the chance of being selected. These individuals then 'reproduce' to create one or more offspring, after which the offspring are mutated randomly. This process may continue until a suitable solution to the problem has been found.

A first approach using a genetic algorithm for a sports-based application example was developed for volleyball (Raik and Durnota, 1995). The genetic simulation of evolution began from a population of randomly generated individuals. The teams in the population then participated in a tournament in which every team played a match against every other team. Based on performance, measured by an accumulated score gained during the course of their matches, teams were then selected and genetically combined to produce a new population of teams. Another tournament was then held using the new population and the process continued. When participating in new tournaments, the chosen team employed constantly evolving strategies to aid in achieving improved results. Better results helped promote the team up the league's ladder, thus enhancing its chance of selection in future tournaments and ultimately the development of even better strategies. More recent work has concentrated on optimising sports technique (see review by Bartlett, 2006), but research output and application again remains limited.

Hybrid intelligent systems

Sports scientists and computer experts are already looking even further to the future by developing hybrid intelligent systems. These systems employ, in parallel, a fusion of artificial models, methods and techniques from subfields such as genetic algorithms and neural networks as it is thought that the human brain also uses multiple techniques both to formulate and cross-check results for usage within the decision-making process. A combination of the above fields has recently been used in aiding the approximation and prediction of centre of mass as a function of body acceleration in maintaining postural stability (Betker et al., 2006).

CONCLUSION

Technology and sports science researchers are leading the way in the development of systems to assess athletic performance. Effective means to improve performance in elite sports are provided by the integrated application of modern information and communication technologies (Baca, 2006). Computer scientists and engineers are cooperating more closely than ever with physiologists, psychologists, biomechanists and match analysts involved in the assessment of performance. Their common aim is to improve systems constantly so as to provide highly innovative and efficient support to coaches and athletes as they attempt to identify and optimise the key elements of elite performance. Whilst the potential of many systems and technologies remains high, research output and practical application are often still relatively low and future advances need to be developed sufficiently to be directly useful for coaches and athletes. Similarly, the validity and reliability of emerging systems need to be verified scientifically and independently to confirm the often substantial claims of manufacturers on how these advances in technology can assess and enhance performance.

REFERENCES

Armstrong, S. (2007) Wireless connectivity for health and sports monitoring: a review. *British Journal of Sports Medicine*, 41: 285–289.

Baca, A. (2006) Innovative diagnostic methods in elite sport. *International Journal of Performance Analysis in Sport-e*, 6: 148–156.

Bartlett, R. (2006) Artificial intelligence in sports biomechanics: new dawn or false hope? *Journal of Sports Science and Medicine*, 5: 474–479.

Barton, G., Lees, A., Lisboa, P. and Attfield S. (2006) Visualisation of gait data with Kohonen self-organising neural maps. *Gait Posture*, 24: 46–53.

Berkoff, D.J., Cairns, C.B., Sanchez, L.D. and Moorman, C.T. (2007) Heart rate variability in elite American track-and-field athletes. *Journal of Strength and Conditioning Research*, 21: 227–231.

Betker, A.L., Moussavi, Z.M. and Szturm, T. (2006) Center of mass approximation and prediction as a function of body acceleration. *IEEE Transactions on Biomedical Engineering*, 53: 686–693.

Bideau, B., Multon, F., Kulpa, R., Fradet, L., Arnaldi, B. and Delamarche, P. (2004) Using virtual reality to analyze links between handball thrower kinematics and goalkeeper's reactions. *Neuroscience Letters*, 30: 119–122.

Byrne, C. and Lim, C.L. (2007) The ingestible telemetric body core temperature sensor: a review of validity and exercise applications. *British Journal of Sports Medicine*, 41: 126–133.

Carling, C., Williams, A.M. and Reilly, T. (2005) *The Handbook of Soccer Match Analysis*. London: Routledge.

Chow, L.S., Greenlund, L.J., Asmann, Y.W., Short, K.R., McCrady, S.K., Levine, J.A. and Nair, K.S. (2007) Impact of endurance training on murine spontaneous activity, muscle mitochondrial DNA abundance, gene transcripts, and function. *Journal of Applied Physiology*, 102: 1078–89.

Fehrenbach, E., Zieker, D., Niess, A.M., Moeller, E., Russwurm, S. and Northoff, H. (2003) Microarray technology – the future analyses tool in exercise physiology? *Exercise Immunology Review*, 9: 58–69.

Gayagay, G., Yu, B., Hambly, B., Boston T., Hahn, A., Celermajer, D.S. and Trent, R.J. (1998) Elite endurance athletes and the ACE I allele – the role of genes in athletic performance. *Human Genetics*, 103: 48–50.

Gant, N., Atkinson, G. and Williams, C. (2006) The validity and reliability of intestinal temperature during intermittent running. *Medicine and Science in Sports and Exercise*, 38: 1926–1931.

James, N. (2006) The role of notational analysis in soccer coaching. *International Journal of Sports Science and Coaching*, 1: 185–198.

Katz, L. (2001) Innovations in sport technology: implications for the future. *Proceedings of the 11th International Association for Sport Information (IASI) Congress*, Lausanne, Switzerland (online at http://www.museum.olympic.org/e/studies_center/iasi_e.html).

Katz, L. (2002) Multimedia and the internet for sport sciences: applications and innovations. *International Journal of Computer Science in Sport*, 1: 4–18.

Katz, L., Parker, J., Tyreman, H., Kopp, G., Levy, R. and Chang, E. (2006) Virtual reality in sport: promise and reality. *International Journal of Computer Science in Sport*, 4: 4–17.

Lees, A. (2002) Technique analysis in sports: a critical review. *Journal of Sports Sciences*, 20: 813–28.

Lees, A., Barton, G. and Kershaw, L. (2003) The use of Kohonen neural network analysis to qualitatively characterize technique in soccer kicking. *Journal of Sports Sciences*, 21: 243–244.

Liebermann, D.G. and Franks, I.M. (2004) The use of feedback-based technologies. In M.D. Hughes and I.M. Franks (eds), *Notational Analysis of Sport: Systems for Better Coaching and Performance* (pp. 40–58). London: E & FN Spon.

MacArthur, D.G. and North, K.N. (2007) ACTN3: a genetic influence on muscle function and athletic performance. *Exercise and Sport Science Reviews*, 35(1): 30–34.

McGarry, T. and Perl, J. (2004) Models of sports contests. In M.D. Hughes and I.M. Franks (eds), *Notational Analysis of Sport: Systems for Better Coaching and Performance* (pp. 227–242). London: E & FN Spon.

Memmer, D. and Perl, J. (2005) Game intelligence analysis by means of a combination of variance analysis and neural networks. *International Journal of Computer Science in Sport*, 4: 30–39.

Moor, C., Braecklein, M. and Jorns, N. (2005) Current status of the development of wireless sensors for medical applications. *Biomedizinische Technik*, 50: 241–51.

Passos, P., Araaújo, D., Davids, K., Gouveia, L. and Serpa, S. (2006) Interpersonal dynamics in sport: the role of artificial neural networks and 3-D analysis. *Behavior Research Methods*, 38: 683–691.

Perl, J. (2001) Artificial neural networks in sport: new concepts and approaches. *International Journal of Performance Analysis in Sport*, 1(1): 106–121.

Perl, J. (2002) Game analysis and control by means of continuously learning networks. *International Journal of Performance Analysis in Sport-e*, 2: 21–35.

Perl, J. (2004) A neural network approach to movement pattern analysis. *Human Movement Science*, 23: 605–620.

Perl, J., Memmer, D., Bischof, J. and Gerharz, C. (2006) On a first attempt to modelling creativity learning by means of artificial neural networks. *International Journal of Computer Science in Sport*, 5: 33–37.

Raik, S. and Durnota, B. (1995) The evolution of sporting strategies. *Complexity International-e*, 2.

Rankinen, T., Bray, M.S., Hagberg, J.M., Pérusse, L., Roth, S.M., Wolfarth, B. and Bouchard, C. (2006) The human gene map for performance and health-related fitness phenotypes: the 2005 update, *Medicine and Science in Sports and Exercise*, 38: 1863–1888.

Rasid, M.F.A. and Woodward B. (2005) Bluetooth telemedicine processor for multichannel biomedical signal transmission via mobile cellular networks. IEEE transactions on information theory. *Biomedizinische Technik*, 19: 35–43.

Reed, D. and O'Donoghue, P. (2005) Development and application of computer-based prediction methods. *International Journal of Performance Analysis in Sport-e*, 5: 12–28.

Santiago, C., González-Freire, M., Serratosa, L., Morate, F.J., Meyer, T., Gómez-Gallego, F. and Lucia, A. (2008) ACTN3 genotype in professional soccer players. *British Journal of Sports Medicine*, 42(1): 71–73.

Spurway, N.C. (2007) Top-down studies of the genetic contribution to differences in physical capacity. In N.C. Spurway and H. Wackerhage (eds), *Genetics and Molecular Biology of Muscle Adaptation* (pp. 25–59). Amsterdam: Elsevier.

Ward, P., Williams, A.M. and Hancock P. (2006) Simulation for performance and training. In A. Ericsson, P. Hoffman, N. Charness and P. Feltovich (eds), *Handbook of Expertise and Expert Performance* (pp. 243–262). Cambridge: Cambridge University Press.

Wiemeyer, J. (2003) Who should play in which position in soccer? Empirical evidence and unconventional modelling. *International Journal of Performance Analysis in Sport-e*, 3: 1–18.

Williams, A.M. (2000) Perceptual skill in soccer: implications for talent identification and development. *Journal of Sports Sciences*, 18: 735–750.

Winter, E.M., Jones, A.M., Davison, R.C.R., Bromley, P.D. and Mercer, T. (eds) (2007) *Sport and Exercise Physiology Testing Guidelines: Sport Testing*. The British Association of Sport and Exercise Sciences Guide. London: Routledge.

Zieker, D., Zieker, J., Dietzsch, J., Burnet, M., Northoff, H. and Fehrenbach, E. (2005) CDNA-microarray analysis as a research tool for expression profiling in human peripheral blood following exercise. *Exercise Immunology Review*, 11: 86–96.

INDEX

221

eBooks – at www.eBookstore.tandf.co.uk

A library at your fingertips!

eBooks are electronic versions of printed books. You can store them on your PC/laptop or browse them online.

They have advantages for anyone needing rapid access to a wide variety of published, copyright information.

eBooks can help your research by enabling you to bookmark chapters, annotate text and use instant searches to find specific words or phrases. Several eBook files would fit on even a small laptop or PDA.

NEW: Save money by eSubscribing: cheap, online access to any eBook for as long as you need it.

Annual subscription packages

We now offer special low-cost bulk subscriptions to packages of eBooks in certain subject areas. These are available to libraries or to individuals.

For more information please contact webmaster.ebooks@tandf.co.uk

We're continually developing the eBook concept, so keep up to date by visiting the website.

www.eBookstore.tandf.co.uk